TOWARDS TOMORROW

Canada in a Changing World

Government

T·O·W·A·R·D·S T·O·M·O·R·R·O·W

Canada in a Changing World
Government

BRUCE BARTLETT
RICHARD CRAIG
GREGORY SASS

Harcourt Brace Jovanovich, Canada

TORONTO • ORLANDO • SAN DIEGO • LONDON • SYDNEY

Canadian Cataloguing in Publication Data

Bartlett, Bruce
Towards tomorrow: Canada in a changing world: government

For use in high schools.
Includes index.
ISBN 0-7747-1283-X

1. Canada—Politics and government. I. Craig, Richard G., 1953 -
II. Sass, Gregory. III. Title

JL75.B37 1989 320.971 C88-095006-4

Design and layout: Bob Garbutt Productions
Composition : Trigraph Inc.

Printed and bound in Canada.

93 MMT 5 4 3 2

TABLE OF CONTENTS

ACKNOWLEDGEMENTS

Every reasonable effort has been made to trace the owners of copyrighted material and to make due acknowledgement. Any errors or omissions drawn to our attention will be gladly rectified in future editions.

Text

p. 11, Quotation from AN INTRODUCTION TO GOVERNMENT AND POLITICS; A CONCEPTUAL APPROACH, pp. 75 & 76 by M. Dickerson and T. Flanagan. Reprinted by permission of Nelson Canada. pp. 21-23, Adaptation of How a Bill Becomes a Law by James Gillies: from CHALLENGE OF DEMOCRACY; IDEALS & REALITIES IN CANADA by L. Glassford. Reprinted with permission of Nelson Canada. p. 29, Excerpt from THE GOVERNMENT OF CANADA, by R.M. Dawson. 5th edition. Copyright © University of Toronto Press 1970. Reprinted by permission. p. 33, Table 2:1 "A Week in the House" from POLITICS IN CANADA by R. Jackson et al. Copyright © 1986 by Prentice-Hall Canada Inc. Reprinted by permission. pp. 39-40, Excerpt from pp. 271-272 THE STRUCTURE OF CANADIAN GOVERNMENT, Revised edition by J.R. Mallory. Copyright © 1984 Gage Publishing Limited. Reprinted by permission of Gage Educational Publishing Company. pp. 40-41, Excerpt from "Why Canada's Loyal Opposition should be Disloyal to Itself" by George Bain. Reprinted from *The Globe & Mail, Report on Business Magazine*, March, 1985. George Bain is a writer on politics and the media for various publications. pp. 41-42, Excerpt from STRAIGHT FROM THE HEART by Jean Chrétien. Reprinted with permission from Key Porter Books. Copyright © 1985 Jean Chrétien. pp. 78-80, Excerpts from an article "Court Paints a Portrait of Life's Bottom Rung" by Sara Cox. Reprinted by permission from *The Vancouver Sun*, 10 August 1985. pp. 80-81, The Miners' Ten Commandments: from THE MAN FOR A NEW COUNTRY: SIR MATTHEW BEGBIE by P.R. Williams. Reprinted by permission Sono Nis Press, Victoria B.C. pp. 83-85, Excerpts from an article "Herculean Job for the Highest Judges Who Decide if Our Laws are Valid" by David Vienneau. From the *Toronto Star*, 23 April 1985. Reprinted with permission - The Toronto Star Syndicate. p. 93 Table 5.1, p. 95 Table 5.2, and p. 101 Table 5.3, adapted from PARTY POLITICS IN CANADA, 5th edition by H. G. Thorburn. Copyright © 1985 Prentice-Hall Canada Inc. Reprinted by permission. pp. 110-111, Excerpts from THE CANADIAN POLITICAL SYSTEM, 3rd edition by R.J. Van Loon and M.S. Whittington. Copyright © 1981 McGraw-Hill Ryerson Limited. Reprinted by permission. p. 111 Table 5.4 and p. 112 Table 5.5, compiled by Bruce Bartlett. Reproduced with permission. pp. 116-117, Excerpt from ABSENT MANDATE; THE POLITICS OF DISCONTENT IN CANADA by Harold D. Clarke, et al. (Canadian Controversies Series). Copyright © 1984 Gage Publishing Limited. Reproduced with permission of Gage Educational Publishing Company. p. 118, Excerpts from RACE FOR THE ROSE by Charles Lynch. Copyright © 1984 Charles Lynch. Reprinted by permission. p. 120, Gallup Poll Results: Reprinted with permission from Canadian Gallup Poll, p. 121 Quotation from an article "Pollsters Predicted Tory Triumph": by Kevin Scanlon from the *Toronto Star* 5 September 1984. Reprinted with permission - The Toronto Star Syndicate. pp. 129-132, Excerpt from HOW CANADIANS GOVERN THEMSELVES. 1988 by Eugene A. Forsey. Reproduced with permission of the Minister of Supply & Services Canada. p. 135-137, Excerpt from THE CHARTER OF RIGHTS AND FREEDOMS: A GUIDE FOR CANADIANS. Reprinted with permission of the Minister of Supply & Services Canada. pp. 146-147, Excerpt from THE NEW CANADIAN CONSTITUTION by David A. Milne. Copyright © 1982 by James Lorimer & Company Publishers. Reprinted by permission. pp. 146-147, Excerpt from AND NO ONE CHEERED; FEDERALISM, DEMOCRACY AND THE CONSTITUTION ACT edited by K. Banting & R. Simeon. Copyright © 1983 Methuen Publications. Reprinted with permission of Nelson Canada. p. 147, Excerpt from CANADA...NOTWITHSTANDING: The Making of the Constitution 1976-1982 by Roy Romanow et al. Copyright © 1984 Carswell/Methuen. Reprinted with permission of Nelson Canada. pp. 152-157, Excerpts from *The Revised Statutes of Canada*,

1970. Reprinted with permission from Justice Canada and the Minister of Supply & Services Canada. p. 165, Excerpt from an article "Judge's decisions becoming political, Regina lawyer says." by Kirk Makin, 20 August 1986. Reprinted by permission from *The Globe & Mail*, Toronto. pp. 181-182, Excerpt from an article "Fringe Parties Still Fighting", 10 October 1986. Reprinted with permission from The Province, Vancouver. p. 186 Table 8.2 and p. 188 Table 8.3, used by permission of the Union of British Columbia Municipalities (Fact Sheets #3 and #9).

Photographs

CP-Canapress Photo Services.
MS-Miller Services.
MSS-Ministry of Supply and Services.
PAC-Public Archives of Canada.
PBC-Province of British Columbia.
VS-Vancouver Sun.

Cover Photograph–Courtesy of the Province of British Columbia, Tourism, Recreation, and Culture.

Chapter 1 p. 3 (left) MSS-Neville Bell-1973 73-3806, (top right) CP, (bottom right) CP; p. 4 CP; p. 9 CP; p. 10 (all photos) CP; p. 12 CP; p. 13 Metropolitan Toronto Central Library - Fine Art; p. 14 (all photos) Metropolitan Toronto Central Library - Fine Art.

Chapter 2 p. 19 (all photos) CP; p. 21 (all photos) CP; p. 23 CP; p. 27 CP; p. 28 CP; p. 30 (left) MSS-George Hunter 1973 73-1928, (top right) MSS-Chris Lund-1967 67-161917, (bottom right) MSS-T. Grant-1966 67-309; p. 32 CP; p. 37 CP; p. 38 (all photos) CP; p. 42 CP.

Chapter 3 p. 47 Toronto Public Libraries - Picture Collection; p. 48 CP; p. 50 CP; p. 52 CP; p. 53 CP; p. 55 CP; p. 56 CP; p. 61 CP.

Chapter 4 p. 65 MS S20683W; p. 69 Metro Public Library - Picture Collection; p. 70 (top) MSS Hans Blohm-1972 72-3440, (bottom) Worker's Compensation Board; p. 71 (top) MS, (bottom) CP; p. 73 CP; p. 75 MS S20721; p. 77 MS; p. 78 Francine Geraci; p. 80 Provincial Archives of British Columbia A-8953; p. 81 Ministry of Provincial Secretary and Government Services - B.C.; p. 83 CP; p. 85 MSS Terry Waterfield-1968 68-18998.

Chapter 5 p. 89 MSS Chris Lund-1968 68-16751; p. 91 CP; p. 92 (all photos) CP; p. 93 MSS Crombie McNeill-1972 72-5799; p. 94 CP; p. 99 PAC C-26400; p. 100 CP; p. 101 CP; p. 102 CP; p. 103 Metro Toronto Library Bd.; p. 105 CP; p. 107 CP; p. 108 CP; p. 113 CP; p. 115 CP; p. 117 CP; p. 119 CP.

Chapter 6 p. 127 (all photos) CP; p. 128 CP; p. 130 CP; p. 133 CP; p. 134 CP; p. 135 CP; p. 136 (top) CP, (bottom left) MS, (bottom centre) CP, (bottom right) CP; p. 137 MSS J.M. Versteege-1973 73-4220; p. 139 CP; p. 141 CP; p. 142 CP; p. 143 (all photos) CP; p. 144 CP; p. 146 CP.

Chapter 7 p. 152 CP; p. 153 (all photos) CP; p. 154 (top) CP, (bottom left) Brantford Expositor, (bottom right) The War Amputations of Canada; p. 155 (top) MSS Pierre Gaudard-1967 67-5881, (bottom) The North York Board of Education and Elizabeth Varghese; p. 156 (all photos) CP; p. 157 The Province-John Thompson Photography; p. 160 CP; p. 162 CP; p. 163 (large ad) used by permission of Idomo Furniture, (small ad) used by permission of Paul Magdar Furs.

Chapter 8 p. 171 (all photos) CP; p. 172 CP; p. 173 CP; p. 174 (all photos) CP; p. 175 PBC Cat. #HP42778 Neg. #B-8226; p. 178 VS-George Diack; p. 179 (all photos) CP; p. 181 PBC Cat. #HP25603 Neg. #H-1532; p. 182 (left) The Province-David Clark, (top and bottom right) VS-Bill Keay; p. 183 PBC Cat. #HP42715 Neg. #B-8203; p. 184 PBC Cat. #HP71107 Neg. #F4290; p. 185 (left) CP, (right) VS-Peter Battistoni; p. 187 (top) PBC Cat. #PH9144 Neg. #A-3263, (bottom) VS-Deni Eagland; p. 189 (left) VS-Deni Eagland, (top right) CP, (bottom) CP; p. 190 (left) CP, (right) The Province-David Clark; p. 191 (left) VS (right) VS-Peter Battistoni; p. 194 VS.

Cartoons and Illustrations: pp. 2, 5, 6, 15 Paul McCusker; p. 151 Avril Orloff.

Shown here and on the cover of this book is the interior of the dome of British Columbia's Legislature. The building was designed by a 25-year-old British architect, Francis Mawson Rattenbury, who came to B.C. only a year before he submitted the winning design for this building in a contest open to all architects in North America.

The building of the B.C. Legislature began in 1893 and was completed in 1897. As far as possible, native varieties of stone and wood were used in its construction. The painted panels in the dome, executed by Victoria artist George Southwell, depict the province's major industries: lumbering, mining, fruitgrowing, and fishing. Ornate gilded plasterwork completes the ornamentation of the dome.

CHAPTER 1

Selected Political Systems

Nancy was right to conclude that politics affect her life. Consider her typical morning routine on a school day:

- □ *7:30: Got up when her radio alarm came on, playing one of her favourite songs.*
- □ *7:30–7:55: Showered and put on a pair of imported jeans.*
- □ *7:55–8:15: Had a breakfast of buttered toast and milk.*
- □ *8:15–8:30: Rode her bicycle to school, stopping for three red lights on the way.*

During this hour, law and government entered Nancy's life in several ways:

- □ *The radio station she was listening to was broadcasting under a licence from the Canadian Radio-Television and Telecommunications Commission (CRTC), an agency of the federal government. The CRTC requires that a certain number of the songs played by any Canadian station must be written, played, or produced by Canadians.*
- □ *The water for her shower was heated with electricity provided by B.C. Hydro, a provincial government company.*
- □ *Nancy's imported jeans came into Canada under the regulations of a complex international agreement known as the General Agreement on Tariffs and Trade (GATT).*
- □ *The bread bag, butter wrapper, and milk carton on the breakfast table were labelled in both French and English, as required by federal language legislation. The labels listed the ingredients in each food, as required by the federal* Food and Drugs Act. *The bread, butter, and milk themselves were produced in accordance with regulations laid down by the British Columbia Ministry of Agriculture.*
- □ *The red lights at which Nancy stopped on the way to school had been placed in those locations by the traffic division of her local government.*
- □ *The fact that Nancy went to school at all was the result of a provincial law requiring school attendance.*

Canadian radio stations, such as this one in Ottawa (left), are regulated by the Canadian Radio-Television and Telecommunications Commission (CRTC), a federal government agency. Why do you suppose the CRTC regulates the percentage of Canadian content in broadcast material?

The Bennett Dam (top right), is owned and operated by B.C. Hydro, a Crown Corporation, which oversees the province's use of water and electricity.

Many imported goods (bottom right), come into Canada under the regulations of the General Agreement on Tariffs and Trade (GATT). This garment worker is producing shirts for export to Canada.

These are only a few examples of the overwhelming impact of politics and government on the lives of Canadians. Most of the activities in Nancy's morning were influenced by laws or regulations made by government. Indeed, politics and government are so intertwined with our daily existence that we take them for granted most of the time. An understanding of politics leads to a better understanding of its effect on our lives.

This chapter presents a broad introduction to politics and government. You will first examine some basic ideas about the nature of government. Next, you will consider three perspectives on ***ideologies****—that is, political doctrines. Finally, you will learn about the features and the evolution of ideologies. As you read through the chapter, keep the following questions in mind:*

- *What is the purpose of government?*
- *What are the three main branches of government?*
- *What is the difference between freedom and equality?*
- *What are the different kinds of freedom and equality?*
- *What are the major ideologies of the twentieth century, and what are the features of each?*
- *How can ideologies be compared?*

The Nature of Government: Some Basic Concepts

To get a broad picture of the nature of government, you must examine three essential concepts: the need for government; the relationship between government, freedom, and equality; and the structure of government.

Many students ride bicycles to and from school. Why do governments pass laws to regulate traffic flow? What traffic laws apply to bicycle riders in your municipality?

The Need for Government

Do you think there is a need for government in people's lives? To answer this question, imagine what Nancy's morning would have been like if no government of any kind existed. Consider her bicycle ride to school. Without the laws passed by government, she and all other cyclists, as well as automobile drivers, would be free to do whatever they wanted. There would be no traffic lights, no signs, no right-of-way rules; in fact, there would be no rules of the road at all. Traffic would likely slow down, or even become paralyzed. It is highly probable that the number of accidents would increase.

Government therefore provides organization and security. It is true that people give up some of their freedom to obey laws such as traffic regulations. It is equally true that obedience to these regulations results in a safe, orderly traffic system. In other words, people accept certain restrictions on their freedom so that society may have order.

Intellectual Freedom

Government, Freedom, and Equality

You read above that order in society is accompanied by certain restrictions on freedom. In fact, order rests largely on the balance between freedom and equality. You have probably heard such statements as, "Everyone should be free," "Everyone should be equal," and "Everyone has rights." But what are freedom and equality? What do they have to do with rights?

Intellectual Equality

Basically, **freedom** has to do with a belief that the rights of the individual are most important. **Equality** has to do with the belief that all individuals have the right to be dealt with in the same way. In some situations, people's **rights** are linked more closely to freedom; in others, they are more closely related to equality. In most everyday situations, government allows people to exercise both kinds of rights. Think again of Nancy's bicycle ride to school. She was free to use any type, make, and colour of bike she wanted, but she was not free to ride it through a red light. She and the other drivers were equal in that they were all obliged to stop at red lights. People's right to be free and their right to be equal are balanced by government, so that society may be orderly.

Economic Freedom

There are many different kinds of freedom and equality. Perhaps the most important types are intellectual and economic. The right of individuals to believe in and think about what they wish has to do with **intellectual freedom**. The right of everyone in society to be protected by law from unacceptable expressions of intellectual freedom, in books or movies for example, has to do with **intellectual equality**. The right of individuals to own property, run a business, invest money, or advertise a product has to do with **economic freedom**. The right of everyone in society to have an adequate level of food, clothing, and shelter has to do with **economic equality**. As you will see in the next sections, these rights are valued differently by governments which follow different political ideals.

Economic Equality

The Structure of Government

Within any political system, government can be divided into three branches. The first is the **legislative branch**, which makes laws. The second is the **executive branch**, which implements (carries out) laws. The third, the **judicial branch**, adjudicates (interprets and applies) laws. In different political systems, these branches may overlap or be separate.

For now, consider a simple example of how the three branches might work at the local level. Suppose that in your community there is a by-law which limits smoking in certain public places. The by-law requires one-half of the seating in restaurants in your community to be designated as non-smoking areas. When your town or city council passed this by-law, it was acting as the legislative branch of government. When local inspectors visited the restaurants to make sure that non-smoking areas were being provided, they were acting as the executive branch. If someone violated the non-smoking by-law and was charged and found guilty, the local court which ordered that person to pay a fine was acting as the judicial branch of the local government.

QUESTIONS

1. How do labels on Canadian food products demonstrate the influence of law and government on our daily lives?
2. Which branch of government interprets and applies laws?
3. Within which of the three branches of government do you think the police should be included? Why?
4. **(a)** What are freedom and equality?
   (b) What relationship do they have to government?

Ideologies in Perspective

All governments follow, to some degree, a certain set of ideologies or political ideas. In the past two centuries, some ideologies have been particularly significant. Five of them are liberalism, conservatism, socialism, communism, and fascism. (As you will see, there are two forms of liberalism, classical and reform.) All five originated in western Europe, but in some form have had influence throughout the world.

The names of political parties do not always correspond precisely to ideological labels. Liberalism, for instance, should not be automatically equated with Canada's Liberal Party, conservatism with Canada's Progressive Conservative Party, nor communism with the modern governments of the Soviet Union and China. A political party may have its roots in one ideology, but also have policies which reflect other ideologies.

The five ideologies named above can be examined from three perspectives: philosophical, political, and economic. Ideologies may be very similar when looked at from one perspective, but poles apart when seen from another perspective.

The Philosophical Perspective: Left Wing and Right Wing

Ideologies can be compared on the basis of attitudes towards or beliefs about the nature of human beings and the desirability of progress. Supporters of some ideologies believe in the capacity of society to use new ideas and technology to improve itself and advance. In varying ways, communism, socialism, and liberalism all advocate progress and have an optimistic view of human nature.

Supporters of other ideologies tend to look back to a past, usually more imagined than real, in which they believe society worked better. When these ideologies call for change, the changes are seen not as a means of progressing, but rather as a way of restoring past values and institutions which have been lost, or are in danger of being lost. In very different ways, both conservatism and fascism serve as examples of ideologies which uphold traditions and have a cautious view of human nature.

Ideologies which support progress are sometimes referred to as **left wing**, while those which support traditions are labelled **right wing**. These terms were used in the late eighteenth century, during the French Revolution. In the French National Assembly, the group that wanted the Revolution to move ahead rapidly sat to the left of the Speaker of the Assembly. Their opponents, who wanted the Revolution slowed or even halted, sat on the right.

The Political Perspective: Democracy and Dictatorship

Ideologies can also be compared on the basis of attitudes towards the relationship between a government and its people. Some governments are the responsibility of large groups of people, while other governments are entrusted to a few leaders or to just one.

The term **democracy** comes from the Greek words *demos*, "people", and *kratos*, "power" or "rule". Literally, therefore, it means "people power" or "rule by the people". Today, the word is generally applied to any system of government in which citizens can freely elect representatives.

While free elections are perhaps the feature that most clearly distinguishes a true democracy, others are important as well. If its newspapers are free to criticize the government, if political parties are allowed to exist, if its courts are not subject to interference by political leaders, then a country can be described as democratic.

Most of the varieties of conservatism, liberalism, and socialism practised today could be termed "democratic" to one degree or another. It would be difficult to say whether any of the three is necessarily more democratic than the others. In historic terms, however, conservatism has tended to be somewhat less democratic than the other two ideologies. For instance, nineteenth century conservatives often argued that only property owners should be allowed to vote because only they had a vested interest; they were therefore the only ones entitled to have a political voice. (Classical liberals sometimes made the same argument, however.) Reform liberals and socialists were the first to urge **universal suffrage**, the right of all adult citizens to vote, regardless of their wealth, status, or sex.

The term **dictatorship** is derived from the Latin verb *dictare*, "to declare repeatedly", "to order". In classical Roman times, a single leader was sometimes temporarily appointed to guide the state in time of crisis. Whatever the leader said became the law of the land; hence the word **dictator**, "the one who orders". "Dictator" refers to a person in power who rules as he or she sees fit, without being answerable to the people. A dictatorship is a system of government in which the leader, who usually has a small group of powerful supporters, rules according to personal decisions and suppresses opposing opinions.

Modern fascist and communist governments are types of dictatorships. Both are examples of what political scientists call **totalitarian** government, that is, a system in which government is in total control of all aspects of political, social, and cultural life. In schools, clubs, and all other forms of social gathering, the official ideology of the state is constantly visible. A good example of this was seen in the Hitler Youth movement of Nazi Germany. From an early age, student members wore uniforms, chanted slogans, and otherwise participated in special clubs and events designed to make them willing supporters of Nazism, a form of fascism. Citizens are often not free to move about

The Hitler Youth movement of Nazi Germany participated in highly visible events to promote the ideology of the state.

in search of a new job or home, but are assigned specific locations and employment. The media are given little choice about what they may report. Totalitarian governments justify the enforcement of such controls with the argument that the needs of the community (*i.e.*, the state) are more important than individual liberties.

Ironically, virtually all communist countries refer to themselves as "people's democracies". While there may be elections, there is only one legally recognized party—the Communist Party. A choice is available to voters; it usually is a choice among candidates of that one party. Communist regimes assert that their elections do allow citizens to signal their approval of the government, so that each regime is in fact a democracy.

The Economic Perspective: Private Ownership *versus* Public Ownership

Ideologies can be compared as well on the basis of attitudes towards the role of government in a country's economic life and the actual control the government exercises over the economy. Economic freedom and economic equality are valued to differing degrees by each ideology. Economic freedom is closely linked to the idea of **private ownership** or **capitalism**. Under this system, business, rather than government, is the major producer of goods and services. Economic equality embodies the concept of public ownership, a system in which government, rather than business, is the chief producer.

This family farm at Niagara-on-the-Lake, Ontario, is privately owned but is subject to government regulations.

Collective farms in Communist China are cultivated to produce maximum yields.

No country in the world has a government which is true democracy or total dictatorship; likewise, no country has an economic system which is true public ownership or completely private ownership. Most countries, however, clearly favour one kind of ownership over the other. In communist countries, the presence of public ownership is overwhelming. In socialist countries, public ownership is prevalent, although private ownership may exist and be regulated by government. Reform liberalism favours private ownership, but will accept government ownership in certain situations. Where conservatism or classical liberalism dominates, so does private ownership. Private ownership exists under fascism, but it is subject to many government restrictions and controls.

Two philosophers, Adam Smith and Karl Marx, are identified with ideologies which advocate opposing economic systems. Smith, a leading classical liberal thinker, is usually regarded as the chief exponent of private ownership. Marx is considered the primary advocate of public ownership.

Smith's book, *The Wealth of Nations*, first published in 1776, put forward the idea of an economic system governed by an "invisible hand", the metaphor he used to describe capitalism. Smith claimed that the supply of goods and services needed by society would naturally match the demand. Sellers would see a need, attempt to fill it, and try to make a profit. Buyers would determine the need and the price they were willing to pay for the goods or services. Thus, in seeking their own private interests, buyers and sellers would create an economic system. These private interests of individuals, in other words, the "invisible hand", would render government interference unnecessary. The system would work of its own accord. The term *laissez-faire* is often used to describe this system.

Nearly three-quarters of a century later, in 1848, Karl Marx expressed the opposite view in *The Communist Manifesto*, which he wrote in collaboration with Friedrich Engels. Marx and Engels argued that the "invisible hand" had not benefitted all of society, as Smith had forecast. Instead, capitalism had allowed the bourgeoisie—the capitalists—to concentrate in their own hands a hugely disproportionate amount of land, wealth, industry, and political power.

In Marx's view, the common good could not and would not result from the existence of any "invisible hand". It would be attained only when the revolution of the proletariat put the workers in charge of government, and of the instruments of production. In other words, having gained political power, the proletariat would also gain economic power. With this power would come economic equality: no-one would be the economic servant of anyone else.

Neither Smith's nor Marx's ideas have ever been practised exactly as they were expressed. Yet the spirit of both men's ideas is still very much alive; the concepts of private and public ownership are still competing in today's world.

QUESTIONS

1. What is implied when a person is described as being "left wing"? How would such a person be likely to vote in British Columbia?
2. What is universal suffrage?
3. What is totalitarian government?
4. Is fascism an example of a right wing or a left wing ideology? Why?
5. **(a)** Is private or public ownership more common in Canada?
   (b) Name one example of each which is found in British Columbia.

The Evolution of Ideologies

Now you will examine the historical roots of the five ideologies, to see how they have evolved over time. It is important to keep in mind as you read that ideologies are not concrete physical entities. Two political scientists, M. Dickerson and T. Flanagan, have expressed this idea well:

> . . .remember that all ideologies are abstractions. They do not really exist; what exists are real people with their individual thoughts and organizations that adopt statements or programs. It is unlikely that the beliefs of any person or organization perfectly fit the description. . .of particular ideologies. Yet there are tendencies and common concerns that unite diverse thinkers, even if they do not agree on every point. Think of ideologies as broad tendencies of thought existing over long periods of time. . . .

Liberalism

"Liberal" comes from the Latin adjective *liber*, meaning "free". "Liberalism" is a very broad, sweeping term which means different things to different people. Essentially, however, two forms of liberalism can be identified. The older, original version is called **classical liberalism**, while the newer, modern type is called **reform liberalism**.

The term "liberal" first came to be widely used during the late eighteenth century in western Europe. Classical liberals were strong believers in both economic and intellectual freedom. In their view of human nature, people were basically good creatures, capable of improving their lot in life through their own efforts. The idea of progress—the belief that social, economic, and political conditions would get better with each generation—was central to classical liberalism. Classical liberals believed that government should not get involved in the economic and intellectual life of the community any more than necessary. They were not particularly concerned with economic or intellectual equality.

Reform liberalism has its roots in the late nineteenth and early twentieth centuries. When the term "liberal" is used today, it is this type of liberalism which is meant. Reform liberalism differs from classical liberalism in its much stronger commitment to economic equality, which supporters believe can be brought about by limited government intervention in the economy. Nonetheless, reform liberalism maintains classical liberalism's commitment to progress and intellectual freedom.

The change in liberal ideology was affected most profoundly by the writings of the economist John Maynard Keynes (1883–1946). Keynes argued that governments should become involved in the economy by controlling the supply of money, even if this meant that governments would spend their way into debt. Such spending was seen as necessary to ensure that all citizens would have access to the basics of life: decent food, housing, and employment. Reform liberalism might be regarded as an important focus of the modern Liberal Party of Canada.

Children outside a Swedish movie theatre protest the decision of the Swedish Board of Film Censorship to restrict their viewing of "E.T.". Their signs say "Let us see E.T.", and "Films for kids should be seen by kids". What is the purpose of government censorship?

Conservatism

"Conservative" comes from the Latin verb *conservare*, meaning "to save". Conservatism emerged in the late eighteenth century in Britain, as a reaction against the excesses of liberalism. Perhaps the major thinker of the conservative tradition was the British statesman Edmund Burke (1729–97).

Early conservatives, such as Burke, believed that the monarch should have authority over the elected Parliament, and that the traditional organization of society and politics should be preserved. Later conservatives agreed that gradual, progressive change was acceptable, whereas radical, abrupt change should be avoided.

Supporters of conservatism have a strong commitment to intellectual equality and believe that moral issues are sometimes a matter of public, not merely private, concern. They may, for example, favour some kind of censorship in order to protect what are perceived to be community standards.

Like classical liberals, conservatives are strong believers in economic freedom. Unlike both classical and reform liberals, conservatives have only a moderate commitment to intellectual freedom.

Some representatives in Canada's Progressive Conservative Party, when they were elected in 1984, tended to advocate economic freedom and intellectual equality. For example, certain government members argued for tax advantages to corporations, and stronger anti-pornography measures. These positions paralleled the traditional conservative position. Yet it is worth noting that other members of the same Conservative government advocated contrary positions.

Socialism

The ideas that gave rise to socialism have been traced by some political scientists to the works of Plato, the great Greek philosopher of the fourth century B.C. Modern socialist ideas are more closely linked to

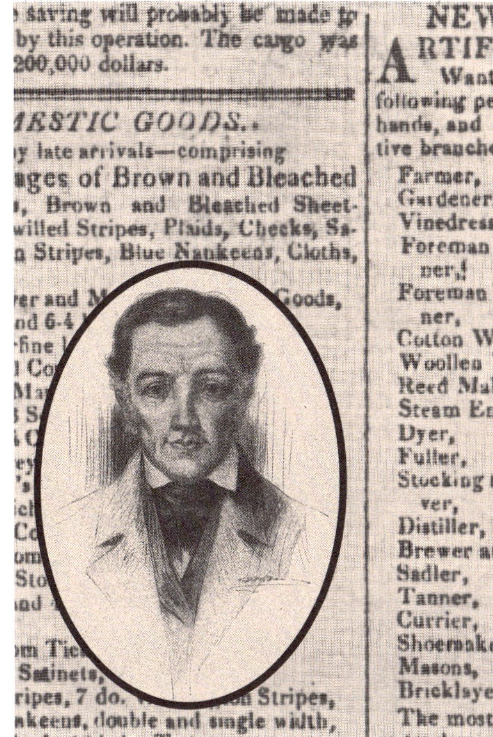

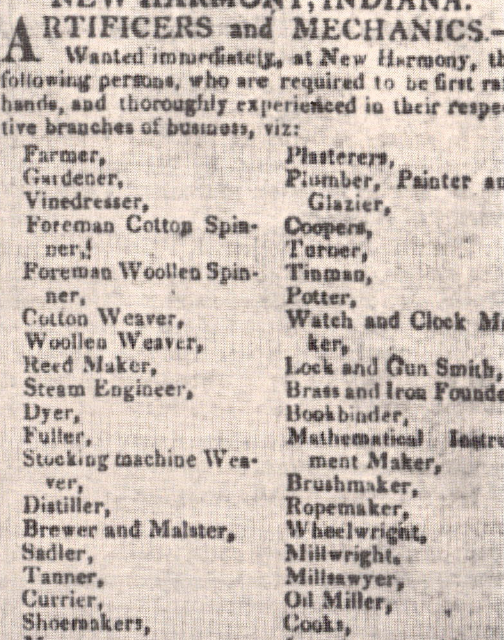

NEW HARMONY, INDIANA.

ARTIFICERS and MECHANICS.– Wanted immediately, at New Harmony, th following persons, who are required to be first rat hands, and thoroughly experienced in their respec tive branches of business, viz:

Farmer,	Plasterers,
Gardener,	Plumber, Painter an Glazier,
Vinedresser,	Coopers,
Foreman Cotton Spinner,	Turner,
Foreman Woollen Spinner,	Tinman,
Cotton Weaver,	Potter,
Woollen Weaver,	Watch and Clock Ma ker,
Reed Maker,	Lock and Gun Smith,
Steam Engineer,	Brass and Iron Founde
Dyer,	Bookbinder,
Fuller,	Mathematical Instru ment Maker,
Stocking machine Weaver,	Brushmaker,
Distiller,	Ropemaker,
Brewer and Malster,	Wheelwright,
Sadler,	Millwright,
Tanner,	Millsawyer,
Currier,	Oil Miller,
Shoemakers,	Cooks,
Masons,	Laundresses and Wash erwomen.
Bricklayers,	

The most satisfactory references and testimonial

Robert Owen (1771–1858)

Robert Owen put his socialist ideals into practice by establishing experimental communities. He placed this advertisement in a New Harmony, Indiana, newspaper to recruit the population for one of these communities.

Could a modern self-sufficient community be created by persons engaged in the above occupations? Explain your answer.

the theories of Jean-Jacques Rousseau, Henri de Saint-Simon, and Robert Owen. The term "socialism" itself first became used extensively in the early nineteenth century, in the writings of commentators upon the Industrial Revolution. During the Industrial Revolution, manual tools were replaced by powerful machines, and the manufacturing operations were concentrated in large factories. Socialist theorists of the time believed that the community, not wealthy individuals or small groups of individuals, should own these industrial enterprises. Government intervention in the economy, they claimed, would produce economic equality. This, in turn, would make the individual truly free.

Like both classical and reform liberals, early socialists were believers in progress and the capacity of innovative ideas and institutions to improve society. They were generally in agreement with the liberal view that human beings were basically good. The essential difference between liberalism and socialism was that liberals believed individuals could be truly free with limited government, while socialists believed government itself could make individuals free.

In Canada, the dividing line between socialism and reform liberalism, as represented by the New Democratic Party (NDP) and the Liberal Party, is sometimes unclear. Both parties have policies which support the economic equality of individuals in society. However, because the NDP also has policies which advocate the economic equality of workers in the workplace, it could be said to be more deeply rooted in socialism.

Posters such as this one were displayed by the leaders of the Russian Revolution, who believed that private ownership of land contributed to social inequality. This particular poster urged farmers to join publicly owned collectives.

Communism

The thinkers most closely associated with early communism are Karl Marx (1818–83) and Friedrich Engels (1820–95). Like the socialists, Marx had economic equality as his ideal. However, he thought that it would come about not by the cooperation of groups sharing property voluntarily, but rather by violent conflict, because the people who held power would not give it up voluntarily.

Marx and Engels concentrated on the negative effects of capitalism. They saw history as a record of the struggle between the oppressors and the oppressed. The most recent oppressors were the wealthy capitalists—the bourgeoisie—and the oppressed were the mistreated, underpaid workers—the proletariat.

Marx and Engels predicted that, in the industrialized nations of western Europe, the proletariat would eventually rise up and destroy the capitalist system. A new system would gradually progress through a number of stages, with the final and permanent one being communism. In theory, a truly communist society would see not only the abolition of private property, but also the disappearance (in Marx's phrase, the "withering away") of government. These two developments would bring about the economic equality of all people.

In fact, the various communist regimes in the world today bear very little resemblance to the future society envisioned by Marx. For one thing, the first communist revolution, which took place in 1917, did not occur in industrialized western Europe (as Marx had predicted) but rather in czarist Russia, a country which, at the time, was still largely agricultural. In modern communist countries government has not withered away, as Marx suggested; on the contrary, it intrudes into every aspect of economic and intellectual life.

Socialist and communist ideologies resemble each other in that both advocate economic equality. However, socialists believe this is to be achieved peacefully, through government intervention.

Karl Marx (left), believed that economic equality would come about through violent conflict between capitalists and workers. He and Friedrich Engels wrote The Communist Manifesto *in 1848.*

Friedrich Engels (right), a friend and collaborator of Karl Marx, was a philosopher, economist, and historian.

Fascism

Historically, fascism is largely regarded as a phenomenon of the period from the early 1920's to the end of World War II in 1945. The word "fascism" is Italian in origin, and was first used by the Italian leader Benito Mussolini (1883-1945), who headed his country's government from 1922 to 1943. Individual freedoms were permitted only if and when they contributed to the good of the nation.

In Mussolini's view, all the economic and intellectual resources of the Italian state were to be directed towards the building of a militarily strong and fiercely proud, united country. In a fascist state, there was no room for intellectual freedom, and only limited room for economic freedom. While private property and private businesses existed, they were tightly regulated by the government which they were supposed to serve.

In virtually all countries of Europe except the Soviet Union, fascist movements of varying strength existed between the early 1920's and 1945. (Indeed, there were fascist movements in Canada at the time.) Italy was the first self-proclaimed fascist state. Others soon came into being, of which the most notable one was Germany, where Adolf Hitler and his National Socialist (Nazi) Party took power in 1933.

Communism can be described as an ideology linked to a vision of the future. Fascism, on the other hand, can be described as an ideology which is linked to the past. It is based on the notion that a mythical, ideal age once existed which could be reborn. In this mythical era, the citizens were "racially pure" and were ranked in a strict social order ruled by a strong father figure. The Nazis also saw the Germans as a superior race descended from ancient Aryan warriors. Nazism was to be a process of recreating the ethnic purity and military supremacy which Germany had lost since that mythical time.

The fascist ideology found in Germany or Italy in the 1930's is no longer practised. However, the term is still used occasionally to describe countries with a military government that keeps a tight rein on intellectual and economic life. The regime of General Augusto Pinochet Ugarte, who in 1973 took over the government of Chile, is sometimes described as an example of modern-day fascism.

The Fasces

The term comes ultimately from the Latin **fasces**, *which denotes a bundle of rods bound together around an axe. In ancient Rome, the rods and axe symbolized the government's power to keep law and order (the rods to control and correct the people) and, if necessary, to mete out punishment and death (the axe of execution).*

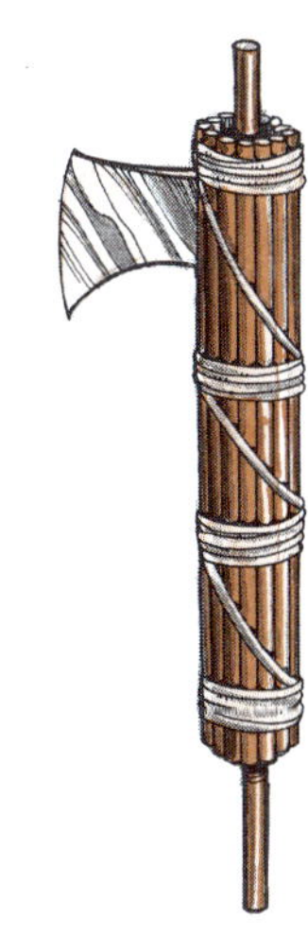

QUESTIONS

1. **(a)** What is the position of classical liberalism on **(i)** economic freedom and **(ii)** intellectual freedom?
   (b) How does reform liberalism differ from classical liberalism?

2. **(a)** What is the position of conservatism on **(i)** change and **(ii)** intellectual equality?
   (b) How does conservatism differ from reform liberalism? from classical liberalism?

3. What contribution to political ideology was made by each of the following individuals: **(a)** Keynes; **(b)** Burke; **(c)** Marx?

4. What is the basic difference between liberalism and socialism?

5. How are socialism and communism similar? How do they differ?

6. What are the differences between communism as an ideology, and communism as a label for the type of government in the Soviet Union?

Chapter Summary

Politics and government influence our lives in many ways. This influence comes largely from laws that are made, implemented, and adjudicated by the three branches of government: legislative, executive, and judicial. Laws exist so that human society may have order.

Order in society depends largely on the balance between freedom and equality. Both freedom and equality have to do with individuals' rights. Presented here are four basic kinds of rights: economic freedom, economic equality, intellectual freedom, and intellectual equality. The different rights sometimes conflict with one another. Furthermore, they are not all valued to the same degree within every ideology.

The five major ideologies we discuss in this chapter are liberalism (classical and reform), conservatism, socialism, communism, and fascism. They can be compared from three perspectives. An examination of attitudes towards human nature and progress forms a philosophical perspective. A survey of forms of government and relationships between government and people provides a political perspective. A look at attitudes to the role of government in economic life gives an economic perspective.

Ideologies are supported by groups of people who agree upon the same broad concepts. They are not static, concrete things; rather, they change over time as society changes.

IN REVIEW

1. Identify each of the following as an example of economic freedom, economic equality, intellectual freedom, or intellectual equality:
   (a) subscribing to the newspaper of your choice;
   (b) the banning of a film by a censor;
   (c) increasing your income by having two jobs;
   (d) paying the same university tuition fees as other students;
   (e) starting a business.

2. Compare the view of human nature according to liberalism with that held in conservatism.

3. Is Canada a true democracy? Explain your answer.

4. Which ideologies support progress? Which support tradition? Place the ideologies on a scale of political perspectives, from left wing to right wing.

APPLYING YOUR KNOWLEDGE

1. Which of the following policies could form part of a political party's ideology? Explain your reasoning.
   (a) Tariffs on imported goods should be high.
   (b) The Canadian army should wear green uniforms.
   (c) In weather reports, the temperature should be given in degrees Celsius.
   (d) Small businesses should be helped by government to survive.
   (e) Air Canada (owned by the federal government) should be sold to a private company.

2. State which of the political ideologies described in this chapter can be associated with each of the following:
   (a) a belief that the disappearance of private property and government will lead to economic equality;
   (b) the chief ideology of the Liberal Party of Canada;
   (c) the ideology followed by Italy's Mussolini;
   (d) a belief that government should not get involved in the economic and intellectual life of the community;
   (e) a belief that traditional, tested ideas and institutions are best.

3. What does economic equality imply?

4. Do you think a high level of intellectual freedom makes a society easier or more difficult to control? Why?

5. List the five ideologies in order of commitment to public ownership.

6. Rank the five ideologies, as they occur today, on a scale between the extremes of democracy and dictatorship.

FURTHER INVESTIGATION

1. Give an example from your own experience which demonstrates that governments are concerned with holding power. Give an example that disproves the statement.

2. Adam Smith claimed that "deliberate, precise planning" of the economy is unnecessary and that the economy, if not interfered with, would work of its own accord. Do you agree with this view? Give reasons for your answer.

3. Review the information within this chapter on economic freedom and economic equality. Consider carefully, then state which you think is of greater potential benefit to **(a)** yourself, and **(b)** the community. Give reasons for your answers.

4. Undertake research on one or more of the following topics:
   (a) the theories of either John Maynard Keynes or Adam Smith;
   (b) the origins of either communism or socialism;
   (c) the practice of fascism by either Mussolini or Hitler.

CHAPTER 2

The Legislative Branch

In the previous chapter you learned that in any political system, government can be divided into three branches: legislative, executive, and judicial. The legislative branch is the subject of this chapter.

What is the legislative branch of Canada's federal government? Strictly speaking, the answer is simply, "Parliament". Parliament has three components: the Governor General, the House of Commons, and the Senate. While all three play a part in the legislative process, the House of Commons has the leading role.

The first section of this chapter presents an overview to familiarize you with the three components of Parliament. Next you will look at the mechanics of the law-making process, that is, at the formal stages in getting a law passed. You will then examine in detail the legislative role of each of the three components of Parliament. Finally, you will consider the broad question of how power and influence work in the legislative process. In this chapter, you will find answers to questions such as these:

- *What are the various stages in the law-making process?*
- *What is the legislative function of each of the three components of Parliament?*
- *How can ordinary citizens influence the making of laws?*
- *How might the House of Commons and the Senate be reformed?*

In the Parliament buildings, in Ottawa, the Governor General, Members of Parliament, and Senators perform the legislative functions of the federal government of Canada.

The Components of Parliament: An Overview

In theory, all three components of Parliament—the Governor General, the House of Commons, and the Senate—have a major part in the lawmaking process. In practice, however, the House of Commons has the most important role in deciding what laws Canada is to have. The legislative role of the other two components of Parliament is, by comparison, of limited significance.

Before considering the lawmaking process and the role of each component of Parliament within it, you will find it useful to have some background information about the three components. First of all, it is important to realize that, in Canada, the **head of state**—the ultimate source of legislative authority—is the **monarch** (the King or Queen).

The **Governor General** is the representative of the monarch in Canada. Although formally appointed by the monarch, the person chosen to be Governor General is always recommended by the Prime Minister of Canada.

In Canada, a government is formed by the political party which wins a federal election by having the greatest number of representatives elected to the House of Commons. The leader of the party which forms the government—the government party—is the **Prime Minister**. The **House of Commons** consists of all the representatives elected to the House, who are called **Members of Parliament** (MP's). MP's of all parties who are not members of the government party make up the **opposition**. The party which has the greatest number of elected representatives next to the government party is called the **Official Opposition**.

From the MP's of his own party, the Prime Minister chooses certain members to form a body known as the **Cabinet**. The members of the Cabinet, called **ministers**, are responsible for the various government **departments** or **ministries**: Finance, Justice, Transport, and so on. The ministers are the Prime Minister's closest advisors. Occasionally, the

Canada's head of state, Queen Elizabeth II, chats informally with Prime Minister Brian Mulroney.

Cabinet includes members of the Senate as well as MP's.

The **Senate** has 104 members, appointed by the Governor General on the advice of the Prime Minister. Since this advice is always taken, it is, in effect, if not in theory, the Prime Minister who decides upon Senate appointments. Until 1965, Senate appointments were for life; now, senators must retire by the age of 75.

QUESTIONS

1. **(a)** Name the three components of Parliament.
   (b) Which has the major role in the lawmaking process?
2. What is the role of Cabinet ministers within the federal government?

The Lawmaking Process

Figure 2.1 is a flowchart summarizing the stages by which the ideas of the government party are transformed into laws. The path shown here is typical, though some legislation may follow a slightly different route. A piece of proposed legislation is called a **bill**. A bill that goes through all the necessary stages becomes a **law**.

FIGURE 2.1 *The Legislative Process*

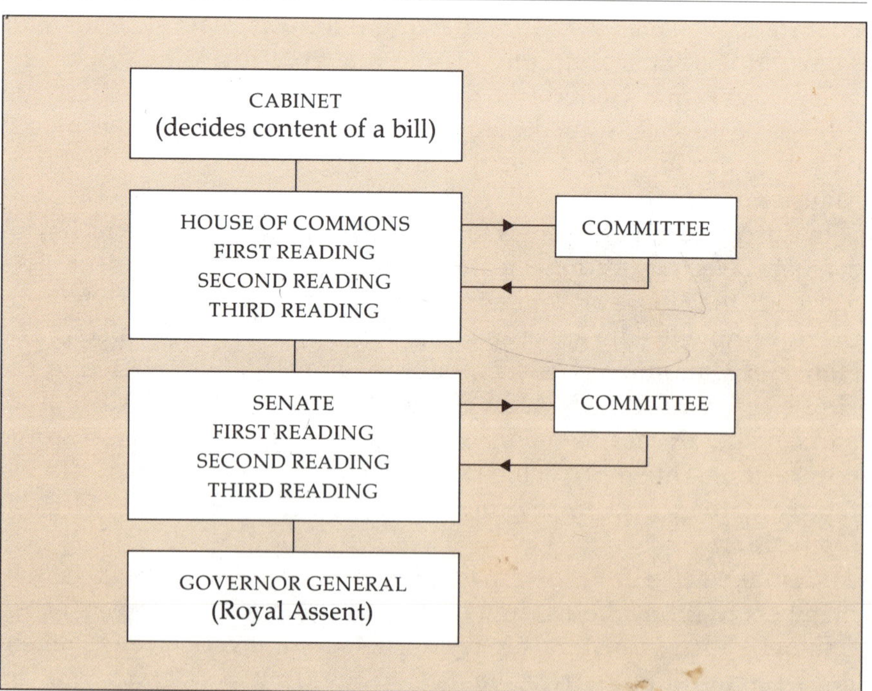

Party Whips stand before the chair of the Clerk of the House to indicate that the Members of Parliament are prepared to conduct the business of the House of Commons.

It is clear from the diagram that all three components of Parliament take part in the legislative process. The idea for a given bill usually originates with the Cabinet. The bill goes first to the House of Commons, and then to the appropriate **House of Commons committee**. These committees consist of 10 to 15 MP's, from all parties in the House, who have special knowledge of or interest in the subject of a certain bill. Because the government party has the greatest number of MP's, however, most committee members will come from that party. From the House of Commons, the bill goes to the Senate and then to the appropriate **Senate committee**. Senate committees are structured in the same way as House of Commons committees. If the bill is passed, it goes to the Governor General for Royal Assent: that is, the Governor General agrees to and signs the bill on behalf of the Queen; this gives it the force of law.

Now you will examine the workings of the legislative process in detail. James Gillies, who was a Toronto-area Progressive Conservative MP from 1972 to 1979, describes the process as follows.

> It is the function of Parliament to govern the country through the making of laws. But how does Parliament do this? What is the procedure through which an idea is converted into legislation?
>
> Before tracing the steps followed in the making of a law, it is important to remember two facts about the way our parliamentary system works.
>
> First, legislation involving the spending of money may only be introduced in the House of Commons. The Senate cannot originate any laws that require use of taxpayers' dollars. Since almost everything requires some spending of funds, this means that practically all legislation starts in the House of Commons.
>
> Secondly, practically all legislation considered in Parliament originates with the government...party. ...The rules of the House of Commons permit individual members of Parliament to introduce legislation so long as it does not involve the spending of money. But an individual, or private, member's bill seldom becomes law. So it is the responsibility of the party in power to make Parliament work, and to bring forth legislation for consideration by all the members of the House of Commons.

James Gillies was a Toronto-area Progressive Conservative MP from 1972 to 1979.

The actual process of converting the ideas (of the government) into law begins when specific legislation is placed on what is known as the **Order Paper**. The Order Paper is simply the agenda of the House of Commons—it states what the House is going to do.

Let us suppose that the government decides it wants to establish a Food Prices Review Board. The House leader, the MP in charge of organizing formal House procedures for the governing party, gives notice to the clerk of the House of Commons—the person who handles the printing of information, sending out of notices, and so on—that the government intends to introduce a law establishing a Food Prices Review Board. The notice of this intention is printed in the Order Paper so that all members know it is coming forward.

Within the next day or so, the cabinet minister responsible for the legislation stands up in the House and asks permission to introduce a bill calling for the establishment of the Board. Such permission is given almost automatically. The minister gives a short statement of what the legislation is intended to do, and asks that the bill, which describes precisely what is to be done, be printed. This is known as **first reading**. At this stage there is no debate—it is basically a time for the presentation of information. The bill is printed and circulated to all members of the House for examination and study.

The real debate about the bill comes at **second reading**, which occurs when the bill is once again placed before the House by the government. At second reading, the minister responsible for the legislation gives a major speech on why the legislation is needed and what it will do. Those who oppose the bill give their reasons for thinking that it is unnecessary or ineffective. Debate may last for several days, with many people speaking, although no one may speak more than once. Also, except for the cabinet minister introducing the bill and one opposition critic, no one may speak for more than an agreed upon time—usually twenty minutes. Eventually a vote is taken. If the vote passes, it means that the majority of the members of the House of Commons has approved the bill in principle; in this case, they approved the establishment of a Food Price Review Board.

However, although the bill is passed in principle, there may be many details in the legislation which are not clear or must be modified. Consequently, the vote at second reading, as well as approving the bill in principle, sends it to a committee for further study.

The committee work is extremely important; it is in the committee that the exact meaning of a particular paragraph in a proposed law is clarified, and that problems the bill may have are solved. It is also possible for changes to be suggested and agreed upon. While the general purpose of the legislation cannot be changed, it can generally be improved in committee. The minister responsible for the legislation appears before the committee and answers questions that may be raised about the legislation.

Once all the sections have been agreed to by the committee, the bill is formally placed before the House of Commons for **third reading**. Third

A Senate legal affairs committee conducts a hearing on a bill in front of cameras for the first time in 1978.

reading is usually rather routine, although there may be debate. Once the bill is given third reading, the House of Commons is finished with their consideration of the proposed legislation.

Before the legislation becomes law it must be passed by the Senate, which follows substantially the same procedure as the House. When the Senate reports to the House of Commons that it has passed the bill, all that remains before it becomes an act of law is for it to be given royal assent. This is done by the Governor General, and is a purely formal step. Royal assent is never withheld.

And so through this process a Food Prices Review Board with very specific powers and responsibilities can be established. In exactly the same way all our other legislation is made. It may seem like a cumbersome process and at times it is. But think of the great protection that it provides everyone. The government cannot do anything without creating laws, without going through a process that ensures that its proposals are throughly debated and discussed. Legislation is improved in the process and, more important, power is checked.

CLOSE-UP

The Legislative Process in Action: The Case of Investment Canada

A key policy difference in recent years between the Conservatives and the Liberals has been in the area of foreign investment. In 1974, a Liberal government created the Foreign Investment Review Agency (FIRA). FIRA's mandate was to monitor the Canadian operations of foreign-based companies. When elected ten years later, the Conservatives under Brian Mulroney moved quickly to replace FIRA with a new agency, Investment Canada. While it would still monitor foreign investment, the new agency would make it much easier for foreign companies to do business in Canada.

Defenders of the proposed Investment Canada argued that it would attract much-needed funds from abroad, and in doing so would create new businesses and new jobs for Canadians. Critics contended that it would allow foreign domination of the Canadian economy.

Bill C-15, the *Investment Canada Act*, was without a doubt the most hotly debated piece of legislation passed by the Conservative government during its first year in office. The huge Conservative majority elected in September 1984, virtually ensured passage of the legislation from the outset. However, rather than be labelled dictatorial, the government allowed delaying tactics from the opposition. The vastly outnumbered Liberals and New Democrats mounted a spirited and lengthy attack on the bill. For Bill C-15 to get from first reading in the House of Commons to Royal Assent took seven months. Lengthy debate, a motion to stall debate, detailed committee examination, and proposals for numerous amendments—all delayed the process of turning Bill C-15 into the law which created Investment Canada.

The bill was introduced on December 7, 1984 by Regional Economic Development Minister Sinclair Stevens, who asked the House "for leave to introduce Bill C-15, an Act respecting Investment in Canada". The motion was agreed to, and Bill C-15 passed first reading.

A few days later, Stevens again addressed the House to "move that the bill be read a second time and referred to the Standing Committee on Regional Development". A lengthy debate ensued, with Liberal Lloyd Axworthy and NDP member Ian Deans attacking the bill. More opposition speeches on the bill occupied the next few days in the House until, on December 17, Liberal Herb

Gray, the Opposition House Leader, made an amending motion that the bill "be read a second time six months hence".

Gray used a common opposition tactic, known as the "six-months' hoist", to stall further debate, and hence a second-reading vote, on the bill. Whether or not his motion would pass, the introduction of the motion succeeded in delaying debate for a full month; the House of Commons adjourned for the Christmas break. When the House resumed sitting on January 21, debate continued on Gray's "six-month hoist" amending motion. Three days later a vote was taken; not surprisingly, Gray's motion was defeated.

Conservative MP Monique Tardif, who was parliamentary secretary to Sinclair Stevens, noted that 56 of the 70 opposition members had spoken on Bill C-15, and made a motion for a vote to stop debate. This motion was voted on and passed, 162 to 34. The House then voted that the Bill proceed to second reading itself, and that vote passed 164 to 41.

On January 30, Bill C-15 officially went to the Standing Committee on Regional Development (SCRD). Of the 17 members of the committee, 13 were Conservatives, two were Liberals, and two were from the NDP. All members of the committee had the opportunity to recommend witnesses from various sectors of the Canadian economy who would present their views on the proposed Investment Canada. In total, 12 groups of witnesses were heard over the course of two months. After this, on April 2, the committee members began a detailed study and discussion of each of the bill's 50 clauses. The SCRD report on Bill C-15 was officially presented to the House of Commons two weeks later.

By May 2, second and third reading debate on Bill C-15 had consumed 80 hours of the House's time. Opposition members had moved a total of 99 amendments to the bill. Sinclair Stevens threatened but did not officially move to invoke **closure**. This device would have allowed the government to use its majority to pass a time limit on further debate on Bill C-15. After Stevens' threat, the opposition temporarily withheld further discussion of the bill. Neither the Liberals nor the NDP wanted to gamble that Stevens would call their bluff, and so they decided to postpone the few remaining hours of House time which seemed to be all that was to be left them for the Bill C-15 debate. In the interim, they searched for an obscure ruling in the Standing Orders that would permit the debate to continue without a fixed time limit. If they had found such a ruling, they could have persuaded the Speaker to disallow closure, if and when Stevens made a motion on it. However, their tactic failed, and on May 21, Stevens made a motion to restrict further debate on the bill to two days of House time. The motion passed 182 to 50.

A total of 43 amendments to Bill C-15 was then put forth by the opposition. When voted on, all but one were defeated. After seven months, at midnight on June 30th, the *Investment Canada Act* officially became law.

QUESTIONS

1. What basic difference of opinion exists between the Liberal Party and the Conservative Party on the subject of foreign investment?
2. Why is it not surprising that Herb Gray's "six-months' hoist" motion on Bill C-15 was defeated?
3. How did the composition of the Standing Committee on Regional Development make it unlikely that Bill C-15 would be altered much when in committee?
4. Why did the SCRD listen to witnesses during the deliberations on Bill C-15?

QUESTIONS

1. In legislative terms, what is a bill?
2. What is the Order Paper?
3. What is "first reading"?
4. If a bill passes second reading, why is a third reading necessary?
5. How may the work of a committee affect a bill before third reading?

The Role of the Governor General

What is known as a **session of Parliament** usually lasts a year or more. The opening of each new session of Parliament is accompanied by ceremonies in which the Governor General is a central figure. On this occasion, the chief function of the Governor General is to read the Speech from the Throne. This speech, prepared by the Prime Minister's staff with input from key Cabinet ministers and their staff, announces in general terms what legislation the government hopes to have passed during the session. Both senators and MP's gather in the Senate chamber to hear the address. The topics covered in the Throne Speech are usually prefaced with such statements as "in this session, my government intends to..." or "my government hopes to accomplish...". The use of "my" signifies that, in theory, it is the Governor General, as the representative of the monarch, who has appointed the Prime Minister and the members of the Cabinet.

Once the Throne Speech is over, the Governor General does not normally visit the Senate until the session comes to a close. While it is the Prime Minister who decides when this is to take place, it is the Governor General who, in the Senate, **prorogues** Parliament: that is, declares the session over.

Between the opening and prorogation of Parliament, the Governor General's legislative role is the giving of Royal Assent. The signing of the bills, which symbolizes Royal Assent, takes place in the Governor General's offices in Rideau Hall. The Governor General is not allowed to enter the House of Commons at any time, nor is the Queen or King during visits to Ottawa. This rule dates back to 1642, when King Charles I of England was barred from the House of Commons as he tried to arrest some members.

In addition to ceremonial and legislative duties, the Governor General has other responsibilties which will be discussed in the next chapter.

Governor General Jeanne Sauvé reads the Speech from the Throne during the opening ceremonies of a session of Parliament.

QUESTIONS

1. Describe the functions of the Governor General in the opening and closing of a session of Parliament.
2. In general terms, what are the contents of the Speech from the Throne?
3. **(a)** What is the Governor General's role in the lawmaking process?
   (b) Why do you think the Governor General's legislative role is not more extensive?

The Role of the House of Commons

To understand the part played by the House of Commons in the legislative process, you must know about the different roles of MP's within the House. First of all, most MP's belong to political parties. The very few who do not are known as **independents**. Second, a select group of the government party's MP's belong to the Cabinet. Third, certain MP's from all parties belong to committees. Fourth, one MP (usually from the government party) acts as the **Speaker of the House**. In this section, you will consider each of these roles of MP's in turn, then look at the schedule of a typical week in the House of Commons.

The Parties

The members belonging to different parties are grouped on opposite sides of the Commons chamber, which is located at the west end of the

Centre Block of the Parliament Buildings in Ottawa. On the government side, the front rows or **benches** are reserved for the Prime Minister and the Cabinet. The ministers holding major **portfolios** (departmental responsibilities) sit closest to the Prime Minister. On the opposition side, directly across from the Prime Minister, sits the **leader of the Official Opposition**. Each opposition party has a **shadow Cabinet**, a group of MP's selected by each party leader to be critics of a specific minister on the government side. MP's on both sides of the House who occupy seats in the rear areas of the chamber are termed **backbenchers**.

The Progressive Conservative caucus room is closed to visitors while a meeting is in progress.
Why do you suppose caucus meetings are not open to the public?

Not all party activity related to Commons business takes place within the chamber itself. One morning a week is set aside for caucus meetings. The **caucus** is simply the gathering of all of a party's MP's. Each party gathers in a separate meeting room to discuss policy, problems, and public opinion. The proceedings of caucus meetings are not made public. If an MP or group of MP's has a disagreement with the party leader, the issue will be thrashed out behind the closed doors of a caucus meeting, not on the floor of the Commons chamber. During meetings of the House, a party's members are supposed to show **solidarity**, that is, to present a united front. Should it happen that an MP votes against his or her own party on one of the readings of a bill, that MP may be expelled from caucus. In other words, the dissident member will continue to be an MP, but will no longer be considered a member of the party. In cases of exceptionally strong disagreement, an MP may voluntarily leave the caucus or even resign his or her seat.

Once the caucus reaches agreement on an idea from the Cabinet, the idea is drafted into a bill. When there is a majority government—in other words, when one party has over half the total number of seats in the House of Commons—party solidarity ensures that the government party's bills get more than half the votes on any reading. Hence, the bills become law. The situation is different when there is a minority government. The party in power needs some opposition support for any bill to get the required majority of votes on its various readings. During the 1972–74 Liberal minority government, for example, the Liberals tailored some of their legislation to satisfy the NDP in order to secure their support. Once the NDP withdrew that support, the government fell, and an election had to be called.

The practice of party solidarity has come in for criticism from many quarters because the making of a party policy is dominated by a handful of MP's on both sides of the House. On the government side, policy is, for all intents and purposes, drawn up by Cabinet ministers and their staff. If a certain minister has the support of the Prime Minister and most of the Cabinet on a policy issue, it is usually the case that the policy will be transformed into a bill and then become law. The policy may be slightly modified in caucus, but the Cabinet generally, though not always, achieves its objectives.

The Cabinet

The Cabinet has a vital role in both the creation and the implementation of government policy. In other words, the Cabinet wields both legislative and executive power. This combination of powers makes the Cabinet the most important group in the legislative and executive branches of government. The selection of the Cabinet, which is an executive responsibility of the Prime Minister, is discussed in the next chapter. For now, only the lawmaking role of the Cabinet within the House of Commons will be considered.

A leading Canadian political scientist, R. M. Dawson, has summed up the significance of the Cabinet's legislative power as follows:

> The cabinet wields extensive authority over all legislation and exclusive authority over the initiation of all financial legislation; the cabinet controls the time, regulates the business, and apportions the energies of the House almost from hour to hour during every day of its meeting. There is virtually nothing which the House does or discusses in which the cabinet has not some interest, and in most of these matters it exercises a paramount control. The functions of Parliament would seem to have degenerated until all that it does is to pass on the measures which the cabinet chooses to offer within the time which the cabinet chooses to allow; to raise and spend the money which the cabinet desires without the opportunity of increasing either revenue or expenditure; to fall in constantly behind the majority, which in turn automatically falls in behind the cabinet. Responsible government would appear to have suffered a strange and alarming inversion: the cabinet is no longer responsible to the Commons; the Commons seems instead to have become responsible to the cabinet.

Most Canadian political scientists would agree with this assessment. There are, however, some restraints on the legislative power of the Cabinet. Occasionally (if not often), an idea devised in the Cabinet will run into objections from the other MP's of the government party. If they object strongly enough, the Cabinet will abandon the idea. For example, in the autumn of 1986, Brian Mulroney's Conservative Cabinet considered the idea of a massive increase in postal rates. Many of the party's non-Cabinet MP's, aware that their constituents would strongly oppose the increase, argued against it. Faced with such resistance from its own party colleagues, the Mulroney Cabinet dropped the proposed postal rate increase.

The Committees

At any given time during a sitting of the House of Commons, it is likely that fewer than half of the MP's will be present. Those absent are often involved in the many other duties of a Member of Parliament, one of the most important of which is attending committee meetings. As you have read, the committees are most active between the second and third reading of a bill.

In 1969, and again in 1982, reforms made to the committee system significantly increased the workload and importance of committees. We shall look later at these reforms. The result is that the formal debates in the House now have even less influence on legislation. At the Commons stage, it is committees outside of a minister's office which are responsible for the polishing and refining of bills.

Proposed legislation on specific matters such as employment, transportation, and immigration is carefully studied by standing committees before recommendations concerning bills are made.

Steel Mill, Selkirk (top right), Manitoba

Logging truck (below), Nanaimo, B.C.

Immigration procedure (bottom right), Vancouver, B.C.

While there are several types of committees—for instance, special, joint, striking, and legislative committees—perhaps the most important are the committees of the whole and standing committees. **Committees of the whole** are composed of the entire House of Commons. Their meetings are held in the Commons chamber, and all MP's present are considered to be committee members. During sessions of the committee of the whole, normal rules of parliamentary procedure are relaxed, and so the meetings are fairly informal. These sessions are reserved for consideration of special sorts of legislation; for instance, clause-by-clause study of the government's annual budget.

In the mid-1980's, there were 13 **standing committees**, which tended to be matched with the major ministries. For example, in the

1984–85 session of Parliament there were committees on Justice and Legal Affairs; Labour, Manpower and Immigration; and Transport and Communications, among others. While the committees themselves are more or less permanent, their members are not; normally, membership is rotated among MP's every two sessions of Parliament. As noted previously, all parties are represented on committees, but the government party dominates.

Standing committees have several tasks, the two most important of them being the study of legislation and the study of public expenditures. The first involves the clause-by-clause study of bills, after which committee members may suggest amendments. If a majority of committee members favours the amendments to a given bill, they are included in the committee's report. Once the report is finished, it goes back to the House and is presented. The report's recommendations form the basis of the third reading debate on the bill.

The study of public expenditures involves standing committees in the review of government departments' spending plans. For example, the Committee on Transport and Communications would study the budgets of both the Transport and the Communications departments, and recommend ways in which their budgets could be better arranged. Standing committees cannot recommend an increase in spending; they can only accept, reject, or reduce the spending estimates already drawn up by the various departments.

The Speaker

The Speaker acts as the "referee" of the House of Commons. He or she sits at one end of the House of Commons on a large raised chair. If the speaker is absent, a Deputy Speaker takes charge. The tables in the center aisle are for the clerk of the House and assistants, who *transcribe* (write down) the proceedings of the House.

Until 1986, the Speaker was appointed by the Prime Minister, who, in consultation with the other party leaders, would select an MP from the government party. Their choice would then be confirmed by a vote of the House. Since 1986, a new, more complicated procedure is used; the entire House of Commons votes for different MP's, until the choice of candidates is narrowed down to one.

The Speaker is responsible for applying and enforcing the rules of Commons' procedure, by which parliamentary business is conducted. In enforcing the rules of parliamentary "fair play", the Speaker must be entirely neutral and impartial. For instance, if a member—even one from the Speaker's own party—violates these practices, the Speaker will rule the MP "out of order", and instruct the person to sit down. In some cases, the member may be expelled from the House for the remainder of the day's sitting, or even the entire session.

The House of Commons Speaker ensures that parliamentary procedure is followed. Here, a frustrated John Bosley, Speaker in 1984, asks Liberal MP Jean-Claude Malepart to withdraw his comment that Prime Minister Brian Mulroney was a liar.

The Speaker and the Members of Parliament in the House of Commons are guided by a set of rules known as Standing Orders which govern the procedure of the House and enable the M.P.s to carry on the business of the House of Commons. The Standing Orders, like the rules of sports, are changed from time to time, to help ensure that they fit the needs of the Members of Parliament and the Canadians who elected them.

Questions and comments may be made in either English or French. The Speaker is expected to be able to make rulings in whichever official language is in use at the moment. Simultaneous translation ensures that MP's who are not bilingual are able to understand what is being said at all times. Each MP's desk is equipped with earphones hooked up to the translator's booth, to be used as needed.

The Speaker's most difficult single task is refereeing the 45-minute time slot in the early afternoon known as **Question Period**, the liveliest event of a typical Commons day. During this time the opposition parties dominate the proceedings. The procedure is that an opposition MP will direct a question, usually to the Prime Minister or another minister. The Speaker does not have to be notified of the question in advance. The question cannot be about a specific bill on the agenda; rather, it will usually concern a current event within the jurisdiction of a particular minister. For example, a question regarding the recent arrival of refugees will normally be directed to the Minister of Employment and Immigration. Since television coverage of the Commons began in 1977, many critics have observed that Question Period resembles a shouting match, with many MP's performing more for the cameras than for the House. As a result, the Speaker sometimes has trouble maintaining discipline during Question Period.

CLOSE-UP

A Week in the House of Commons

Table 2.1 shows the schedule for a typical week in the House of Commons according to a schedule set up in 1982. A representative from each party, known as the party House Leader, meets weekly with the Speaker. Between them they draw up a list of members who will speak at a given time on a certain day, and in what order. These prior arrangements are necessary to ensure that each day's proceedings will be orderly.

As you can see, the bulk of the Commons agenda is devoted to government business. These are essentially, if not entirely, the periods during which specific bills are being debated.

TABLE 2.1 *A Week in the House of Commons*

HOUR	MONDAY	TUESDAY	WEDNESDAY	THURSDAY	FRIDAY
11:AM	Government Business	Government Business	(Party Caucus Meetings)	Government Business	S.O. 21 / Question Period / Routine Government Business
12:00 NOON					
1:00 PM	Suspension (Lunch)	Suspension (Lunch)		Suspension (Lunch)	Suspension (Lunch)
2:00 PM	S.O. 21 / Question Period	S.O. 21 / Question Period	S.O. 21 / Question Period	S.O. 21 / Question Period	Government Business
3:00 PM	Routine	Routine	Routine	Routine	
4:00 PM	Government Business	Government Business	Private Members' Business	Government Business	
5:00 PM					
6:00 PM	Adjournment Debate (Late Show)	Adjournment Debate (Late Show)		Adjournment Debate (Late Show)	
Evening	Possible Emergency Debates OR Sittings Beyond Normal Hour of Adjournment (Mondays, Tuesdays, Thursdays) →	→	→	→	

Note: *The daily and weekly timetable outlined in this Table is that which operated under the experimental Standing Orders adopted by the House of Commons to take effect in December 1982 (subsequently renewed in December 1983). This schedule was outdated in 1986.

S.O. 21 refers to a **Standing Order**, under the 1982 schedule, that enables the Speaker to allow members to make statements of no longer than 60 seconds on issues of importance to them. Fifteen minutes are set aside each day for these statements.

Routine refers to the times when the Speaker normally makes rulings on the proceedings so far, and on those which are to come next. The contents of this period are not unlike the morning announcements on your school's public address system.

The **Adjournment Debate**, or "Late Show", is generally the last event of the parliamentary day, unless for some reason the sitting is extended. From 6:00 p.m. to 6:30 p.m., any three MP's are given up to 7 minutes each to raise issues which, for the most part, concern unresolved items from Question Period. One 3-minute reply to each item is allowed.

As you will notice in the Table 2.1, the Wednesday schedule contains two items not on the other days' agenda: party caucus meetings and private members' business. The time allotted for **private members' business** gives backbench MP's a further chance to air their views. Many political observers have suggested that the role of government party backbenchers in the Commons chamber is often reduced to applauding a minister's speech or voting with the party on one of the readings of a bill. On the opposition side, too, these observers note, backbenchers are often little more than echo chambers for the speeches of the party leaders or the shadow Cabinet.

On Wednesday afternoons, any MP—usually a backbencher—may attempt to introduce a bill or motion on his or her own initiative. For example, a backbench MP who feels strongly about changing the law on an issue such as capital punishment or abortion may use the occasion to set forth a bill on the topic. However, the parliamentary rules on private members' business make it nearly impossible for such bills to get beyond first reading; as a result, these bills almost always "die". The real purpose of private members' business is, then, not so much to introduce legislation as to allow backbenchers to express an opinion, or to raise matters which concern them or their constituents.

The schedule shown in Table 2.1 is departed from during certain special periods in a session of Parliament. During these periods, generally known as **opposition days**, the time normally reserved for government business is given to the opposition. For example, the eight days following the Throne Speech and the six days following the government budget speech are set aside for opposition speeches. A minimum of another 25 **supply days**—so called because they are "supplied" to the opposition—is also set aside during each session.

QUESTIONS

1. What are the four roles of MP's within the House of Commons?

2. **(a)** What is a shadow Cabinet?
(b) What is the purpose of a shadow Cabinet?

3. Why are disagreements among the MP's of the same party resolved in caucus?

4. Why do minority governments have to be aware of the views of MP's of other parties within the House of Commons?

5. What is the committee of the whole?

6. How is the detailed study of public expenditures carried out within Parliament?

7. What is the main role of the Speaker of the House of Commons?

The Role of the Senate

Since the creation of the Senate in 1867, members have been required to be at least 30 years of age and to own property worth at least $4000 in the province where they reside. When senators die or retire, it is the privilege of the Prime Minister, with the formal approval of the Governor General to decide who will be appointed to replace them and at what time.

At the time of Confederation, the primary purpose of the Senate was to act as a second legislative house providing regional, rather than popular, representation. That is, the Senate would give equal representation to all regions of the country in order to balance the large number of Commons seats held by Ontario. Today, of the 104 Senate seats, Ontario and Québec have 24 each. The four western provinces also hold 24 Senate seats (six apiece), as do the Maritimes (ten each for New Brunswick and Nova Scotia, four for P.E.I.). Newfoundland has six Senate seats, while the Yukon and the Northwest Territories have one.

The Senate's second major purpose is to give "sober second thought" to legislation coming from the House of Commons. In theory, the Senate has always had the power to **veto** (forbid) legislation from the House. A bill that has successfully passed three readings in the House of Commons must also pass three readings in the Senate. However, only in extremely rare cases has the Senate ever voted down legislation passed by the House, though it may occasionally stall bills. In 1987, for instance, the Senate seemed to reflect the views of a large number of Canadians when it stalled a drug patent bill. On the other hand, when the Liberal-dominated Senate tried in 1985 to block a spending bill already passed by the Conservative majority in the House of Commons, the outcry from the public and the MP's was such that the Senate backed down.

A third purpose of the Senate is to "polish" legislation from the Commons. On occasion, some bills may already be under study by a Senate committee before third reading in the Commons. As a general practice, the Senate does not make significant changes in the actual content of bills. Rather, its committees help to clean up the precise wording or technical details of bills. Such tasks are unglamorous, routine ones which are often overlooked, but they are very important.

Another function of the Senate, although it is a "last resort", is to supply Cabinet ministers when MP's are not available. A Prime Minister will always, by tradition, have at least one representative from each province in the Cabinet. In 1979, however, the Conservatives had only two MP's elected in Québec; in 1974, the Liberals had no elected representatives in Alberta, and in 1980, they had none in any of the three westernmost provinces. In these cases, Prime Ministers Joe Clark and Pierre Trudeau, respectively, appointed senators as Cabinet ministers in order to give Cabinet representation to the provinces which had failed to elect enough, or any, MP's from the government party.

QUESTIONS

1. What are the four main purposes of the Senate?

2. Describe the legislative functions of the Senate.

3. Explain the public reaction to the Senate's attempt in 1985 to block a spending bill that had been passed by the House of Commons.

4. Under what circumstances might a senator serve as a Cabinet minister?

Power and Influence in the Legislative Process

The legislative process within the Canadian parliamentary system has been criticized on several grounds. One objection is that the average citizen seems to have little or no influence over what happens in the House of Commons. Another is that MP's have too little influence through committee work, and reforms are needed to balance the power of the Cabinet with the rest of the Commons. A third argument is that the Senate is irrelevant, outdated, and needs reform. Each of these criticisms is considered in turn below.

Influencing the Lawmakers

There are at least three ways in which citizens can, to some degree, influence events in the House of Commons.

The first and probably most important way is through elections. Any

Bob White, leader of the National Auto Workers Union, speaks out against the proposed Free Trade Agreement between Canada and the United States.

How do you suppose leaders of large organizations can influence government policy?

government that passes legislation which proves unpopular with large segments of the population does so at its own peril. When the next election comes around, that government may well find itself out of office. For this reason, controversial legislation is generally passed at least a year prior to an election, in the hope that the voters will have either accepted it or forgotten about it by election time. This strategy works only sometimes. For example, the short-lived Progressive Conservative government of 1979–80 attempted to pass a budget that would have allowed petroleum prices in Canada to rise significantly. Before the legislation could be passed, the government fell on a non-confidence vote. The return of the Liberals to power in the 1980 election was largely attributable to the loss of Conservative support in Ontario, where many voters would have been hurt by the proposed price increase.

Citizens can also exercise some influence over legislation through direct or indirect contact with their MP's. Many MP's take regular polls or telephone surveys in their constituencies in order to find out the public's opinion on various issues. If enough MP's of the government party discover that a certain policy is unpopular, and if enough of them speak out in caucus, the Cabinet will have to rework or reject that policy. Such was the case with the rejected postal rate increase of 1986.

Another way of affecting legislation involves **special interest groups**, which will be discussed in greater detail in the chapter on elections. These groups are active between, as well as during, elections. Sometimes they arise almost spontaneously in a reaction against government policy. If their protest is forceful enough, the Cabinet backs off. A good example of a spontaneous special interest protest occurred in 1984–85. In late 1984, the Conservative Cabinet decided to **de-index** old age pensions, that is, to do away with the practice of raising

This war veteran protested that the Québec government's Bill 101 would take away his right to speak English in Québec. In 1977, the bill became law. In 1981, however, the Supreme Court of Canada ruled that both official languages must be used in the legislature and courts of Québec.

Canadian senior citizens protest the Progressive Conservative 1985 proposal to de-index pensions. The government quickly dropped the highly unpopular plan.

pensions to keep pace with inflation. Across the country, newspaper editorials and letters to the editor, radio phone-in shows, and angry mail to MP's made it clear that the measure was highly unpopular. The protest against de-indexation climaxed in June 1985, with a massive demonstration of senior citizens on Parliament Hill. Within a week, the government announced that the plan to de-index pensions would be dropped.

Reforming Parliamentary Committees

Many parliamentary observers believe that the legislative and executive roles of the Cabinet have become too closely interrelated, with the result that the Cabinet has too much power and ordinary MP's have too little. Committee membership is perhaps the most significant way in which most MP's can have some effect on the government. It follows, therefore, that increased power for the committees should lead to increased power for ordinary MP's.

The recommendations set out in the 1984–85 *Report of the Special Committee on Reform of the House of Commons* included a redefinition of the power of parliamentary committees. Their effect would be to make the executive branch, as represented by ministers and their departments, more accountable to the legislative branch, as represented by the committees.

One recommendation suggested that parliamentary committees be given more power to examine departmental documents currently unavailable to them. Suppose, for example, that the Minister of Regional Economic Expansion intended to grant subsidies to companies willing to locate in regions of high unemployment. The Standing Committee on Regional Development would be empowered to collect and analyze sensitive departmental documents having to do with the proposed subsidies. As well, the committee would have more power to call witnesses to committee hearings, including public servants working in that department.

Another recommendation was that parliamentary committees be allowed to question persons nominated to be deputy ministers or directors of Crown corporations. Since these nominations are often matters of patronage, such a measure would, in effect, make some patronage appointments subject to the scrutiny of committees. For example, persons nominated by the Cabinet to be directors of such Crown corporations as Air Canada or Via Rail would be obliged to appear for questioning before the Committee on Transport and Communications.

As of the late 1980's, these recommendations have not been acted upon. Reform of the House of Commons remains an unresolved issue.

CLOSE-UP

What Purpose Does the House of Commons Serve? Three Views

"The first view of the purpose of the House of Commons and its members which you will read here comes from a leading scholar on Canadian political life, Professor J. R. Mallory of McGill University in Montréal. The second is that of George Bain, a noted journalist who has written for numerous newspapers and magazines. The third view comes from Jean Chrétien, a former Liberal MP and senior Cabinet minister with more than 20 years of parliamentary experience.

A Political Scientist's View

"The first function of the House of Commons is... to act as an electoral chamber; to give a government authority, to sustain it and thus make stable government possible; and, lastly, to withdraw confidence from a government which no longer deserves to rule. . . . Most of the time we know, as soon as the election results are in, which party is to govern and that this will not change until the House is dissolved and a new election is held. Sometimes. . . no party has a majority. In that case the party which can negotiate the support of third parties can carry on as a government. When that third party support is withdrawn. . . a government will be forced to either resign or, most probably, seek a new election to settle the matter. Most of the time a government can control the House through its majority so that it is an illusion to think of the House of Commons being able to make or destroy a government at any time. Members of the House of Commons are not players in this game: they are part of the scoreboard.

"The second function of Parliament is legislation, but the role nowadays is not to make the law, but to approve what the government has proposed. This is not quite the mere formality that it sounds. Opposition parties can drag their feet, and obstruct progress until a government will either modify its proposal to get it through or abandon it. . . .

"The third function of Parliament is to act. . . as the nation's congress of opinions and committee of grievances. Ministers must answer on the floor of the House at question time, and defend in detail the operation of their departments against the criticism of opposition members. Governments today profess to pay a great deal of attention to opinion polls as a means of knowing what the public thinks, but inability to perform effectively before parliamentary criticism is still one of the most fatal faults in a minister."

—Professor J.R. Mallory

A Journalist's View

"Parliamentary government or, more correctly, Cabinet government is extraordinarily wasteful of talent and a bit of a fraud.

Think back to the last election campaign. Remember the constituency profile in the local paper, or on the local television news, containing brief sketches of the three—or was it four?—candidates from whom you could choose? However many of them there were, all but one did not make it and went back to whatever they were doing before, and disappeared from the political scene. The one went off to Ottawa to scrutinize public spending, inquire into matters of public concern, lend his or her best judgment to the modification or the strengthening of legislation, and help make the laws of the land—and also disappeared from the political scene. In any case, he or she was heard of no more in the papers or on TV.

"Most MPs are good people. They are conscientious and work

hard. They are driven, most of them, by an irrational urge to Do Something for the country. They interrupt their careers, uproot their families or live apart from them, take a lot of abuse, and are too often accused of being in it for what they can get out of it. Apart from their legislative and public-watchdog roles, they also serve as personal ombudsmen for constituents in their dealings with government bureaucracy.

"...Once the full crop of MPs is delivered to Ottawa, however, the news media show very little interest in telling the public what the non-Cabinet ones do there.

"Why? Because they know that nothing much is going to be affected by anything that is said by a backbencher in the House of Commons—or even in the committees, where there is a little more room for independent initiative. The Cabinet, made up of 40 elected people out of 282, will get its way with very little call on the brainpower of the other 242, who were elected ostensibly to help run the country. The Cabinet may take some political advice from its own backbenchers, although even there the MPs increasingly are supplanted by the quasi-scientific head-counters of the polling organizations as sources of advice on what the country can or cannot be made to swallow without gagging. For ideas about policy and legislation, the real stuff of government, the Cabinet relies on the bureaucrats."

—George Bain

A Former Cabinet Minister's View

"The most effective contributions of many MPs go unreported because they often take place in the party caucuses, which are secret. There are regional caucuses and special caucuses on various subjects, such as agriculture or regional development, but the key one is the general caucus that meets every week when Parliament is sitting. It's a chance for questions and complaints, reports and policy development, topical problems and general discussions. The caucus of the governing party includes the prime minister and his cabinet, of course, so it's a place for significant back-bench input. Sometimes MPs don't get much press attention because they don't make much use of the House of Commons, but they'll get up now and then in the caucus and speak so much sense that their views are noted; and ministers are often more devastated by a frank, well-reasoned attack from one of their own MPs than from a slew of opposition critics and reporters....

"...Many good MPs never get the recognition or the reward their influence deserves. Those who have achieved a stunning coup in caucus are the least likely to boast about it in public,

Jean Chrétien has held many Cabinet posts during his long career as a politician.

Should the selection of Cabinet ministers be left entirely to the Prime Minister? Give reasons for your answer.

because they know they would be the prime suspects in any breach of confidentiality. Many times they don't even realize that they have changed a decision by convincing a minister with a pertinent intervention. Seldom does the minister go back to them and say, 'It's because of your little speech that I decided to do things this way.'

"...Because some MPs are selected to be in the cabinet in the parliamentary system, two classes of politician are created. That's discouraging.... No doubt many more MPs want to go into the cabinet, and they often fail for reasons that have nothing to do with their capabilities or intellects. On the one hand, I like to argue that anyone who wants to be a minister badly enough, works hard, and has the talent usually becomes a minister. On the other hand, I have to recognize that because of regional representation or representation by age, sex, and ethnic background, the cabinet frequently contains people who aren't first-rate and excludes talent that should be there....

"More and more... elections are fought among party leaders. In a sweep such as the Tory victory in 1984, good members are swept out with the same broom as the bad ones, while bad ones are carried in on the coattails of the victorious party. So the work, personality, and intelligence of MPs count for less and less in the riding campaigns. In my judgment maybe no more than fifty MPs make a personal difference in the outcome of their elections. The rest tend to rely on the appeal of their leader and the luck of belonging to the winning party. The risk is that MPs will become more marginal, more expendable, and at the mercy of the leadership. Certainly fewer back-benchers will be prepared to give their leaders frank advice or tell them to go to hell if they know they can be replaced."

—Jean Chrétien
Straight From the Heart

QUESTIONS

1. Why, according to Professor Mallory, is it "an illusion to think of the House of Commons being able to make or destroy a government at any time"?
2. Why might the House of Commons be called a "committee of grievances"?
3. Why, according to George Bain, do the news media "show very little interest" in telling the public what the MP's who are not in the Cabinet are doing?

4. What are Jean Chrétien's criticisms of the Cabinet?
5. Why might an MP's influence within caucus go unrecognized by the people who elected him or her? Why might such recognition be important?
6. Which of the three points of view presented do you consider the most expert? Give reasons for your choice.

Reforming the Senate

Three major criticisms of the Senate are that it over-represents the business leaders of the country, that it serves as a patronage device for the government party, and that the distribution of seats does not give equal representation to all regions of the country on the basis of population, physical area, or regional interest. Roughly two-thirds of all senators have backgrounds as either corporate executives or corporate lawyers. The Senate is therefore suspected of being too favourable to the interests of the business community. As for the second criticism—five out of every six senators have been party executives or fundraisers, or actively involved with the party they represent. With regard to the third objection, it may be noted that British Columbia has six Senate seats, while the Atlantic provinces, which are smaller in both area and population, hold a total of 30.

The most persistent of these criticisms is the second: that because its members are appointed, the Senate is used as a patronage device. Many Canadians believe that, unless this aspect of the Senate is reformed, the institution has no place in a country which makes a claim to democratically elected representation.

Senate reform was debated during the 1980–81 constitutional negotiations, but as other issues came to predominate, the question faded. The *Constitution Act, 1982* left the Senate virtually as it was.

The issue has not died, however. The 1984 *Report of the Special Joint Committee on Senate Reform* suggested a number of changes. One would have modified the Senate's legislative power to that of a **suspensive veto**. That is, instead of having the power to reject legislation outright (a power which it almost never uses), the Senate would only be able to suspend or delay its approval for 120 days. Another proposal was that no Cabinet ministers be appointed from the Senate. A third recommendation, perhaps the most important, was that senators be elected. A senator's term of office would be nine years, after which he or she could not stand for re-election.

Like the 1984–85 recommendations for Commons reform, the recommendations for Senate reform had not been acted upon as of the late 1980's.

QUESTIONS

1. Why do governments try to pass controversial legislation at least a year before an election?
2. What did scrapping the plan to de-index old age pensions demonstrate about special interest groups?
3. What two measures are being considered to reform the House of Commons?
4. **(a)** List three Senate reforms suggested by the *Report of the Special Joint Committee on Senate Reform*.
   (b) For each, write one argument supporting the reform and one argument opposing the reform.
   (c) Which, if any, of these reforms do you support? Give reasons for your decision.

Chapter Summary

Parliament, which consists of the Governor General, the House of Commons, and the Senate, forms the legislative branch of Canada's federal government.

The lawmaking process in Parliament normally begins with the introduction by a Cabinet minister of a bill into the House of Commons. After a brief, formal first reading, the bill is debated by MP's. After this debate, which is known as second reading, the bill goes to a standing committee for study, then returns to the Commons for a third-reading debate. Once the bill passes third reading, it goes to the Senate. There, it normally follows a process parallel to the one carried out in the Commons. After third reading in the Senate is passed, the bill receives Royal Assent from the Governor General and officially becomes law.

Within the Commons, MP's have several roles. The MP's who form the Cabinet are the most powerful Members of Parliament. They introduce bills and guide them through the House. Party solidarity within the Commons ensures that backbenchers usually support their leader. Parliamentary committees are the main way in which MP's of all parties become involved in the study of bills. Presiding over the activities of the House of Commons is the Speaker, an MP who acts as a referee for the House proceedings.

The Senate's original purpose was to give "sober second thought" to bills passed by the Commons and to provide regional representation that would offset the large number of Ontario seats held in the Commons. Many observers believe that the Senate no longer effectively serves these purposes.

Critics of our legislative system argue that average citizens have little input into Parliament, and that both Houses of Parliament are in need of reform. Elections, contacts through MP's, and special interest groups do offer citizens a measure, albeit limited, of influence in government. In the mid-1980's, recommendations of parliamentary committees called for reforms of both the Commons and the Senate, but these recommendations have not been acted on.

IN REVIEW

1. What is meant by the comment that "power is checked" by the process through which bills must pass to become law?

2. Why does the Cabinet have so much legislative power?

3. Rank the duties of a Member of Parliament from most important to least important. Give reasons for your choices.

APPLYING YOUR KNOWLEDGE

1. **(a)** Why do bills go to committees during the lawmaking process?
(b) Why are members of opposition parties included on the committees?

2. Do you think it is fair that a bill proposed by an opposition member is almost always defeated? Give reasons for your answer.

3. **(a)** Explain why some Canadians prefer minority governments over majority governments.
(b) Which do you prefer, and why?

4. Why are certain days during a session of Parliament set aside for opposition speeches?

5. Closure is a method available to the ruling party to set a time limit for debate on a bill. Is this a justifiable technique? Give reasons for your answer.

FURTHER INVESTIGATION

1. Why would the withholding of Royal Assent by the Governor General create a political crisis in Canada?

2. Make a list of interest groups found within your community. Write a brief description of the concerns of each. Discover which, if any, of these groups have been successful in influencing government policy.

3. Undertake research on one or more of the following topics:
(a) why the monarch is still represented in Canada's Parliament;
(b) the pattern of federal election results in your riding during the past four elections;
(c) the senators who represent British Columbia: who they are, and when they were appointed;
(d) the names, ridings, and political party affiliations of the MP's of B.C.;
(e) what the federal budget is spent on;
(f) controversial bills currently being considered in Parliament.

CHAPTER 3

The Executive Branch

- □ *A Petro-Canada service station attendant fills your family car with gas.*
- □ *A clerk at the local post office sells you stamps.*
- □ *A counsellor at the local unemployment insurance office shows your unemployed neighbour how to file a claim for benefits.*
- □ *You turn on the CBC television news. The Governor General is seen welcoming a new ambassador to Canada.*
- □ *Later in the same broadcast, the Prime Minister is seen announcing a Cabinet shuffle.*

What do all these situations have in common? They are all examples of direct or indirect activities of the **executive branch** *of Canada's federal government. The four main components of the executive branch are the Governor General, the Prime Minister, the Cabinet, and what might loosely be called the federal* **bureaucracy**.

"Bureaucracy" is the collective term for the huge network of public service departments, Crown corporations, agencies, boards, commissions, directorates, and so on which make up the government's administrative structures. Some of these structures are within the direct control of the executive branch; others are only indirectly so. The federal bureaucracy is by far the largest part of Canada's federal government, and usually of any government. It is the sector of government with which Canadians most often come into contact in their day-to-day lives. The bureaucracy employs more Canadians and consumes more of our tax dollars than any other part of the government.

In this chapter, you will examine in turn the roles of the four main components of the federal government's executive branch. While reading the chapter, keep the following key questions in mind:

> *What is the function of each of the four components of the executive branch of our government: the Governor General, the Prime Minister, the Cabinet, and the bureaucracy?*

- *Into what three categories do Cabinet ministers fall?*
- *What is the role of Cabinet committees?*
- *What are the four main kinds of structures within the federal bureaucracy, and what is the role of each?*

The Role of the Governor General

The head of state is the person who represents the supreme executive authority of the nation. In Canada, this person is the monarch. Elizabeth II is the Queen of both Great Britain and Canada. The executive position of the monarchy in Canada is recognized by a 1952 Act of Parliament confirming Elizabeth II as Queen of Canada. It is also recognized in Canadian political vocabulary in the use of the word "Crown". For example, government-owned forests or parks (provincial as well as federal) are described as "Crown lands". Government-owned companies such as Air Canada or Canadian National (CN) are "Crown corporations". Evidence of the monarchy is visible on some Canadian postage stamps and coins, which bear likenesses of Queen Elizabeth.

In Canada, the Crown is represented by the Governor General. At first, the Governor General for Canada was chosen by the British government, subject to the monarch's approval, and was drawn from

New Brunswick received the right to produce coins from copper in 1843, and imprinted them with the head of Queen Victoria, Canada's head of state at the time. Queen Elizabeth II, Canada's current monarch, is portrayed on all of the coins minted in Canada today.

Governor General Jeanne Sauvé returns the traditional Brownie salute to a young Canadian.

Why are the ceremonial duties of the Governor General important to Canadians?

the British nobility. Later, the British government consulted with the Canadian government about the choice. Ultimately, the British government lost all say in the matter. Since 1952, Canada's Governor General has been a native-born Canadian nominated by the Prime Minister, and then officially appointed by the monarch. A Governor General's term lasts a maximum of six years, but usually five. It has been a practice since 1952 to alternate francophone and anglophone Governor Generals. Jeanne Sauvé, appointed in 1984, was the first woman to be Governor General.

The Governor General performs many ceremonial duties in his or her executive role. One of these duties is to receive new ambassadors formally to Canada. Another is to act as host to visiting heads of state. A third ceremonial duty of the Governor General is to bestow Canada's official awards, such as the Governor General's Literary Awards, given yearly to a number of Canadian authors. The Order of Canada, which is also presented by the Governor General, recognizes Canadians who have made an outstanding contribution to public life.

It is part of the Governor General's official executive role to "ask" the leader of one party or another to form a government after an election. If this party leader was Prime Minister before the election, that leader continues in office. When a different party has been elected, however, the previous Prime Minister resigns, and the leader of the elected party is called upon by the Governor General to form a government.

In normal circumstances, the leader of the party winning the most seats is asked to form a government. But when an election results in a minority government, the situation could, in theory at least, be different. For example, the 1972 federal election returned 109 Liberals and 107 Conservatives. For a few days after the election, it was uncertain which of the two parties would be supported by the NDP, with its 31 seats. As it turned out, the NDP chose to support the Liberals. It is interesting to wonder what would have happened if the NDP had decided instead to support the Conservatives. Would Liberal leader Pierre Trudeau, who had gone into the election as Prime Minister, have resigned? What would the Governor General have done in this case? And what would he have done if Trudeau had not resigned? Because of the way matters turned out, we shall never know the answers.

QUESTIONS

1. What is the government bureaucracy?

2. Why are government-owned areas called "Crown lands"?

3. Who was Canada's first woman Governor General?

4. Name two duties performed by the Governor General?

5. **(a)** What is the purpose of the Order of Canada?
(b) Why is it presented by the Governor General?

The Role of the Prime Minister

The Prime Minister is the central figure in the Canadian system of government. The powers of the office are enormous. Yet these powers are not written down in any document. Rather, they are powers of convention, ones which have evolved out of British parliamentary practice. Essentially, these powers are of four overlapping types: party leadership, appointment, governmental organization, and dissolution.

The Power of Party Leadership

According to the 1970 revisions to the *Canada Elections Act*, it is up to the party leader to decide who is acceptable as an official party candidate at election time. Although the party leader does not actually *nominate* candidates, all nominations must meet with the leader's approval. A prospective candidate who has disagreements with the party leader may win a nomination, but may fail to receive approval to campaign under the party banner. In that case, the candidate will be forced to run as an independent. The fact that this situation happens so rarely is testimony to the strength of party solidarity in the Canadian system.

When a party wins an election, its leader can claim that it has received a **mandate**. In other words, the leader can say that the voters have shown that they want the elected party to form a government, and its leader to head the government as Prime Minister. As party leader, the Prime Minister can count on the support of the governing party's MP's in the House of Commons. Many of them will owe their seats as much to their leader's popularity as to their own, if not more so. MP's of the government party will, as a rule, vote affirmatively on a bill that has resulted from the policy decisions made by the Prime Minister and the Cabinet. The Prime Minister's control of the party caucus ensures that disagreements among the governing party's MP's will be ironed out behind closed doors.

The Power of Appointment

In theory, making appointments to most major government offices is an executive power of the Governor General. Yet the Governor General always accepts the appointments suggested by the Prime Minister, even if some private disagreement exists. Recall that, in fact, the nomination of the Governor General is itself a power of the Prime Minister (with formal approval from the monarch).

After an election, the most important task a Prime Minister faces is the selection of MP's for the Cabinet. Several factors are involved in this selection, perhaps the most important two being regional and ethnic considerations. Every province is represented in the Cabinet, if possible, with Ontario and Québec having the most representation on

Prime Minister Brian Mulroney and Queen Elizabeth pose with Cabinet ministers, in 1984, at Rideau Hall, Ottawa.

Do the regional and ethnic considerations in Cabinet selection create a balanced or unbalanced representation of MP's in Cabinet? Explain your answer.

the basis of their populations. Major urban regions within each province should also be represented; there will always be Cabinet ministers from the Toronto, Montréal, and Vancouver areas, for instance. In most cases, there will be at least one anglophone minister from within Québec, and one francophone minister from outside of Québec.

Another factor in the selection of MP's for Cabinet is patronage. Prominent Cabinet posts are often given to MP's who have rendered the Prime Minister or the party a valuable service. For example, support given during a leadership convention may be repaid later with an appointment as minister in a major portfolio or department. Michael Wilson's appointment as Finance Minister after the 1984 election could, to some extent, be seen in this light. On the other hand, a Prime Minister may give major Cabinet posts to key rivals for the party leadership, as a means of reconciliation with them. Prime Minister Mulroney's appointment of Joe Clark as his Minister of External Affairs could be interpreted in this way.

An additional factor in Cabinet selection, which balances and supplements the others is competence: a Prime Minister should try to appoint MP's to portfolios which suit their skills and backgrounds. It could be argued that Michael Wilson's close ties with the Toronto business community qualified him to be Finance Minister, or that Joe Clark's international experience while he was Prime Minister in 1979–80 qualified him for External Affairs.

The Prime Minister also has the power to make a great many other appointments, generally associated with patronage. In fact, there are so many patronage positions to be filled that the Prime Minister has time to handle only several dozen or so personally. Others will be handled by the Prime Minister's Office (PMO), by consensus within the Cabinet, or by an individual minister, for postings directly within his or her jurisdiction. When the Conservatives took power in 1984, for instance, there were about 3500 positions to be filled at the discretion of the Prime Minister and/or the Cabinet, and another 10 000 to be filled at the discretion of individual ministers.

The Power of Government Organization

The Cabinet is a key executive organization, of which the Prime Minister is simultaneously both member and chairman. In addition, two other important executive organizations report directly to the Prime Minister: the Prime Minister's Office and the Privy Council Office (PCO). In various interlocking ways, these three organizations both support and extend the Prime Minister's power.

The Prime Minister and the Cabinet

The Prime Minister not only appoints Cabinet ministers, but may also abolish, create, or combine government departments and ministries. He also decides the size of the Cabinet. Joe Clark's government of 1979–80 had 30 ministers; by 1984, Pierre Trudeau's had 37. John Turner's short-lived administration in the summer of 1984 somewhat reduced the size of the Liberal Cabinet. After the election in September of that year, Brian Mulroney appointed 40 ministers to the Cabinet—the largest membership in Canadian history.

Having 30 or 40 ministers is cumbersome for day-to-day decision making. Therefore, the Prime Minister generally has a small group of eight to a dozen Cabinet ministers who serve as the main policy-making body. Depending on the Prime Minister in office, this group is known variously as the "inner Cabinet" or the "Priorities and Planning (P and P) Committee".

Cabinet appointments are by no means permanent. It is customary for a Prime Minister to shuffle the Cabinet roughly every two years, reassigning some ministers to new portfolios, dropping others, and appointing some MP's formerly not in the Cabinet as ministers. For example, Brian Mulroney's Cabinet shuffle in June 1986 gave half of his ministers new portfolios, replaced six others, and left the rest in the same portfolios. The reasons for a Cabinet shuffle are often political rather than administrative: to reinforce regional representation, to remove ineffective ministers, or to put an especially strong minister in charge of a portfolio which needs his or her guidance and leadership.

The Prime Minister's Office

The vast majority of the staff in the Prime Minister's Office is involved in routine matters: answering mail, making up schedules, screening requests for appointments and visits, and so on. But the top people in the PMO play a vital role as advisors to the Prime Minister. The head of

Principal Secretary Jim Coutts and Prime Minister Trudeau discuss the effects of party policy on the government's popularity. Why are Principal Secretaries usually partisans of the Prime Minister?

the PMO is known as the **Principal Secretary**. The person who holds this position is probably one of the half-dozen or so most influential people in the government.

The Principal Secretary is a **partisan** figure: someone closely connected to the party, and most often a close friend of the Prime Minister. Because frank, objective, and reliable advice is invaluable, it is not surprising that the Prime Minister fills this position with a close acquaintance. For example, Brian Mulroney's Principal Secretary, Bernard Roy, was an old friend from Laval University law school and was best man at Mulroney's wedding.

The Principal Secretary's task as head of the PMO is essentially to advise the Prime Minister as to how government policy will affect the party's popularity. For example, the PMO might commission a poll to assess whether the public is in favour of a change in the income tax system or of the sale of a Crown corporation. If the poll suggests that the idea is unpopular, the Prime Minister may have the policy reworked.

The PMO has grown enormously in both size and power over the past three decades. In the 1950's and early 1960's, under Louis St. Laurent and then John Diefenbaker, it had a staff of about 30. Under Lester Pearson in the mid-1960's it grew to about 40 members. By a decade later, Pierre Trudeau's PMO had a staff of nearly 100.

The Privy Council Office

Unlike the PMO, the Privy Council Office is officially part of the federal public service, the bureaucracy. It is, in theory, a non-partisan body made up of career bureaucrats who act as the "eyes and ears" of the Cabinet. In the mid-1980's, it consisted of about 300 officers and support personnel. The top figure in the PCO is the **Clerk of the Privy Council**. This person ranks as the chief public servant in Canada. Like the Principal Secretary of the PMO, the Clerk of the Privy Council is one of the most influential people in government. Unlike his or her PMO counterpart, however, the Clerk is, in theory, a neutral figure, someone without any direct personal connection to the government party. Reporting directly to the Prime Minister, the Clerk is responsible for the coordination of Cabinet meetings (which are kept secret), and for conveying Cabinet decisions to the bureaucracy.

The function of the PCO staff is to provide impartial research and study on proposals made in the Cabinet. For example, if the Cabinet decides to review Canada's immigration laws, PCO staff supplies facts, figures, projections, and other data. On the basis of these data, the PCO then submits several alternative policies to the Cabinet. The Cabinet decides which, if any, of these alternatives to accept.

The impartiality of the PCO Clerk has tended to be more theoretical than factual in recent Canadian history. The Prime Minister can hire or fire the Clerk at will. When there is a change of government, the Clerk of the Privy Council normally changes as well. For example, Michael Pitfield was appointed to the post in 1975 by Prime Minister Trudeau. Rightly or wrongly, it was widely believed that Pitfield had an influence on the Prime Minister that went beyond impartial consideration of policy. Pitfield was fired by the Conservative government which took over in 1979, then was reappointed by the Liberals when they regained power the next year. In a much-criticized move, the Liberals appointed Pitfield to the Senate in 1982. Many observers believed that it was improper for a supposedly non-partisan public servant to be awarded a Senate seat, even if Pitfield did sit as an independent.

Michael Pitfield, Clerk of the Privy Council during Trudeau's government, was appointed to the Senate in 1982. Why was this a widely criticized appointment?

The Power of Dissolution

It is the Prime Minister's role to advise the Governor General when to dissolve Parliament so that an election may be called. In theory, the power of dissolution belongs to the Governor General. In practice, however, the Governor General generally grants the Prime Minister's request for dissolution. Therefore, in reality, the Prime Minister can seek dissolution at will. The power of dissolution is, in effect, the power to set the timing of an election.

When a majority government is in power, the Prime Minister normally waits until sometime during the government's last two years of Parliament's maximum five-year term before calling an election. The election date is normally set at a time when the polls show a rise in the popularity of the government.

When a minority government is in power, the situation is less certain. Prime Ministers naturally prefer to lead a majority, rather than a minority, government. Thus, an election may be called within the first two or three years of Parliament's five-year term, as soon as the polls suggest that the governing party can secure a majority in the Commons. Such a "premature" election call is always a gamble for a

Prime Minister, but, if carefully planned, can work and produce the desired majority government. For example, in 1974, Pierre Trudeau provoked the NDP to withdraw support from his 20-month-old minority Liberal government. The Liberals were subsequently defeated in the House of Commons; Trudeau asked for dissolution and called an election. The gamble paid off, since the election returned a Liberal majority.

There are, however, limits on the power to time an election. Elections must be held every five years. A Prime Minister who waits too long may pay the price, as Trudeau did five years after his 1974 majority victory. Polls in late 1977 and early 1978 showed a large Liberal lead, and the Prime Minister's advisors urged him to call an election. But Trudeau waited another year, and, by early 1979, had little time to manoeuvre. He was required to call an election in spite of sagging Liberal support in the polls, and a minority Conservative government was brought to power.

The short life of this minority government also illustrates the limits on the Prime Minister's power to set the timing of an election. The defeat of the Conservatives after only nine months in office was totally unexpected. It resulted from a non-confidence motion organized by opposition MP's. A vote of non-confidence in a government's ability to pass legislation can occur if the opposition outnumbers the government party. In this instance, several Conservative MP's were absent during a budget debate in the House. The Conservatives found themselves outnumbered by opposition MP's who strongly objected to certain provisions in the budget, and who quickly organized a non-confidence motion, which passed. Prime Minister Clark had no choice but to ask the Governor General to dissolve Parliament and call an election, which returned a Liberal majority, again under Pierre Trudeau.

QUESTIONS

1. **(a)** List the four types of powers held by the Prime Minister.
   (b) What gives the Prime Minister the right to hold these powers?
2. How does a leader of a political party win a mandate?
3. Name and describe factors that determine Cabinet appointments.
4. Why do most Prime Ministers form an "inner Cabinet"?
5. What is the major purpose of the Prime Minister's Office?
6. The Clerk of the Privy Council is supposed to be non-partisan, but may not in fact be so. Explain.
7. How do polls influence the timing of elections?
8. Describe the collapse of Joe Clark's government.

The Role of the Cabinet

Cabinet ministers are not equal in importance or power. At the time of writing, there are three categories of Cabinet minister. The first and most important category consists of **ministers** in charge of permanent, regular government departments: Finance, Justice, and Regional Industrial Expansion, among others. The second group is comprised of **ministers of state**, who are usually in charge of relatively small, often temporary, departments linked to a larger, major one. For example, the Minister of State for Small Business and the Minister of State for Tourism are "junior" ministers whose areas of jurisdiction are in effect subdepartments of the Department of Regional Industrial Expansion. The third category is made up of **ministers without portfolio**. Such ministers have no specific areas of responsibility; they are often in the Cabinet so that a particular province or region may have its quota of Cabinet representation.

As already noted, Cabinet ministers are in almost all cases drawn from the House of Commons, although in special circumstances they may be senators. Yet there is no strict written provision that at the time of appointment a minister (even the Prime Minister) *must* be a member of either the House of Commons or the Senate. An appointee who is not in Parliament will, however, seek a Commons seat as quickly as

Otto Jelinek, discharges his responsibility as Minister of Fitness and Amateur Sport by launching Sneaker Day and National Fitness Activity Week, in 1986.

possible. An example of this relatively rare situation occurred in 1975. Pierre Juneau, head of the Canadian Radio-television and Telecommunications Commission (CRTC), was appointed by Prime Minister Trudeau as Minister of Communications. In an attempt to get a seat in the House of Commons, Juneau ran in a Montréal-area by-election. On losing the by-election, he resigned from the Cabinet.

Jean Chrétien, seen here as President of the Treasury Board in 1976, carries into the House of Commons folders containing estimates for the next fiscal year.

CLOSE-UP

The Career of a Cabinet Minister

Since elections sometimes put a new political party in power, and since between elections there are Cabinet shuffles, Cabinet ministers' jobs are temporary. From the mid-1960's to the mid-1980's, the average time in office of a Cabinet minister was from two to two-and-a-half years.

One of Canada's most famous political figures during that period was Jean Chrétien, whose views on the purpose of the House of Commons were stated in Chapter 2. Chrétien was a Québec Liberal MP from 1963 to 1985, when he retired from politics. His long and varied career shows clearly that a talented and versatile political figure can serve in a great many portfolios. It is a measure of his expertise that he was the first francophone to be Minister of Finance, a position denied to *Canadiens* since Confederation. The following list of Cabinet portfolios held by Chrétien up to the 1984 election demonstrates his political skill.

April 1967	Minister without portfolio, attached to Ministry of Finance
January 1968–July 1968	Minister of National Revenue
July 1968–August 1974	Minister of Indian Affairs and Northern Development
August 1974–September 1976	President of the Treasury Board
September 1976–September 1977	Minister of Industry, Trade and Commerce
September 1977–June 1979	Minister of Finance
March 1980–September—1982	Minister of Justice and Attorney General of Canada; Minister of State for Social Development
September 1982–July 1984	Minister of Energy, Mines and Resources
July 1984–September 1984	Deputy Prime Minister and Secretary of State for External Affairs

Since the mid-1960's, full Cabinet meetings have played an increasingly minor role in government business. Nowadays, it is rare for the entire Cabinet to meet more than once a week. Most meetings of ministers take the form of a **Cabinet committee**, the most important of which is the Priorities and Planning Committee. Since the 1970's, Canada's Cabinet structure has generally had about ten Cabinet committees, each with a half-dozen to a dozen ministers. Each committee meets approximately once a week. Priorities and Planning is generally made up of the Prime Minister and the ministers of major departments. The other Cabinet committees have a narrower focus. Because there is a considerable overlap of responsibilities among committees, it is likely that a key figure such as the Minister of Finance would sit on several committees.

Cabinet solidarity is central to the executive process of Canadian government, just as party solidarity is central to the legislative process. Cabinet decisions are always collective, despite the numerous committees. For example, if legislation were introduced to change the income tax system, the Minister of Finance and the Minister of National Revenue would probably be the key figures involved in the planning. Yet the Cabinet as a whole would take responsibility for the decision. A Cabinet minister who disagreed with his or her colleagues would have to keep the disagreement private, and, in public, accept the decision made by the group. In cases of extreme, irreconcilable disagreement, the minister would resign.

Cabinet secrecy is also a vital aspect of the executive process. Unlike House of Commons and Senate debates and the proceedings of parliamentary committees, the records of Cabinet meetings are not made public. Sometimes, though, there may be a "leak": a minister may tell a newspaper reporter what was said in a Cabinet meeting, on the promise that he or she will not be identified in the article. Such leaks were not uncommon in the time of John Diefenbaker and Lester Pearson. Since the era of Pierre Trudeau, however, Cabinet secrecy has become stronger.

Most Cabinet decisions are carried out through a device known as an **order-in-council**. This is a Cabinet document, signed by the Governor General, which orders a particular course of action based upon a particular law. In effect, an order-in-council has the force of law. When a newspaper says "the government has decided such-and-such", it is likely an order-in-council, not the passage of legislation, which is being discussed. Appointments to government office, for example, are normally made through orders-in-council. During the mid-1980's, Cabinet orders-in-council numbered around 5000 a year.

In another example, issues involving foreign investment in Canada are resolved through orders-in-council made under the authority of the *Investment Canada Act*. Suppose the question of the ownership of a specific company operating in Canada came up. In this case, the government would not need to introduce a bill in the House of Commons to rule on whether or not the company had to be sold to

Canadian owners. Rather, the Cabinet would examine what courses of action were open to it under the Investment Canada guidelines, study the suggestions of Investment Canada personnel, and make a decision accordingly. The documents setting forth the decision would be formally written up by the staff of the Privy Council Office and sent to the Governor General for signature.

A key executive agency linked with the Cabinet is the **Treasury Board**. Its head, the President of the Treasury Board, has the status of a Cabinet minister. In effect, the Treasury Board is a Cabinet committee. Besides the President, five ministers sit on the committee, the Minister of Finance always among them. The role of the Treasury Board is to monitor and evaluate the budgets of the various government departments.

The Treasury Board Secretariat is the government department which provides administrative support for the Treasury Board. It is the official employer of public servants, sharing with the Public Service Commission the complex task of fixing job classifications and salaries for the tens of thousands of Canadians who work directly for government departments of the federal bureaucracy.

QUESTIONS

1. Name and describe the three categories of Cabinet ministers.

2. Why is Cabinet solidarity central to the executive process of Canadian government?

3. What is Cabinet secrecy?

4. What is an order-in-council?

5. What is the basic function of the Treasury Board?

The Role of the Bureaucracy

If all three levels of government—federal, provincial, and local—are considered together, then it can be said that about one in every five working Canadians is part of the bureaucracy, which carries out the daily tasks and services of government. About one-quarter of the total number were employed directly or indirectly by the federal government in the mid-1980's.

The federal bureaucracy is an immensely complex organization divided into several hundred branches. To simplify the picture, it is possible to identify four major bureaucratic structures within the federal government: government departments, Crown corporations, regulatory agencies, and advisory bodies. Each of these structures has a unique relationship with the executive branch of the federal government. Crown corporations, in particular, have a legal status that is partly independent of, yet still linked to, the executive branch.

Government departments employ about half of the approximately 600 000 Canadians in the federal bureaucracy, while Crown corporations employ about a third. The two smaller structures, regulatory agencies and advisory bodies, share the remaining one-sixth of the employees of the federal bureaucracy between them.

Government Departments

As of 1986, there were 23 officially designated government departments, each of them under the authority of a Cabinet minister. Government departments can be broken down into two broad types. The first might be called "vertical" departments, because their function is to administer and supply various services "down" to the public. The other type could be called "horizontal" departments, since they provide services "across" to other departments. (See Table 3.1.)

TABLE 3.1 *Government Departments as of November, 1986*

VERTICAL	HORIZONTAL
Agriculture	External Affairs
Communications	Finance
Consumer and Corporate Affairs	Justice
Employment and Immigration	Revenue
Energy, Mines and Resources	Public Works
Environment	Science and Technology
Fisheries and Oceans	Supply and Services
Indian and Northern Affairs	
Labour	
National Defence	
Health and Welfare	
Regional Industrial Expansion	
Secretary of State	
Solicitor General	
Transport	
Veterans' Affairs	

Because the running of government is so complex, and because Cabinet ministers are only temporarily in office, no minister can learn everything about his or her department. In fact, a Cabinet minister will never see or even know about the vast majority of routine documents, files, and decisions that are passed daily through the department. For such day-to-day administration, the minister must rely on public servants.

Within a department, the top public servant is known as the **deputy minister**. Typically, this person has 20 or more years of experience in the public service and has made a career of serving in a particular department. As the real expert in the department, it is the deputy minister to whom the minister must turn for advice. Reporting to the deputy minister are several **assistant deputy ministers**, each with a specialized area of responsibility. In turn, various directorates, branches, and divisions report to the assistant deputy ministers, and so on down the line. The organizations of the middle and lower levels of government departments differ according to the needs and responsibilities of a given department.

Crown Corporations

A Crown corporation is essentially a business that is owned by the government. The precise legal definition of a Crown corporation is obscure; even political scientists disagree about exactly how many organizations within the federal bureaucracy could be classified as Crown corporations. To complicate matters, some Crown corporations, such as CN, are broken down into many smaller corporations. Considering just the major ones, there are approximately 70 Crown corporations. If the smaller ones are taken into account, there are about three times that number.

In some respects, Crown corporations function in the same way as private businesses. They have boards of directors, they create and sell goods or services, and they attempt to make a profit. Nevertheless, some vital distinctions between Crown corporations and private companies do exist. The former are accountable to a particular government department. The presidents of CN and Via Rail report to the Minister of Transport, for instance. As well, the presidents and directors of Crown corporations are in almost all cases appointed by order-in-council of the Cabinet.

Regulatory Agencies

Regulatory agencies are the government organizations that set the rules and regulations by which businesses in Canada, both public and private, must operate. Like Crown corporations, these agencies are linked to specific government departments and their top personnel are appointed by order-in-council. For instance, the CRTC, which sets guidelines for radio and television broadcasting in Canada, falls under the Department of Communications. Investment Canada, which rules on applications by foreign companies to do business in Canada, comes under the Department of Regional Industrial Expansion. The Canadian Transport Commission, which, among other things, regulates the fares charged by Canada's airlines, is responsible to Transport Canada.

Advisory Bodies

Advisory bodies are organizations within the federal bureaucracy whose role is to study and make recommendations on certain special issues. They are generally of two kinds: temporary and permanent.

Temporary advisory bodies are called either **Royal Commissions** or **Task Forces**. A commission or task force is appointed by order-in-council for a term of about three years. During this time, the members travel across Canada to sound out public opinion on a particular issue, then publish a report. The government may or may not act upon the report's recommendations. Temporary advisory bodies address issues of concern to many sectors of government, and they are unconnected to any particular department. Instead, they are directly responsible to the Cabinet.

An example of a temporary advisory body was the Task Force on Canadian Unity (1977–79), co-chaired by Jean-Luc Pépin, a former Liberal Cabinet minister, and John Robarts, a former Conservative Premier of Ontario. It was appointed after the *Parti Québécois* won the 1976 election in Québec. This victory once again raised the issue of French-English relations in Canada. The task force recommended, among other things, that language rights should remain a provincial responsibility, and that the composition of the Senate should be changed. Neither recommendation was acted upon by the Liberal government of Pierre Trudeau.

Permanent advisory bodies, as their name suggests, provide ongoing recommendations to the government on particular issues. While their advice applies to the government in general, these organizations report either to particular departments or directly to the Prime Minister. Examples of the first type are the Canadian Advisory Council on the Status of Women, which reports to the Secretary of State, and the Science Council of Canada, which reports to the Ministry of State for Science and Technology. An example of the second type is the Economic Council of Canada, which reports to the Prime Minister.

Judge Thomas Berger conducts an informal hearing in the northern community of Inuvik as part of the investigations made during the Mackenzie Valley Pipeline Inquiry. Why do you suppose the Federal government wished to consult these people?

QUESTIONS

1. Name the four major structures within the federal bureaucracy.

2. What is a vertical government department? A horizontal department?

3. What is the title of the top public servant within a department?

4. How do Crown corporations and private companies differ in the way the top executive (usually a president or director) is appointed?

5. **(a)** What are the two types of advisory bodies?
(b) How do their tasks differ?

Chapter Summary

The four main components of the executive branch at the federal level are the Governor General, the Prime Minister, the Cabinet, and the bureaucracy.

The Governor General's executive role is largely ceremonial. One of the most important functions of the position is exercised when a Prime Minister resigns after an electoral defeat. In such a case, the Governor General must ask another party leader to form a government.

The Prime Minister has four main types of power. The power held as party leader ensures that the PM has the support of MP's in the governing party. The power of appointment enables the PM to select MP's for a Cabinet and to make patronage appointments. The power of government organization allows the PM to modify both the size and the structure of the Cabinet, as well as to choose the heads of two important executive agencies: the Prime Minister's Office and the Privy Council Office. Finally, the PM also holds the power, in practice, of setting the date of an election.

Cabinet ministers are normally (though not necessarily) MP's. The most influential Cabinet ministers are in charge of permanent government departments, ministers of state are in charge of temporary departments, and ministers without portfolio act in an advisory capacity. Cabinet committees conduct most of the Cabinet's business. Cabinet decisions are made on the basis of solidarity and secrecy. Most of these decisions are made in the form of an order-in-council.

The federal bureaucracy has four main structures. Government departments, the largest in terms of employees, may be either "horizontal" or "vertical". Crown corporations, the next largest bureaucratic structure, are semi-independent of the executive branch. They are essentially government-owned businesses. Regulatory agencies, the third type, set up the rules of operation for public and private businesses. Advisory bodies, the fourth type of federal bureaucratic structure, make recommendations to the government on broad issues of public concern. These bodies may be either permanent or temporary.

IN REVIEW

1. Why would a Prime Minister choose to increase the size of the Cabinet or to expand the staff of the Prime Minister's office?
2. Why are orders-in-council not debated and voted upon by the House of Commons?
3. Why are the departments of External Affairs and Finance considered horizontal departments?
4. **(a)** Which power of the Prime Minister allows him to set the date of an election?
   (b) Describe the process by which this power is exercised.

APPLYING YOUR KNOWLEDGE

1. Why did the Canadian government press for, and win, the right to name Canada's Governor General?
2. Why has the practice been established of having at least one francophone Cabinet minister from outside Québec and one anglophone Cabinet minister from inside Québec?
3. When can an opposition party have a "stranglehold" on the government?
4. Do you agree or disagree with the Cabinet's use of orders-in-council in making government decisions? Explain.

FURTHER INVESTIGATION

1. Traditionally, persons running as independents in an election have had little hope of being elected. Why do you think this is so? Do you think this should concern Canadians?
2. State one advantage and one disadvantage of Cabinet solidarity being "central to the executive process of Canadian government".
3. Some Canadians believe strongly that Crown corporations should be privatized, or sold to private concerns. Find out some of the reasons for this opinion. Do you agree or disagree with it?
4. Undertake research on one or more of the following topics:
   (a) the recipients of last year's Order of Canada;
   (b) the members of the current federal Cabinet, their portfolios, and their home ridings;
   (c) the standing of the leader of each of Canada's federal parties in the latest opinion poll.

CHAPTER 4

The Judicial Branch

The third branch of Canada's government is the judiciary. The courts and judges that make up the judicial branch are considered to be independent of the other two branches. They "govern" in that they resolve legal disputes by interpreting and applying the laws made by Canada's elected representatives.

The administration of justice is both a federal and a provincial responsibility. The names of courts vary from province to province, but their overall operation is similar. The substance of Canada's laws, found in statutes and in decisions of Judges, varies from province to province.

In this chapter, you will examine the structure and operation of Canada's legal system. You will begin by considering the foundation of law, the principles which underlie the operation of the courts. Then you will look at the principal sources of Canadian law: the French Civil Code, the English common law and the Parliament of Canada. Next you will examine the division of the vast body of law into its various categories, of which the two main ones are public law and civil law. The following section reviews the nature of the judiciary: the role of judges in Canada's legal system. The last section discusses the structure of the Canadian legal system; it looks at courts in the Province of British Columbia and at courts at the national level. As you progress through the chapter, keep these questions in mind:

- *What is the rule of law, and why is it so important to Canada's legal system?*
- *What are the sources of Canadian law?*
- *What are public law and civil law?*
- *What are the nature and the role of the judiciary in the Canadian legal system?*
- *How does the judicial branch interact with the other branches of government to maintain social order?*

The Foundations of Law

The judicial branch of government includes Canada's judges and courts and deals with the administration of justice. Its purpose is to interpret and apply laws, protect society from criminals, resolve private disputes, and ensure that our constitutional rights are enforced. The foundation of law in Canada, the dispensing of justice, is based on the principle of the rule of law and theories of law and justice.

The Rule of Law

Society has government so that it may have safety and order. The law is the instrument by which safety and order are maintained in Canada. The rule of law is the fundamental principle of Canada's system of government in general, and of the law in particular.

Central to the concept of the rule of law is that everyone, regardless of social position or power, must obey the laws of the land. Nobody is above the law, including those who govern us; the rule of law limits the power of the government. Under the rule of law, everyone is equal before the law; all laws affect all people in the same way, whether they are rich or poor, male or female, Canadian-born or new citizens. In addition, the rule of law guarantees everyone fundamental justice: the right to a fair and impartial trial before independent judges who apply the laws of the land.

Equality before the law and the right to a fair trial are considered by many to be cornerstones of the Canadian legal system. This system has been built on the rule of law and is designed to promote the peaceful resolution of conflicts in Canada.

A gavel is used by judges to call a court to order or attention. It has become a symbol of a judge's role.

Law and Justice

In studying the judicial branch in Canada, it is important to consider the meanings of the words "law" and "justice", as well as the relationship between the two. In simplest terms, law is a set of rules or procedures. But justice cannot be defined so easily. The Hon. James C. McRuer, Chief Justice of the Supreme Court of Ontario during the 1960's, stated that "justice" is a term that can be no more precisely defined than love or hate or charity, but is something that the human heart acknowledges. However, human attitudes and values, including the sense of justice, have changed through the ages. For instance, slavery was an accepted part of many human societies until scarcely a century ago. Today it is unthinkable. Such changes in the human sense of justice are reflected in changes in the law. It is therefore possible to define "law" somewhat more precisely by saying that it is a set of rules or procedures which evolves as a result of the changes in a society's sense of justice. Notice that this definition expresses a relationship between law and justice.

"I am not here to dispense justice, I am here to dispose of this case according to law. Whether this is or is not justice is a question for the legislature to determine."—Sir Thomas W. Taylor, Chief Justice of Manitoba, 1887–1899.

These complex and yet rather vague definitions of law and justice become further complicated when you consider that not all societies have the same sense of justice. Nor, for that matter, do all people in a single society necessarily have the same view of what is just. The Close-up which follows presents a range of viewpoints on law and justice.

CLOSE-UP

Theories of Law

From the time of the earliest societies to the present, the nature of law and justice, and the relationship between the two, have been matters of debate. Many Greek and Roman philosophers argued that law and justice were the same. This view was still held by most clerics and lawyers of the Middle Ages. By the eighteenth century, however, the majority of philosophers held the opposite point of view: that law and justice were different matters. The judges and lawyers of today are still engaged in this debate. Their personal values and attitudes influence the positions they take in the controversy, and, therefore, the way in which they approach legal problems.

Below are the facts of a real case heard in the English courts in 1884. The accused were convicted of murder and sentenced to death but requested a pardon. The fictitious judgments which follow, passed by three imaginary judges, reflect different schools of legal thought.

Regina* vs. *Dudley and Stephens England, 1884, 14 L.R. 273

THE CHARGE "Murder of Richard Parker on the high seas within the jurisdiction of the Admiralty."

THE FACTS Three men, Dudley, Stephens, and Brooks, and a seventeen-year-old boy, Parker, were caught in a fierce storm about 2500 km from the Cape of Good Hope. Forced to abandon their ship, they set out in an open boat with no water and only two one-pound (half kilogram) tins of turnips for food. They managed to capture a small turtle on their fourth day, but the entire turtle was consumed by the twelfth day. For the next eight days, they were without food. Using oilskin capes, they were able to catch some rainwater to drink but this, too, soon ran out.

On the eighteenth day, Dudley and Stephens talked to Brooks about what should be done if no more food or water was to be found. They suggested that lots should be cast to determine who should be put to death to save the others. Brooks disagreed, and

Parker was not consulted. Later, Dudley and Stephens suggested that it would be best to kill Parker, as he was suffering the most and had no family to return to.

On the twentieth day, while Parker was asleep, Dudley, with the consent of Stephens but not of Brooks, approached the boy and put a knife to his throat, killing him. The three men then fed on the body of Parker for three days. On the fourth day, they were rescued and carried to England, where Dudley and Stephens were committed for trial on a charge of murder.

Several months later, a jury found both men guilty of the murder of Parker. They were sentenced to be hanged. Their lawyer then requested that they be pardoned because of the unusual nature of the circumstances.

THE POSITIONS OF THE IMAGINARY JUDGES One judge, who supports what is called the **positivist** school of thought, interprets the written language of the statue on murder literally. Dudley and Stephens deliberately took the life of Parker and thereby committed murder and so they should suffer the consequences of their action. This judge rejects the idea that the circumstances of the crime should be considered.

The second judge, whose position is the **natural law** approach, looks to the "state of nature", the circumstances in which the men found themselves. He rejects the idea that the men were bound by the regular law of the land concerning murder. Thus, this judge argues against a simple interpretation of the law on murder and is willing to support the request for a pardon.

The third judge, who follows the school of law called **legal realism**, argues that the situation in which Dudley and Stephens found themselves and the opinions of the public and government authorities on the matter must be considered. This judge supports the request for a pardon, in the belief that most members of the public think that Dudley and Stephens have suffered enough during their ordeal, and that society would gain very little by executing them.

The three judges, reflecting three different legal theories while examining the same facts, vote 2 to 1 to pardon Dudley and Stephens.

QUESTIONS

1. (a) With which school of legal thought do you agree most closely?

(b) What judgment would you pass on Dudley and Stephens?

(c) Although Brooks ate of Parker's body, he was not tried for murder. Was this just? Explain your answer.

2. Dudley and Stephens were found guilty of wilful murder, since the circumstances were deemed to be no legal justification for killing. They were granted Royal Mercy by Queen Victoria, and their death sentences were commuted to life imprisonment. The legal authorities decided to release Dudley and Stephens after six months' imprisonment. Do you think this was a just solution?
3. Name an issue today which might be as difficult for the courts to decide as the *Dudley and Stephens* case, and then describe how supporters of the three schools of legal thought would review the issue.
4. How do the three viewpoints on law presented in the Close-up differ?
5. What do you think judges of the positivist school would think of the statement, "An unjust law is not a law"?

QUESTIONS

1. Which branch of government is responsible for the administration of justice?
2. What are considered by many to be "the cornerstones of Canada's legal system"?
3. Refer to the Sidebar on page 65. Which school of legal thought does Sir Thomas Taylor follow? Explain.

The Sources of Canadian Law

Canada's laws are based mainly upon two legal systems: the Civil Code tradition introduced by French settlers, and the common law tradition introduced by British settlers. These systems take different approaches to the creation and interpretation of legal principles. A third source of laws in Canada is the government, which originates and passes legislation in the form of **statutes**.

The Civil Code System

The Civil Code system is used today in Québec only. The older of Canada's two legal systems, Québec's Civil Code has its origins in Roman law. The first **codified** (systematized) set of Roman laws dates back to about 500 B.C. Nearly 1000 years later, the Emperor Justinian decided to consolidate these early Roman laws and all those which had been passed later. The resulting document is known as the **Justinian Code**.

In the Middle Ages in France and other parts of Europe, the Justinian

Code was used as the basis for other codes of laws. One of them was the **Custom of Paris**, the law that the earliest French settlers brought with them to Québec. These two codes of law, along with others which have been passed since the early nineteenth century, influenced the development of the Québec Civil Code.

It is important to note that only those matters which fall under provincial jurisdiction are covered by the Civil Code. Laws pertaining to areas of federal jurisdiction apply across Canada, including Québec. Thus, the legal system of Québec is unique only in certain areas of law.

In a Civil Code system such as that of Québec, the laws are in the form of an accepted set of principles put forth in a written code. Judges decide individual legal cases by referring to the codified principles.

The Common Law

The common law system is used in all provinces and territories of Canada, except Québec. This system developed in England after the Norman Conquest of 1066, when William the Conqueror introduced the use of the French language and the Norman system of laws. The judges appointed by William and his heirs had their choice of using the Norman laws, the old Anglo-Saxon laws, church law, surviving Roman laws, and local laws. The judges were directed to travel throughout the kingdom to hear and decide legal cases, using their choice of the various legal systems.

At the end of their journeys, the judges returned to the capital of the kingdom. Inevitably, they compared notes on their cases. As years and decades passed, a new system of law began to develop. Instead of resorting to the confusion of old legal traditions, judges started to base their decisions on the judgments previously made by other judges in similar situations. These prior decisions were called **precedents**. The practice of deciding cases in a common way on the basis of common principles is known as following the **rule of precedent**. The rule of precedent is a cornerstone of the common law system. Gradually, the new system came into use throughout England.

In Canada today, the common law approach examines the decisions of judges in previous cases, then extracts general principles, which are applied to the specific legal problem before the court. A degree of interpretation may be necessary when a new case deals with a situation which has never previously been before the courts. Thus it is that the common law constantly evolves and remains flexible, unlike the Civil Code system, which is rigidly defined.

The coronation of William the Conqueror heralded the beginning of the common law system in England. During his reign, judges began to decide individual cases on the basis of precedent or custom.

Statute Law

In Canada, all three levels of government—federal, provincial, and local—pass legislation, a collective term for laws or statutes. These laws, together known as **statute law**, represent by far the greatest proportion of the laws used in Canada.

The Library of Parliament was the only Parliamentary building to survive the fire of 1916. Its large collection of books and documents, including Canada's statutes, and its research services are of particular use to Canada's MP's.

IN ALL CASES OF INJURY

The employer shall

1. Make sure that first aid is given immediately, in accordance with the Regulations.
2. Record the first aid treatment or advice given to the worker.
3. Complete and give to the worker a Treatment Memorandum (Form 156) if health care* is needed.
4. Provide immediate transportation to a hospital, a doctor's office, or the worker's home if necessary.
5. Submit to the Board, within three days of learning of an accident, an Employer's Report of Accidental Injury/Industrial Disease (Form 7) and any other information that may be requested.
6. Pay full wages and benefits for the day or shift on which the injury occurred.

The worker shall

1. Promptly obtain first aid.
2. Notify the employer immediately of any injury requiring health care* and obtain from the employer a completed Treatment Memorandum (Form 156) to take to the doctor or the hospital.
3. Choose a doctor or other qualified practitioner, with the understanding that a change of doctor cannot be made without permission of the Board.

...nd promptly return...
...ed from the B...

The Workers' Compensation Board is regulated by administrative laws which outline the relationship between employers and employees in the work place.

Disputes sometimes arise, however, over the precise meaning and legal application of a given statute. It is the responsibility of judges to resolve such controversies. The decision in such cases forms a precedent, which is then used by other lawyers and judges. Judges then interpret and apply the legal principles developed in such cases to extend the common law.

QUESTIONS

1. What are the three sources of law in Canada?

2. What are precedents? What is the "rule of precedent"?

3. What is the main difference between the Civil Code system and the common law system?

4. How do statute law and common law reinforce each other?

The Types of Law

The Canadian system of law has had a complicated growth, with many roots and branches. It is therefore helpful to classify it into various categories. The two major groupings into which all law can be divided are **public law** and **civil** (or **private**) **law**.

Public Law

Public law, as its name suggests, covers all laws that concern the general public. It deals with the relationships between individuals and the government, as well as those among the various branches of government.

Public law can be further broken down into three areas: constitutional law, administrative law and criminal law. Constitutional law forms the topic of Chapter 6. **Administrative law** regulates the activities of various government agencies, including Crown corporations, and prescribes the relationship between these agencies and the public. For instance, a worker injured on the job would contact the Workers' Compensation Board, which pays benefits to workers injured on the job. Or a union trying to sign up new members would follow the regulations on certification, which are included in the *Industrial Relations Act*.

Criminal law is the area of law concerned with offences against the public interest. It deals with human conduct which is considered harmful both to society as a whole and to its individual members. Such offences as homicide, sexual assault, theft, and impaired driving, which the government of Canada has prohibited by law, fall into the category of criminal law. Over the years, Parliament has enacted a

Judges may impose prison sentences on criminal offenders to protect society from harmful behaviour. From the reign of William I, serious crimes have been considered to harm the state and not just injure individuals.

number of federal statutes which define these crimes, and set out procedures for trial as well as for possible penalties which a judge may impose on a convicted offender.

Most of Canada's criminal law is set out in the federal act, or statute, known as the *Canadian Criminal Code*, which is modified and added to as necessary. Other important federal laws include the *Narcotics Control Act*, which controls the use of narcotic substances in Canada, and the *Food and Drug Act*, which regulates the use of foods and drugs.

Canadian criminal cases are tried in the name of the Crown, the head of state, acting as the representative of society. To indicate this fact, the Latin word for "Queen", *Regina*, is used in every criminal **case citation** (case title), as you saw in "*Regina* vs. *Dudley and Stephens*".

Civil Law

Civil law incorporates all laws affecting the relationships between individuals, between individuals and private organizations, and between organizations. It is therefore sometimes called "private law". Like public law, civil law can be divided into categories: contract law, property law, labour law, family law, and intellectual law, among others.

The change of ownership of this land is governed by property law, which is a type of civil law.

QUESTIONS

1. Into which three areas can public law be broken down?
2. In what document is most of Canada's criminal law written?
3. Why is civil law sometimes called "private law"?

The Nature of the Canadian Judiciary

The term "judiciary" refers collectively to all judges at all levels of courts in Canada. You have seen that the role of the judiciary is to interpret and apply laws. Three important aspects of this role in the Canadian legal system will be examined: the impartiality and independence of judges, the appointment of judges, and the limitations placed on judges.

Canadian judges and juries make their decisions in an adversarial setting, that is, one in which the two sides in a trial are seen as being actively opposed. The adversarial system is discussed at the end of this section.

The Impartiality and Independence of Judges

In England, where many Canadian legal traditions originated, the monarch was responsible for appointing judges, as well as for supervising and removing them as he or she saw fit. This remained true until 1701, when the *Act of Settlement* was passed. This *Act*, which decreed that judges were to hold their appointments during good behaviour, rather than at the Sovereign's pleasure, was the major landmark in the struggle of judges to free themselves from the monarch's control and gain what are now considered the two key characteristics of the judiciary: impartiality and independence.

Today, it seems obvious to us that judges must be impartial. Neither individuals nor groups should be able to get special treatment from the courts. Otherwise, the principle of the rule of law breaks down.

Over the years, two traditions have developed to ensure that judges are fair and unbiased. The first is the rule against **conflict of interest**: no judge should preside over any case in which he or she has a personal interest, financial or otherwise. Thus, judges usually will not hear either cases involving people who were formerly their clients when they themselves were lawyers practising law, or cases being presented by their former legal partners.

The second tradition is the **passive role** that judges are expected to play in court cases. That is, judges must be neutral, completely open-minded observers who listen to all the evidence presented to them by the lawyers and witnesses on both sides. This tradition helps them maintain a distance from the dispute that they are hearing, and thereby allows them to be as objective as possible in making their decisions. For this reason, judges rarely take an active role during a trial.

The independence of judges, their freedom from government interference or influence, is fundamental to Canada's legal system. It ensures that every case that comes before a court will be heard by a judge who is free of any pressure from the government or any other source which might affect his or her ability to render a fair, unbiased decision. The tradition is so essential to the Canadian legal system that even the appearance of interference is not tolerated. The famous saying, "Not only must justice be done, it must be seen to be done," comes out of this tradition.

Two safeguards exist to promote both the impartiality and the independence of judges. First, judges are appointed for life, though most retire by the age of 75. Secondly, it is very difficult to expel judges from office because they can be removed only by a vote of both the House of Commons and the Senate. In fact, this has never happened, and it could occur only if it could be proven that the judge was unable to perform his or her duties adequately because of age or such misconduct as breaking the law. This high degree of job security means that judges do not have to be concerned whether their decisions please the government.

The second safeguard is that judges are free from prosecution for anything they do in the handling of a dispute. Freedom from prosecution allows them to administer the law without fear of suffering personally for the decisions they make in cases which are often very complex.

Judge Rosalie Abella, head of the 1984 Royal Commission on Equality in Employment, shows the report which recommended that work of equal value should receive equal compensation.

The Appointment of Judges

In Canada, judges are appointed by the government. The provincial government of each province appoints judges to the Provincial Courts. Eligibility for this position requires a person to have practised law for at least five years. The federal government appoints judges to all federal courts and to the higher levels of courts in each province. Eligibility for this position requires a minimum of ten years of legal practice.

When a judge is needed, representatives of the provincial government (for Provincial Court) or the federal and provincial governments (for all other courts) search out names. They also ask lawyers, law schools, judges, and others to suggest candidates. The leading candidates are scrutinized for their integrity, personal and work habits, and ability. Next, they are asked whether they would be willing to serve. If the answer is affirmative, then, as a rule, the names of strong candidates are sent to the Canadian Bar Association (CBA), the national organization of Canadian lawyers. A CBA representative will state whether each candidate is "well qualified", "qualified", or "not qualified". After this, a decision is made whether or not to appoint a given candidate.

Over the years, there has been much public debate about whether appointments to the bench are used as a patronage device, to reward members or supporters of political parties. Many legal writers say that the growing complexity and the workload of court cases today has made this less and less likely, since it is very important for the government to try to get the best qualified people to serve. Others, however, have argued that the very fact that the decision as to who becomes a judge is left to politicians in the federal or provincial Cabinets ensures that political patronage will be a factor in the selection of at least some judges.

The Limitations on Judges

All new judges are expected to sever connections with their former law firms and to resign any directorships of companies which they might hold. While serving as judges, they are allowed to vote in municipal, provincial, or federal elections but rarely do so; to show their neutrality, they hesitate to express public support for any political candidate, party, or ideology. On occasion, some judges in Canada have criticized one or more of these limitations. Mr. Justice Berger, a judge of the Supreme Court of B.C. until he resigned in 1983, stated that there do exist rare occasions when members of the bench should speak out on matters of public interest. At that time, Judge Berger criticized the federal government and nine of the ten provincial premiers for agreeing to a new Constitution for Canada which did not include guarantees of Native rights or veto power for Québec. Chief Justice Bora Laskin of the Supreme Court of Canada responded in these words to Judge Berger's criticisms: "A judge has no freedom of speech to address political issues which have nothing to do with his judicial duty."

The Adversarial System

Judges make decisions on disputes in an adversarial setting. The adversarial system of resolving conflicts is based on the notion that the best way to obtain a fair decision in a dispute is to structure trials as competitions between two sides. This system has its origins in ancient trials by combat, where might proved right. Both sides of a dispute have the opportunity to present evidence and arguments in court to which the judge or the judge and jury listen passively. A decision is then made by a neutral and independent judge, or by a jury.

In some instances Canadian law gives accused persons the right to choose between trial by jury and trial by judge. In other cases, the Criminal Code states that they should be tried by jury.

Juries decide the guilt or innocence of the accused on the basis of the facts presented during a criminal trial. The unbiased nature of their decisions is ensured by the mechanism for creating juries. Juries are composed of members of the community who have been selected arbitrarily, placed in a panel, and then either eliminated by either side or sworn in by the court clerk. The fairness of a jury's decision is also ensured; for example, all 12 members of a jury must come to a unanimous decision in a criminal trial. If they cannot, a new trial with another jury is ordered.

The adversarial system found in Canada differs from the **inquisitorial system** common to many European countries. There, the court regards itself as responsible for discovering the truth of the cases

Lawyers present evidence and arguments to a judge or jury in court. Both sides of a case are heard to enable the jury to reach a fair and unbiased decision.

before it. Thus, in the inquisitorial system, judges question witnesses carefully and ensure that all the important evidence is heard.

QUESTIONS

1. **(a)** How is conflict of interest avoided in the Canadian judiciary?
   (b) Why is it important for judges to avoid even the appearance of conflict of interest?
2. What two safeguards promote the impartiality and the independence of Canadian judges?
3. **(a)** What is the difference between the adversarial system and the inquisitorial system?
   (b) Which do you think is more likely to result in justice? Explain your reasoning.

The Structure of the Canadian Legal System

The legal system of Canada can be imagined as a pyramid. The base of the pyramid consists of the Provincial Courts of each province. The next level is occupied by the County and District Courts (the name varies from province to province). In some provinces, the highest level is the Supreme Court of the Province, which has both a trial division and an appeals division. In British Columbia, however, the Supreme Court and the Court of Appeal are at separate levels, with the Court of Appeal being the highest provincial court.

The remaining levels of the pyramid are occupied by federal courts. First come the Federal Court and the Citizenship Court. The Federal Court deals with matters involving the federal government and its employees, while the Citizenship Court, as its name indicates, deals with cases involving citizenship.

At the apex of the pyramid is the Supreme Court of Canada, the highest court of appeal for cases from all courts. The Supreme Court deals only with cases of national concern or those involving important legal issues.

Below, the various courts of British Columbia will be used as examples of the Canadian legal system at the provincial level. Then the three federal courts will be examined in detail.

The Court Structure of British Columbia

The B.C. court system is modelled on that of Great Britain. It consists of three trial courts—the Supreme Court, the County Court, and the Provincial Court—and a Court of Appeal.

FIGURE 4.1 *The Courts of British Columbia*
Cases may be appealed to the Supreme Court of Canada.

APPEAL COURT OF B.C.
(Not a trial court.) Hears matters appealed from the decisions of Lower Courts.

SUPREME COURT OF B.C.
Hears civil cases of any amount, normally over $50 000. Hears very serious criminal offences, and some appeals from Lower Courts.

COUNTY COURT OF B.C.
Hears criminal cases such as robbery, theft over $1000 etc., where an accused elects a higher court trial, as well as civil cases involving claims of less than $50 000. Also hears some appeals from Lower Courts.

PROVINCIAL COURT
Hears 90 per cent of B.C.'s criminal matters, conducts preliminary inquiries and handles youth offences, traffic offences and minor civil disputes. Also handles family matters.

Criminal Division **Family Division** **Small Claims Division**

Both the federal and the provincial governments are involved in the B.C. court system. The federal government appoints the judges of the Supreme Court, the County Court and the Court of Appeal, and their salaries are paid from federal revenues. The provincial government appoints and pays the judges of the Provincial Court. In addition, because the administration of justice was delegated to the provinces at the time of Confederation, the provincial government pays the staff salaries and other operating costs for all four levels of courts.

Provincial Court

Provincial Court is the first level of the B.C. court system. It was created in 1969, when the B.C. government passed a statute to consolidate all courts at the municipal level—Small Debts, Family and Children's Courts, and Magistrates Courts—which had existed previously. Today, there are Provincial Courts in most B.C. communities.

The criminal trial process in B.C. usually begins in the criminal division of the Provincial Court. When an accused makes a first appearance before a judge, one of several results may follow. The accused may be given time to obtain a lawyer. If the accused has been arrested, the judge may order either release, under certain bail conditions, or detention (keeping the accused in custody until trial). For a large number of criminal offences, such as theft under $1000 or driving while disqualified, the trial will be held in Provincial Court, at a later date. For more serious offences, however, the accused will usually be able to elect (choose) the type of trial he or she wants. If an accused elects trial by jury, a **preliminary hearing** will be conducted in the

Most provinces in Canada have a Criminal Court, which is usually a division of the Provincial Court.

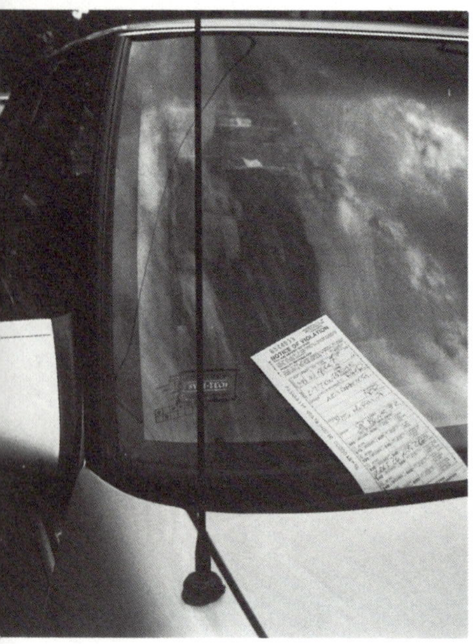

Parking offences are dealt with in Provincial Court.

Provincial Court to determine whether there is enough evidence for the case to go to trial in a higher court. For example, an accused murderer who elects trial by jury will normally be tried in the Supreme Court of British Columbia.

The **Family Division** of Provincial Court has authority over matters related to family disputes, including applications for child support and criminal charges arising out of family conflicts such as assault.

The **Youth Court Division** hears criminal trials of young persons between the ages of 12 and 17 years, under the special procedures which Parliament has established for young offenders.

The **Small Claims Division** hears civil disputes in which the sum involved is fairly small (under $3000, in 1986). The monetary limit changes over time to reflect inflation. People usually present their own case in Small Claims Court.

Traffic violations such as parking and speeding offences, breaches of municipal by-laws on noise or pollution, and other minor matters are also dealt with in Provincial Court. In the large metropolitan centre of Vancouver, they are handled by a separate division of the Provincial Court, to avoid a backlog of cases. Small B.C. cities and towns usually have one judge, who hears everything from small claims to criminal cases.

Judges of the Provincial Court are called "Your Honour" while in court.

CLOSE-UP

Courtroom 101

The article quoted below describes a typical day in Courtroom 101 at the Provincial Courthouse in Vancouver, where most persons accused of breaking a criminal law first come into contact with the judicial system.

Court paints a portrait of life's bottom rung
By Sarah Cox, *Vancouver Sun*, Aug. 10, 1985

They call it a zoo, a circus, a meat grinder or just the Skid Road of Canada's legal system.

It's a never ending parade of colorful characters—two brothers charged with throwing a mailbox at a city bus, a self-confessed heroin addict who stole lipstick from London Drugs, a man who ripped a telephone out of the Columbia Hotel when the broken cigarette machine failed to return his money. The real name is Courtroom 101—where more than 2500 people each year plead guilty or not guilty to everything from shoplifting to murder.

For duty counsel Neil Sacks, every working day last week began with an early morning elevator ride from the alley behind 312 Main up to the fifth floor of the police station. Hired by the Legal Services Society, Sacks and 140 other Vancouver lawyers take weekly turns acting for those who can't afford to pay fees demanded by private lawyers. Judge Keith Libby, who presided last week over Courtroom 101, says he often wonders what the system must look like from the bottom up, instead of from his viewpoint high above the courtroom.

"We're terribly misunderstood. A lot of people have an image of a judge as an older person who climbs into the closet at five at night and doesn't get out until ten the next morning."

But passing judgment in Courtroom 101 requires compassion, energy, and a good sense of what the community will tolerate, says Libby, a judge for five and one-half years.

"You have to go to great lengths to explain why you are giving a certain sentence. You're leaving yourself wide open to criticism."

August 1: A woman on welfare with three young children is charged with stealing food from a Safeway store.

She leaves her children—two boys and a girl—in their seats half-way up to the visitors' section, and walks to a microphone at the front of the courtroom.

Libby reads the charges—obtaining merchandise under a false pretense (with a false cheque), theft over $200, and a failure to appear.

"Guilty," she replies to all three.

Dressed in black pants and a white top, she looks frightened. Her little girl had fallen asleep, propped up against her brother.

Libby leans back in his seat and frowns. He asks for a pre-sentence report from a probation officer and tells her to return Sept. 5 for sentencing.

She was only one of at least seven shoplifting cases Aug. 1. A welfare recipient was given six months for stealing $23.45 worth of food from a Woodward's store last June. Another welfare recipient told Libby he had arthritis and couldn't afford to buy pain killers so he "decided to take the chance."

Libby says "it becomes very difficult to be fair" when he sometimes has to sentence up to 20 people a day. . .About one-half of the people who appear each day in 101—like those charged with sexual assault or murder—are in court to fix a trial date. And 10 to 15 percent of the daily flood of people through 101 plead guilty, says Libby. "A lot of them are real characters—the ones that come late, the spunky ones who aren't cowed by the whole process."

Judge Matthew Baillie Begbie in 1858, was appointed the first permanent judge of the Supreme Court of Civil Justice *for the colony of British Columbia. He was known for administering justice in an unorthodox but vigorous manner.*

. . . Libby says that there is a whole mish-mash of cases in 101 and it's difficult to say which charges appear most frequently. But he has noticed certain trends depending upon the time of the year or events happening in Vancouver. Most people are arrested when the weather is lousy and immediately after welfare day, he says. Theft charges usually escalate in August during the Pacific National Exhibition and more people are charged with a minor drug trafficking charge when a rock star performs in Vancouver.

Rod Holloway, director of legal aid at 191 Alexander, says the court system would be hopelessly slowed down if legal aid didn't exist.

"Having lawyers down there increases the number of guilty pleas and helps relieve clogging in the system because a lot of cases don't even go to trial."

As it is, 101 deals with so many people each day it's often called a "zoo or a meat-grinder," says Holloway.

QUESTIONS

1. How do you think a judge should deal with cases concerning welfare recipients stealing necessities of life?
2. Why is legal aid important to the operation of Courtroom 101?
3. What do you think Judge Libby means when he talks of giving sentences which the community will tolerate? What factors does he have to consider in passing sentence?

County Court

County Court is the next level in the B.C. court system. County Court judges are appointed to one of the eight judicial counties of the province. They sit mainly within the counties in which they reside, hearing both civil and criminal cases in major centres and small towns, but they do sometimes travel to other counties.

Most cases heard in this level of court deal with such serious criminal offences as robbery, arson, or possession of a dangerous or restricted weapon. Some of the cases are heard by a judge and jury, others by a judge alone, depending on the type of trial which was elected by an accused in Provincial Court.

Civil cases occupy less of the County Court's time, and usually involve situations in which an amount under $50 000 is in dispute. The County Court also has the authority to hear cases involving construction tradespeople, such as plumbers and electricians, regardless of the disputed amount.

In addition, County Court judges hear appeals of some minor criminal cases which were tried in Provincial Court. They are also local judges of the Supreme Court and are, in that capacity, empowered to deal with certain Supreme Court matters, such as petitions for divorce, applications for child custody and maintenance, and the division of family assets. Like Provincial Court judges, County Court judges are addressed as "Your Honour".

The Supreme Court of British Columbia

The Supreme Court of British Columbia is the highest trial court in the province. Both it and the County Courts were created in 1859, when British Columbia was still a colony.

Supreme Court judges usually hear the most serious civil or criminal cases, although they may hear any case, regardless of the matter or the amount of money involved. Just a few examples of the many types of civil action brought before this court are contract disputes, personal injury claims, divorce cases, and child custody matters.

Among the serious criminal matters tried in the Supreme Court are drug conspiracy, aggravated sexual assault, and murder. An accused who pleads "not guilty" to a charge of murder will be tried in the Supreme Court by a judge and jury. Usually, the accused will have had a preliminary hearing in Provincial Court before being referred to the Supreme Court for trial.

In addition to hearing cases in the large Law Courts complex in Vancouver, Supreme Court judges travel "on circuit" around the province, conducting trials in 14 other major centres. These trials are called **assizes**, from the French word for "a sitting". Finally, Supreme Court judges also have the authority of judges of the Provincial Court and County Court, and sometimes sit as such. Judges at the Supreme Court level are called "My Lord" or "My Lady" while in court.

The Royal Coats of Arms of the Province of British Columbia. The Latin motto means "Splendour Without Diminishment".

To keep order in the days of the gold rush, many mining communities in B.C. adopted "The Miners' Ten Commandments".

The Miner's Ten Commandments

1. *Thou shalt have no other claim but one.*
2. *Thou shalt not make thyself any false claim, nor any likeness to a mean man by jumping one.*
3. *Thou shalt not go prospecting before thy claim gives out. Thou shalt not take thy money nor gold dust to the gambling table.*
4. *Thou shalt remember what thy friends do at home on the Sabbath. Six days thou mayest dig or pick all the body can stand, but on Sunday thou shalt wash all thy dirty shirts and darn all thy stockings.*
5. *Think more of the gold and how thou can make it fastest than how thou wilt enjoy it.*
6. *Thou shalt not kill thy body by working in the rain.*
7. *Thou shalt not grow discouraged and think of going home before thou hast made thy "pile".*
8. *Thou shalt not pick out specimens from the company pan and put them in thy mouth or thy purse.*
9. *Thou shalt not tell any false tales about thy "gold-diggers".*
10. *Thou shalt not covet thy neighbour's gold nor his claim, nor undermine his bank by following a lead, nor move his stake, nor wash tailings from his sluice.*

The Court of Appeal of British Columbia

The Court of Appeal, the highest court in the province, was created in 1909. Its function is to hear appeals of both civil and criminal decisions made by the three trial courts. Up to five judges may hear cases in the Court of Appeal. Appeals of criminal convictions or sentences and civil judgments imposed by lower courts are usually brought before three judges, while constitutional matters are generally heard by all five judges.

Judges of the Court of Appeal regularly sit in the Law Courts complex in Vancouver, and also several times a year in Victoria. They serve as judges of the Court of Appeal for the Yukon as well.

Anyone dissatisfied with a decision of the Court of Appeal of British Columbia has the right to seek permission to apply to the Supreme Court of Canada in Ottawa. The decision to grant permission is usually made by a panel of three judges from the Supreme Court of Canada, though in some cases it is made by judges of the B.C. Court of Appeal.

The National Courts of Canada

As you read earlier, there are three federal courts in Canada: the Supreme Court of Canada, the Federal Court of Canada, and the Canadian Citizenship Court. These courts were created by the Parliament of Canada, and are administered by the federal government.

The Supreme Court of Canada

The Supreme Court of Canada is located in Ottawa. It is the final appeals court in the country for both civil and criminal matters. Like other courts of appeal, the Supreme Court of Canada does not conduct new trials of fact; that is, its function is to review cases which have already appeared before a lower court or courts. The Supreme Court can review any decision made by any court in Canada, and make a final decision in the case. When a decision is made, a new precedent is often set, and all lower courts are required to follow the principles of law established in the case when they are hearing similar cases. For this reason, it is said that the decisions of the Supreme Court of Canada are *binding* on all lower courts.

The Supreme Court of Canada was established in 1875, but did not become the highest court of appeal until 1949, when appeals to the Privy Council in England were abolished. The court is composed of a Chief Justice and eight lesser or **puisne** (Old French for "junior" or "inferior") judges. Appointments to the Supreme Court represent the different regions of Canada. There must at all times be three judges from Québec; the remaining judges are selected from the Maritimes, Ontario, and the western provinces. Usually five judges sit when the court is hearing appeals, but in very important cases seven or as many as the full complement of nine judges may sit. Cases involving constitutional issues are always heard by all nine judges.

This photograph, taken in 1982, shows the Justices of the Supreme Court of Canada sitting on the bench. At the extreme right is Justice Bertha Wilson, the first woman to be appointed to this body.

The parties involved in a case which reaches the Supreme Court almost never appear before the court; rather, they are represented by their lawyers, who present arguments on the legal issues involved. The Supreme Court judges listen to the arguments, review the appropriate sections of the written transcript of the trial in question, then render their decision. All decisions of the court are published so that judges of lower courts throughout Canada may follow them.

CLOSE-UP

New Task of the Supreme Court of Canada

The article which follows comments on the new duty which the patriation of the Constitution in 1982 imposed on Supreme Court judges.

Herculean job for the highest judges who decide if our laws are valid

by David Vienneau, *Toronto Star*, April 23, 1985

OTTAWA—It's a room few Canadians will ever see, but one in which decisions that affect their everyday lives will be made. Dominated by a large, circular oak table and nine red-leather, cushioned chairs, it is the conference room to which the black-robed justices of the Supreme Court of Canada retire immediately after hearing a case.

In this room, lined with shelves containing hundreds of musty old books and the crests of Canada and the provinces, the court had begun the herculean task of interpreting the Charter of Rights and Freedoms...

The job, given the court on April 17, 1982, with the patriation of the Constitution, means the eight men and one woman have the power to strike down unfair or discriminatory laws passed by Parliament and the provincial legislatures. And it means the court will eventually touch the lives of all Canadians and not just those involved in criminal, civil or constitutional battles.

"In the past the court didn't affect every Canadian," Chief Justice Brian Dickson said in an interview. "But all that changed in 1982 with the patriation of the Constitution. That affects every Canadian man, woman and child."

It is Dickson who leads the procession of judges out the back door of the main court room down three red-carpeted steps to the conference room, where collectively they will chisel out changes to Canada's legal history.

After the court has heard a case it immediately retires to the conference room where, in reverse order of seniority, each justice is asked to state his or her opinion on how it should be decided...

Dickson says that while these are only tentative opinions, the justices are unanimous on how a case should be decided in about 70 percent of the cases.

"Usually these are calm meetings but they can become quite heated and quite emotional," he said. "We are independent people and each one's voice carries the same weight and each is free to express himself or herself as forcefully as possible."

...Dickson, who keeps score on his notepad, decides who will write the judgment and any dissenting opinions. He has in front of him a list of the judgments each member of the court is already working on.

"It's an informal procedure," Dickson explained. "Sometimes it's merely a question of asking for volunteers, or some judge may have a particular interest in that particular issue or body of the law, or someone may have less of a load of cases to write."

"The person who is most vociferous in dissent will write any opposing opinion," Dickson said.

Nothing more is said on the case until the judge writing the decision circulates a draft opinion to each member.

In theory, every member of the court can write on every case but in practice this is rarely done, largely because the court believes it speaks with more authority if it is united behind one voice...

A judge has the option of changing his opinion right up until the time the judgment is delivered. The judge who wrote the majority ruling does the reading in open court.

QUESTIONS

1. How did the patriation of Canada's Constitution change the role of the Supreme Court of Canada?
2. How does the Supreme Court arrive at its rulings?

The Federal Court of Canada

The Federal Court, which deals with matters concerning the federal government and its employees, was created in 1972 to replace what was previously called the **Exchequer Court of Canada**, which dated from 1887. It has its headquarters in Ottawa, in the same building as the Supreme Court of Canada. While Supreme Court judges remain in Ottawa, Federal Court judges travel throughout the country to conduct trials or appeals in their areas of authority.

Judges of the trial division of the Federal Court usually hear civil matters involving the federal government, maritime and shipping disputes, inter-governmental disputes, and cases dealing with patent law. Appeals on tax and citizenship decisions are heard by the appeals division of the court.

The Citizenship Court of Canada

The Citizenship Court of Canada is not a trial court. It exists to review and assess applications for Canadian citizenship. The court examines all applications to determine whether they satisfy the requirements of the *Canadian Citizenship Act* and also conducts citizenship ceremonies.

New Canadian citizens pledge an oath of loyalty in one of Canada's Citizenship Courts.

QUESTIONS

1. Name the four courts of British Columbia.

2. Which court has authority over family disputes in British Columbia?

3. What is the purpose of the Small Claims Division of the B.C. Provincial Court?

4. **(a)** Which court is the highest trial court in the province?
(b) Describe the functions of the judges of this court.

5. What is the purpose of the B.C. Court of Appeal?

6. Name the three federal courts of Canada, and describe the functions of each.

7. How do the decisions of the Supreme Court of Canada affect lower courts?

Chapter Summary

The judicial branch of government is an essential part of the system of government in Canada. Independent of the other two branches of government, it has the often difficult task of interpreting laws and applying them to the everyday situations of Canadians. All people in Canada are equal before the law and are guaranteed a fair trial because the cornerstone of our legal system is the rule of law.

Canadian law has three sources: the rigidly set Civil Code system; the common law system which is based on precedents; and statute law, which is made by elected representatives in government. All Canadian laws can be divided into two categories: public law, which covers the relationships between individuals and government, and civil law, which deals with the relationships between individuals.

We expect the interpretation and application of the law by judges and juries to be fair and based on an independent and impartial assessment of arguments presented by the opposing sides of a conflict. Conflicts are peacefully resolved in a level of court within the Canadian legal system.

Each province in Canada has several levels of courts which hear a wide range of public and civil cases concerning provincial matters. British Columbia, for example, has three levels of trial courts and a Court of Appeal. The federal courts of Canada have authority throughout Canada and deal with matters of national interest.

IN REVIEW

1. What is the "rule of law"?
2. With which school of legal thought would you identify a judge who holds each of the following beliefs?
   (a) A judge's duty is to apply the law, not to comment on its validity.
   (b) Reason and moral principles should be the bases of law.
   (c) Judges cannot be totally objective or neutral.
3. What was the result of the *Act of Settlement*?

APPLYING YOUR KNOWLEDGE

1. Rules and regulations such as the "laws" that make up the Miners' Ten Commandments are meant to reflect community needs. Review the Commandments.
   (a) Suggest which commandments a miner could safely ignore.
   (b) Which commandments do you think the community would enforce? Why?
2. Is it possible for a judge to be truly unbiased? Explain your answer.
3. Mr. Justice Berger believes that judges should speak out on matters of public interest. Chief Justice Bora Laskin stated that "a judge has no freedom of speech to address political issues." Which point of view do you support? Why?
4. If you were selected for jury duty, what would be your reaction? Why? What would be your greatest concern in connection with fulfilling your duties?
5. In the United States some judges are elected. Suggest one advantage and one disadvantage of such a judicial system.

FURTHER INVESTIGATION

1. Are law and justice the same when Native rights issues come before the courts? Explain your answer.
2. Research one or more of the following topics.
   (a) The evolution of law in the Roman (or Greek) Empire.
   (b) A recent federal statute.
   (c) The use of computers in keeping track of judges' decisions.

CHAPTER 5

Federal Elections and Political Parties

Earlier in this book, "democracy" was defined as "rule by the people". In a large and complex nation such as Canada, it is impossible for every person to have a daily say in the decisions of the government. However, Canadian citizens play a significant role in the political process when they exercise their right to vote. When Canadians vote in federal elections, they elect people to represent their community in the House of Commons. This system of government is known as representative democracy.

In this chapter, you will examine the Canadian system of elections and party government. First you will be given an overview of the electoral process at the federal level. In the next four sections, the history, regional strength, policy, and structure of Canada's major political parties will be discussed. Finally, you will see Canada's electoral process and political parties "in action" by considering some significant aspects of the 1984 election. While reading this chapter, keep these key questions in mind:

- *What are the major steps in the process by which federal Members of Parliament are elected?*
- *What are Canada's three major political parties today? Which one has been dominant in the government over the past century?*
- *Since 1968, from which region(s) of Canada has each party drawn most of its electoral support?*
- *What have been the chief policy differences among the three major parties?*
- *What are the main features of the organization of Canada's political parties?*
- *How did the 1984 federal election illustrate the influence of the media on the political process?*

Federal Elections: An Overview

You will recall from Chapter 2 that Parliament, the law-making branch of Canada's federal government, has three components: the House of Commons, the Senate, and the Governor General. The first of these is the most powerful. It is also the only one whose representatives are elected. These representatives, the Members of Parliament, are chosen by the people of Canada in federal elections.

At the time of Confederation, there were 181 Members of Parliament. By the time Newfoundland had become the tenth province in 1949, the number had risen to 262. At the time of the 1984 election, there were 282 MP's. Thus, as the population of Canada has grown, so has the total number of MP's. The formula for this adjustment, which is based on census data, has undergone many changes over the years.

Each Member of Parliament represents a **constituency**, the population of a particular geographical area. Constituencies are sometimes also called **ridings** or **seats**. The number of constituencies in a given province is based on that province's share of the Canadian population. For example, British Columbia, with about 10 percent of the total population, had 28 of the 282 constituencies at the time of the 1984 election.

In theory, any Canadian citizen 18 years of age or over, may choose to run at election time as a **candidate** in a federal constituency. Usually, but not always, candidates are representatives of a **political party**. A vote is, therefore, generally a vote for a party as well as for a candidate. The candidate who gets the most votes in a constituency becomes the MP for that constituency. The party which has the most MP's forms the government party, and its leader becomes the Prime Minister. The party with the second-largest number of seats is designated the **Official Opposition**, and that party's leader is the **leader of the opposition**. If a party wins more than one-half of the total number of seats, it forms a **majority** government, while a party which gets more seats than any other party, but less than half the total, forms a **minority** government.

An election can either return to power the party which had formed the government before the election or give the right to form a government to another party.

The process whereby Canadian federal elections are conducted is an elaborate one, formally set out in the *Canada Elections Act*. It can be considered to have six stages: *dissolution, enumeration, nomination, campaigning, balloting, and tabulation.*

Dissolution

You have learned that one of the Governor General's most important executive functions is to *dissolve* the House of Commons at the request

While Canadians support different federal political parties, our national flag is a symbol of Canada's unity.

Nationalism

Nationalism *refers to the common hopes of a group of people who are united by culture, political system, or place of birth, or by combinations of the three. Nationalism is rooted in emotional feelings which are often expressed politically.*

For example, some members of the **Parti Québécois**, *which was in power in Québec from 1976 to 1985, argued that a* **Québécois** *spirit of nationalism related to culture and place of birth, and that Québec deserved political sovereignty. Québec nationalists wanted independence from the rest of Canada because it would preserve, encourage, and advance* **Québécois** *culture.*

of the Prime Minister, that is, to dismiss the MP's and thereby make way for a new election. At the same time, the Governor General fixes an election date suggested by the Prime Minister. This date usually falls on a Monday, and must be within 50 days of the date of dissolution. As you can see, although the power of dissolution belongs in theory to the Governor General, in practice it belongs to the Prime Minister.

A Prime Minister will generally ask the Governor General for dissolution under one of two circumstances: either that the government is near the end of its five-year term, or that the government has been defeated on a major bill in the House of Commons. The first circumstance almost always occurs when a majority government is in power; the second, when a minority government is in power.

In the first case, the government is observing the constitutional rule that an election must be held every five years. In practice, a government often seeks re-election after four years. In the second case, the government seeks dissolution because it has lost on a non-confidence motion, a vote in which Members of Parliament indicate whether they still support the government. It is always one of the opposition parties which makes a motion to hold a vote of non-confidence. Since a majority government can count on the support of its own party's MP's, it is virtually impossible for it to lose on a non-confidence motion. In a minority government situation, however, a combination of opposition MP's outnumber the government MP's, and the non-confidence motion will pass. The Prime Minister then asks the Governor General for dissolution. This situation occurred in 1980, when a Progressive Conservative government had been in power for only eight months.

Enumeration

Following dissolution, the Governor General asks the Chief Electoral Officer, who is a civil servant, to issue **election writs** and thereby put the election machinery into motion. Reporting to the Chief Electoral Officer are the **returning officers**. Returning officers are so called because they are in charge of compiling both the list of voters' names "returned" to the constituency office and the election results "returned" in that constituency on election day.

The preparation of the voters' list is known as **enumeration**, and the people who visit Canadians' homes to record names, addresses, and occupations are known as **enumerators**. Voters who cannot be reached by enumerators can phone or visit an enumeration office to make certain that their names are put on the list. Seventeen days before election day, the lists are finalized.

Within each constituency, there are anywhere from several dozen to several hundred **polling stations**, where the voting occurs. Each polling station has its own list of voters. On average, a polling station's list holds about 250 names.

Nomination

As soon as election writs are issued, that is, at the same time that enumeration begins, each party must decide who will be its candidate in each constituency. The selection of candidates is known as **nomination**. Indeed, even before dissolution and the issuing of election writs, a party may already be in the process of nominating candidates.

In theory, any Canadian citizen 18 years of age or older may be nominated as a candidate. In practice, most candidates are nominated to represent a party, and they tend to be long-time workers for their party. Although there are no specific laws governing nomination procedures, parties generally select a candidate for each constituency at a nomination meeting held in that riding. Party members present at the meeting vote until one of the people seeking the nomination has a majority.

Sometimes, people without any attachment to a political party do become candidates. Those who decide to run in this way are identified as "independents" on the election ballot. It is rare for an independent candidate to get more than a handful of votes in an election, let alone win a seat. However, most constituencies usually have one or more independent candidates on the ballot.

Every candidate, whether independent or affiliated with a party, must make a deposit of $200 with the returning officer for the constituency. The candidate must also present nomination papers containing the signatures of 25 other electors. If the party leader officially endorses the candidate, the latter's name will be listed on the ballot for that constituency on election day. The winning candidate and all others who get at least half as many votes as the winner have their deposits refunded after the election.

Liberal Leader John Turner addresses his caucus in July 1984, with the purpose of introducing the political process to newly nominated candidates for the next federal election. This meeting took place before dissolution of Parliament and the issuing of election writs.

Campaigning

The campaign takes place from the time when election writs are issued to the weekend before election day. During this period, the parties and candidates present themselves to the public through the various media and in public meetings. Later in this chapter, you will look more closely at election campaigns. Next to election day itself, the campaign is the highlight of the election process.

These posters for the leaders of the three major parties in the 1976 Québec election campaign present Robert Bourassa, René Lévesque, and Rodrigue Biron to the public. Which poster is most effective, and why?

Balloting

On the day of a federal election, each polling station is open from 8 a.m. to 8 p.m. Employers are required by law to allow their workers time to vote. In most cases, polling stations are located in a neighbourhood school, church, or community centre. People who for some reason cannot vote on election day may vote in an **advance poll**, usually held a week before the regular election.

The process of recording a vote on a ballot is a simple one. Each polling station is manned by a **deputy returning officer**, who is responsible to the returning officer. When a voter enters a polling station, his or her name is checked by the deputy returning officer against the list of voters prepared for the poll. The deputy returning officer then gives the voter a ballot, to be taken to a curtained booth. There, the voter pencils an "X" in the box beside the name of the candidate he or she favours. The voter then folds the ballot, leaves the booth, and presents the ballot to the deputy returning officer, who drops it into a special locked box.

The deputy returning officer checks voters' names off the enumeration list before they are handed their ballots. Why do you think this is done?

Tabulation

Once the polling stations close, the ballot boxes are opened and the ballots counted by the deputy returning officer. Nowadays, computers tabulate the voting results for many polls in very short order. At the close of voting, local television and radio stations can legally begin to broadcast the results as they come in.

Thanks to computer technology, the media can sometimes predict the outcome of an election very soon after the polls close. Because of time-zone differences, voters in British Columbia are always the last to learn about the election night results. In the 1984 election, for example, the national TV networks indicated a sweeping majority victory for the Progressive Conservative Party nearly three hours before they could even begin their election-night coverage in the Pacific time zone!

Occasionally, the results are so close that it is impossible to predict the outcome of the election. In 1972, the entire country had to wait until the votes from B.C. were in to find out that nationwide, the Liberals had edged out the Progressive Conservatives by only two seats.

TABLE 5.1 *Summary of Federal Election Results, 1968–84. In which of these years did Canadians elect a majority government? A minority government?*

Election Year	*Winning Party*	*No. of Seats Held by Winning Party*	*Total No. of Seats*
1968	Liberal	155	264
1972	Liberal	109	264
1974	Liberal	141	265
1979	PC	136	282
1980	Liberal	146	282
1984	PC	211	282

The election results of the 1976 Québec election are tallied and posted. What is the benefit of using computers for this task?

Sometimes the vote in a particular constituency may be very close. If the margin of victory is roughly 100 votes or less, the runner-up candidate may request a **recount**. A recount usually takes place within a few days of the election, and is supervised by the constituency's returning officers. In other cases, a recount may be undertaken because suspicious circumstances surrounded the voting. Recounts of this sort are carried out by two Supreme Court judges.

It sometimes happens that, between national elections, an MP dies or decides to resign. If this happens, the constituency represented by the MP is declared vacant. A **by-election** is then held, so that voters in the riding may elect a new MP. Customarily, a by-election takes place within a few months after a vacancy occurs.

CLOSE-UP

Are Canadians Fairly Represented?

In Canada's federal elections, the results can be measured in two ways: by the number of seats won, and by the **popular vote**. In terms of determining the winning candidate, the first of these is the only one that matters. As you have seen, the party with the most seats forms a government.

But political scientists generally regard the popular vote as a more reliable measure of which party is most favoured by the public. While the number of seats won is an *absolute* figure, the popular vote is a *relative* figure. The popular vote received by a party is expressed as the percentage of total ballots marked. For example, if 10 million ballots are cast nationally, and the candidates of a certain party get 3 million of them, that party's share of the popular vote is 30 percent. However, the popular vote figures often bear little relationship to the number of seats won by each party. In the 1984 federal election, for example, the figures for seats won and the popular vote were as shown in the following table:

TABLE 5.2 *Figures for Seats Won and Popular Vote, 1984*

Party	*No. of Seats Won*	*Popular Vote*
PC	211	50%
Liberal	40	28%
NDP	30	19%
Other	1	3%
Total	282	100%

In this election, as in others, the percentage of the popular vote for each party did not correspond closely to the number of seats won by each party. The Conservatives won 211 of 282 seats, or 75 percent, though they received only 50 percent of the popular vote. The Liberals won 40 seats, or 14 percent, with 28 percent of the popular vote, and the NDP took 30 seats, or 11 percent, with 19 percent of the popular vote.

Indeed, sometimes the party with the highest popular vote figure does not win the most seats. This situation occurred most recently in 1979. In that election, the Conservatives received only 36 percent of the popular vote, even though they won 136 seats (48 percent), the most obtained by any party. The Liberals, with 40 percent of the popular vote, won only 114 seats (40 percent).

How can there be such a discrepancy between a party's share of the popular vote and its share of parliamentary seats? The answer often lies in the fact that a party may win by huge margins in some constituencies, but lose by relatively small margins elsewhere. The Liberals experienced this situation in 1979. A great many Liberal candidates in Québec won with majorities of 30 000 votes or more. Yet, for winning a seat, a margin of one vote is just as useful as a margin of 30 000. Where the Liberals lost, especially in Ontario, the margin of defeat was often only a few hundred votes or less. When these kinds of figures are tallied up, the discrepancy between seats and popular vote can be very large.

Many Canadians believe that the present system of "winner-take-all" representation by constituency is unfair. They point out that parties are often seriously over-represented or under-represented in relation to their share of the popular vote. Assume for a moment that the 282 seats in the 1984 election had been divided on the basis of the popular vote. The Conservatives would then have won a number of seats equal to 50 percent of 282, that is, 141 seats rather than 211. By the same standard, the Liberals would have won 79 seats instead of 40, and the NDP 54 instead of 30. The 3 percent of the popular vote received by "other" candidates would have resulted in 8 seats instead of 1.

No country in the world today has an electoral system which produces an exact correspondence between the popular vote and electoral representation. However, various forms of **proportional representation**, representation on the basis of the popular vote, exist in most countries of western continental Europe.

One country which mixes a "winner-take-all" constituency system and a system of proportional representation is West Germany. Some critics of the Canadian system have suggested that we might learn from the West German model. Suppose for a moment that in Canada's 1984 election, a version of the West German model had been applied. There would still be 282 constituencies, but twice that number of MP's, *i.e.*, 564. The share of MP's per province would remain the same; therefore, B.C. would have 56 of the 564 MP's (instead of the 28 of 282). Within each province and territory, one-half of the MP's would be elected by **constituency vote**; the other half, by **party vote**. Those elected by constituency vote would be elected in exactly the same way as in the Canadian system: that is, the candidate with the most votes in a constituency would win. Those elected by party vote would be candidates chosen by their parties from a special list. Each party would have a separate list for each province and territory.

QUESTIONS

1. **(a)** What is the popular vote?
   (b) Why does the text call it a "relative figure"?
2. Why, in 1979, did the Liberals win only 114 seats out of a total of 282 while receiving 40 percent of the popular vote?
3. How does the West German electoral system differ from that of Canada?

QUESTIONS

1. Why can Canada be called a "representative democracy"?
2. Why has the number of MP's risen since Confederation?
3. **(a)** What is a constituency?
   (b) How is the number of constituencies per province determined?
4. Name the six stages in the electoral process at the federal level.
5. Describe the tasks in an election of the returning officers.
6. Why is it important for people who are eligible to vote to be enumerated?
7. Describe a polling station, and what happens in it.
8. How are candidates chosen?
9. What is the purpose of an advance poll?
10. What is a by-election?

A Brief History of Canadian Political Parties

The political landscape in Canada in the twentieth century has been dominated by two political parties, the Liberals and the Progressive Conservatives. Of the 26 federal elections held between 1896 and 1984, the Liberals have won 18 and the Conservatives have won the remaining 8.

During this period, four other parties, or **third parties** as they are sometimes called, have known a degree of electoral success at the federal level. Yet none has ever won enough seats to form a government or even the Official Opposition. These four are the Progressives, the Social Credit Party, the *Créditistes*, and the New Democratic Party. Of the four, only the last is active today at the federal level.

Conservatives and Progressives: The Progressive Conservative Party

The modern federal Progressive Conservative Party has its roots in the pre-Confederation coalition of Canada West Tories, led by John A. Macdonald, and Canada East *bleus*, led by Georges-Etienne Cartier. The coalition called itself the "Conservative Party". Except for a five-year term after 1873, when the Pacific Scandal forced his government's resignation, Macdonald served as Prime Minister from Confederation until his death in 1891.

After 1896, the Conservatives found themselves in opposition, remaining there until the leadership of Sir Robert Borden revitalized the party. Returned to power in 1911, they led the country through the next decade. Borden's Union Government of 1917–21 was a coalition of Conservatives and English-speaking Liberals that attempted to guide the country through wartime crises such as the conscription issue.

By 1921, the Union Government coalition had come apart. The election of that year saw the Conservatives reduced to 50 seats and 30 percent of the popular vote. Most of their support came from rural Ontario and the Maritimes. It was the party's worst electoral showing since Confederation.

In that same election, a new party, the Progressives, showed significant strength in western Canada and rural Ontario, winning 65 seats and 23 percent of the popular vote. This showing not only helped create the first minority government in Canada, but also marked the greatest success ever enjoyed by a third party, both in number of seats and in popular vote.

Except for a brief return to power in 1925–26 and again in 1930–35, the Conservatives remained in opposition until 1957. The party's tenure in office under R.B. Bennett during the early 1930's corresponded to the height of the Great Depression. It was the worst possible time for any party to shoulder the responsibility of government. In 1943, the Conservatives formed a coalition with the remnants of the Progressive Party and became the Progressive Conservative Party.

In 1957, under the leadership of the "prairie populist", John Diefenbaker, the Progressive Conservatives came to power with a minority government. The next year saw a smashing PC majority victory with 208 seats out of 265. Yet what had been nation-wide support for the party quickly dissolved, particularly in urban Ontario and everywhere in Québec. After 1963, the PC's were doomed to another two decades in opposition, except for the short-lived government of Joe Clark in 1979–80.

The 1984 election was a victory for the PC's that rivalled the 1957 victory. Under their new leader Brian Mulroney, the party won a majority in every province. The total of 211 Conservative seats marked the highest number ever won by a party in a federal election.

The Liberal Party

The origins of the Liberal Party are found in the pre-Confederation coalition of Canada West Clear Grits led by George Brown, and the *Parti Rouge* led by A.-A. Dorion in Canada East. The first post-Confederation Liberal government, from 1873–78, was that of Alexander Mackenzie. In the early years after Confederation, the Liberals were far less organized and united than the Conservatives. But in 1896, the Liberals came to power federally under the leadership of Sir Wilfrid Laurier. A strong base of support in Québec which had been building for the Liberals ever since the 1885 execution of Louis Riel was solidified in that election. Québec's overwhelming electoral preference for the federal Liberals would prevail almost unbroken until 1984.

Laurier's "sunny ways" policy of conciliation attempted to forge a new harmony between French and English, East and West. It worked well enough to keep his government in power for 15 consecutive years. But by 1911, the Laurier magic had worn out, and the Liberals lost the election. The main issue of the election was reciprocity, currently better known as free trade. Reciprocity was championed by the Liberals but opposed by the Conservatives, as it had been since the days of Macdonald.

Laurier's successor, William Lyon Mackenzie King, headed the first minority government in Canadian federal politics. In 1921, his party won 116 seats, not quite enough to form a majority in a house of 235 seats. To stay in power, King cautiously allied himself with the newly formed Progressive Party and its 65 seats. Over the next decade, King's subtle borrowing of both Progressive ideas and Progressive support proved successful. Except during 1925–26 and 1930–35, King remained Prime Minister until his retirement in 1948. He held office longer than any other Prime Minister in Canadian history to date.

Louis St. Laurent succeeded King, leading the Liberals to majority victories in the elections of 1949 and 1953. Following the Liberal loss of power in 1957, St. Laurent retired, passing the leadership to Lester B. Pearson. Pearson led the party to two election victories in the 1960's, neither of which was quite strong enough to ensure a majority (129 of 265 seats in 1963, and 131 of 265 in 1965). On Pearson's retirement in 1968, the party chose Pierre Trudeau as its new leader.

Trudeau led the Liberals to a majority victory in 1968, a minority victory in 1972, and another majority in 1974. After his government's loss to the PC's in 1979, he considered retirement, but came back to lead the party to one more majority victory in the 1980 election. Trudeau finally retired in 1984, and was succeeded by John Turner. Within days of his winning the Liberal leadership and becoming Prime Minister, Turner called an election, which turned out to be the greatest electoral disaster the Liberals had ever known.

VOTE LIBERAL

1930 BUDGET

BRITISH PREFERENTIAL TARIFF

BRITISH PREFERENTIAL TARIFF

MISS CANADA

"THE GATES ARE MINE TO OPEN"

What do you suppose is the message of this 1930 campaign poster?

The New Democratic Party

The New Democratic Party began as the Co-operative Commonwealth Federation. The CCF was founded in 1933, in Regina, on the basis of a socialist platform. Its first leader was J.S. Woodsworth, a former leader of the small, short-lived Labour Party.

From fewer than 10 seats and less than 10 percent of the popular vote in the elections of 1935 and 1940, the CCF grew to win 28 seats and 16 percent of the popular vote in 1945. The party did not again achieve a similar level of electoral success until the 1960's, after it was reorganized and renamed the New Democratic Party in 1961. The NDP

Retiring NDP Leader Tommy Douglas (right) lifts the arm of the new party leader David Lewis at the party's 1971 leadership convention.

was forged from a coalition of the old CCF with the political wing of the Canadian Labour Congress and other Labour groups. Its first leader was former CCF Premier of Saskatchewan, Tommy Douglas.

While it has never formed a federal government or even the official federal opposition, the NDP has formed provincial governments or the official provincial opposition at one time or another in all the western provinces, as well as in Ontario. Traditionally, all of its significant federal support has come from these parts of the country.

The Social Credit Party and the *Créditistes*

The Social Credit Party, based in western Canada, was active federally from the mid-1930's to the mid-1970's. Its breakaway Québec version, the *Créditistes*, was active from the mid-1960's to the mid-1970's. The peak of Social Credit success was the 1962 election, in which the party won 30 seats and 12 percent of the popular vote. The *Créditistes* enjoyed their best election in 1972, winning 15 seats and 24 percent of the Québec popular vote. Both parties are virtually extinct today at the federal level.

QUESTIONS

1. What are third parties?

2. What historic basis exists for associating the colour blue with the Progressive Conservatives, and the colour red with the Liberals?

3. Review in point form the history of the present Progressive Conservative Party.

4. Which province most strongly and consistently supported the Liberals from 1896 to 1984?

5. Which Prime Minister served longest in office?

6. **(a)** Which is the only socialist party among the major federal political parties?
(b) What was the original name of this party?

Regionalism and Canadian Political Parties

It is customary for political commentators to look at Canada as being composed of four distinct regions: the Atlantic region; Québec; Ontario; and the West, which includes the Yukon and the Northwest Territories. To be sure, there are many distinctions within these regions. In the Atlantic region, for example, Newfoundland has a history, culture, and character quite distinct from those of the Acadians. The traditions and allegiances of rural Québec differ from those of the province's cities. The same kind of contrast exists between heavily urbanized southern Ontario and the other parts of that province. In the West, British Columbia is sometimes considered a region in its own right, apart from the prairie provinces. Despite such intra-regional variety, the four broad regions still form a suitable basis for examining how support for the various federal parties differs across Canada.

Consider the data in Table 5.3. They show that a party often wins an election with massive support from one or two regions and little or no support from the others. Such regional imbalance creates considerable difficulties. When one area of the country gives most of its support to the winning party, that region obtains heavy representation in the federal government. By the same token, a region that elects few members of the winning party has little government representation. The federal elections of 1968 to 1984 all demonstrate some degree of regional imbalance.

Here a woman in traditional Acadian costume makes brooms as her ancestors did long ago. Many regions of Canada have their own traditional heritage and culture. How might this affect their voting habits?

TABLE 5.3 *Federal Election Results by Region, 1968–84*

		Atlantic	*Québec*	*Ontario*	*West*	*National*
1968 (Liberal majority)	Liberal	7	56	64	28	155
	PC	25	4	17	26	72
	NDP	0	0	6	15	21
	Other	0	14	1	1	16
1972 (Liberal minority)	Liberal	10	56	36	7	109
	PC	22	2	40	43	107
	NDP	0	0	11	20	31
	Other	0	16	1	0	17
1974 (Liberal majority)	Liberal	13	60	55	13	141
	PC	17	3	25	50	95
	NDP	1	0	8	7	16
	Other	1	11	0	0	12
1979 (PC minority)	Liberal	12	67	32	3	114
	PC	18	2	57	59	136
	NDP	2	0	6	18	26
	Other	0	6	0	0	6
1980 (Liberal majority)	Liberal	19	73	52	2	146
	PC	13	1	38	51	103
	NDP	0	0	5	27	32
	Other	0	1	0	0	1
1984 (PC majority)	Liberal	7	17	14	2	40
	PC	25	58	67	61	211
	NDP	0	0	13	17	30
	Other	0	0	1	0	1

(Adapted from statistics in Thorburn, H.G., ed., *Party Politics in Canada*, 5th edition. Toronto: Prentice-Hall, 1985, pp. 338–349.)

Premier Allan Blakeney speaks to students during a campaign swing in support of NDP candidates in Manitoba. Why do you suppose Blakeney spends valuable campaign time speaking to people who are too young to vote?

In the election of 1968, the year of "Trudeaumania", the Liberals received very strong support in both Québec and Ontario and moderate support in the West, but won only 7 of the 32 Atlantic seats. Four years later, the Liberal majority was reduced to a minority. The Liberals trailed the PC's in seats in both the Atlantic region and Ontario, and ran behind both the PC's and the NDP in the West, obtaining only 7 of the 70 seats there. Only their strong showing in Québec, 56 of 74 seats, kept them in power. In 1974, the Liberals gained modest increases in seats in the Atlantic and the West. Their seats in the latter area were obtained at the expense of the NDP. Yet, as Table 5.3 shows, the Liberals were still behind the PC's in both those regions. The support they regained in Ontario in 1974 gave them back the majority they had lost in 1972.

As in 1972, the 1979 election saw the Liberals behind the PC's in the Atlantic and in Ontario, and behind both the PC's and the NDP in the West. However, as the figures in Table 5.3 testify, they remained the top party by far in Québec. Support for the PC's in Ontario swelled to 57 of the province's 95 seats. This support from Ontario, coupled with an increase in western support, gave the Conservatives enough seats to form their first government since 1962. Québec had elected only a single MP to the new government. The Liberals regained a national majority in the 1980 election. They won a majority of seats in three regions, but only 2 of 80 seats in the West. In this election, the Liberals reached their highest level in Québec, but fell to their lowest in the West.

Table 5.3 shows that NDP support has been virtually non-existent in the Atlantic region and Québec. As of 1984, the NDP had elected members from the Atlantic region only twice and had never elected a member in Québec. In Ontario, the party's record of 11 seats in the 1972 election was not bettered until 1984. It is from the West that the NDP has drawn most of its federal strength.

The 1984 election was a rarity in Canadian history, in that the winning party got a majority of seats in all regions—in fact, in all provinces and both territories. The greatest surprise of that election was the switch from the Liberals to the Conservatives in Québec. Less surprising but still significant were the heavy Liberal losses in Ontario to both the PC's and the NDP.

QUESTIONS

1. Why did the Liberals' loss of support in the 1972 election not result in a change in government?
2. After which election did the West have the least representation in the federal government?
3. Which election resulted in the most balanced regional representation for the government?
4. There are currently 282 seats in the House of Commons. Is it possible for a party to win enough seats in Québec alone to form a government? In Québec and Ontario combined? In the West?

Canada's interest in Free Trade with the United States has a long history. In 1897, Laurier, a Liberal, actively sought a trade agreement with the United States. This foreign policy proposal was opposed by the Conservatives and eventually lost Laurier the 1911 election. In 1987, Mulroney, a Conservative, actively sought a Free Trade Agreement with the United States, which was opposed by the Liberals, and which, again, became an election issue.

Laurier represents the "Canadian free trader" in this turn-of-the-century cartoon.

The Policies of Canada's Political Parties

What a party proposes to do if it is elected, and what it does do when elected, can be called its **policy**. There are certain policy differences among the parties. Since the economy is generally the issue that concerns voters the most, it will be useful to look at the broad outlines of the economic policies of the three major parties. Two other issues that serve as good points of comparison are federal-provincial relations and foreign policy.

The Economy

Today, the economic policies of all three major parties are to some degree **interventionist**. That is, all the parties believe that the government should take a positive role in the direction and control of the economy. However, none of them wants an economy that is under complete government control. In other words, no party is either wholly capitalistic or completely socialistic. Between these extremes, the parties show some differences. The Conservatives have tended to favour light to moderate intervention; the Liberals, moderate to strong intervention; the NDP, strong to very strong intervention.

Three examples of government intervention in the country's economy are the establishment of Crown corporations, regulations for businesses, and controls on foreign investment.

Each will be discussed below, to illustrate party differences in the matter of intervention. The examples also serve to demonstrate that the parties not only change their own policies, but even adopt one another's.

Crown Corporations

Petro-Canada, a federally-owned oil company, was created by the Liberal government in 1974–75. Before the Liberals proposed the idea of such a company, the NDP had already urged it. When Petro-Canada was set up, the Conservatives claimed that it was too powerful; the NDP, that it was not powerful enough. In the 1979 election campaign, the Conservatives pledged themselves to sell the company. During their short term of office after the election, however, they softened their stance. They would, as Prime Minister Joe Clark put it, **privatize** Petro-Canada; that is, allow private businesses and/or individuals to buy shares in the company. Clark's government was not in power long enough to do anything about the matter. When the Conservatives returned to power in 1984, under Brian Mulroney, they left Petro-Canada more or less as it was.

Regulations for Businesses

The issue of wage and price controls emerged at a time of severe inflation in the Canadian economy. In 1974, the Conservative opposition, led by Robert Stanfield, argued that inflation could be kept down by establishing a government ceiling on the level to which prices and wages could rise. This was a more interventionist idea than many Tories were comfortable with. It was also too interventionist for the governing Liberals. The NDP's answer to economic problems was not to control inflation by controlling wages, but to clamp down on large corporations. Canadians would be best served, the NDP argued, by an increase in taxes on large corporations. The money from these taxes could be redirected to needy Canadians. The minority Liberal government of Prime Minister Trudeau fell, and an election followed. In the 1974 campaign, the Liberals mocked the Conservatives' proposed wage- and price-control scheme. The concept was unpopular with the voters, and this unpopularity helped restore the Liberal majority in 1974. Yet just a year later, the Trudeau government itself enacted a temporary wage- and price-control scheme.

Foreign Investment

The Foreign Investment Review Agency (FIRA) was established in 1973, by the Trudeau government. It was intended to screen foreign companies that wished to set up or change operations in Canada. The Conservatives argued that FIRA was hurting the economy by refusing or over-regulating foreign investors. By contrast, the NDP claimed that FIRA was not doing enough to keep the Canadian economy in the hands of Canadians. When elected in 1984, the Conservatives moved quickly to change FIRA. The agency was renamed Investment Canada. The purpose of the revamped agency was to tell foreign investors, in the words of Prime Minister Mulroney, that Canada was "open for business". Both the Liberals and the NDP have criticized several of the decisions made by Investment Canada.

Federal-Provincial Relations

In Canada, political power is divided between the federal and provincial governments. Whether one of the three major federal parties favours more federal power or less usually depends on the issue in question. A party that calls for increased federal power can be described as **centralist**; one which favours increased provincial power can be called **decentralist**. In general, both the Liberals and the NDP have been quite centralist in recent decades, although neither has ever been as centralist as was the CCF. The Conservatives have tended to be the most decentralist of the federal parties. The respective positions of the parties might best be exemplified by a single issue: the constitutional negotiations of 1980–81. One of the most contentious issues in the negotiations concerned the powers that the provincial governments would hold under the amended Constitution.

The Liberal position on federal-provincial power sharing in the 1970's and early 1980's was closely linked to the political values of Pierre Trudeau. As party leader and Prime Minister, Trudeau brought to his party and to the federal government a marked desire at least to halt,

Prime Minister Brian Mulroney meets with the Provincial Premiers at a constitutional conference held at Meech Lake, Québec.

if not to reverse, what he saw as a dangerous drift towards decentralization in Canada. In Trudeau's view, there had to be no doubt that the federal government led and the provinces followed.

Central to Trudeau's concern was the language issue. He believed that the amended Constitution must reinforce minority language rights, which had an important link with the federal policy of official bilingualism. Minority language rights for education, an area outside of federal jurisdiction, had to be enshrined in the Constitution. Once there, these rights could not be tampered with by any provincial administration.

The Liberals under Trudeau were also alarmed at the strengthening of interprovincial barriers to trade and employment. For example, it had become the practice of some provinces to establish **local-hiring policies**, which allowed only residents of a given province to work in certain industries in that province. Workers from other parts of Canada were thus discouraged from seeking work there. The *Constitution Act, 1982* contains somewhat modified versions of the Trudeau government's views on both language rights and job mobility.

While the federal NDP had some objections to the details of Liberal constitutional proposals, there were no significant disagreements on general principles. However, NDP leader Ed Broadbent had a difficult time persuading certain factions within his party to support patriation of the Constitution over the objections of eight provinces. On the matter of the content of the Constitution, the NDP urged that the document respect the provinces' wishes for increased control over their natural resources.

In the late 1970's and early 1980's, the Conservatives spoke of Canada as "a community of communities", using the words of their leader Joe Clark. While the precise meaning of Clark's phrase was never made clear, the expression was taken to describe a Canada in which the federal government and the provinces would be more like partners, and less like leader and follower. The Conservatives under Clark put up a strong opposition to the Trudeau government during the patriation debate of 1980, arguing that the consent of the provinces was vital. Once patriation was achieved, over the Conservatives objections, the party worked for the acceptance of a version of an amending formula which would acknowledge the provinces' right to dissent on future amendments.

Foreign Policy

A vital issue in Canadian foreign policy has always been Canada's relationship with the United States. Indeed, it is often difficult to separate the broad subject of Canadian foreign affairs from the more specific subject of Canada's dealings with the United States. All three major parties are aware that Canadian interests are tightly linked with those of the U.S.A.

A giant Ronald Reagan puppet manipulates a small Brian Mulroney puppet in a demonstration before a one-day summit between the two leaders in 1988. What do you suppose the demonstrators were saying about Canadian-U.S. relations?

However, the parties have not always agreed on how close Canada-U.S. ties should be. Until the late 1960's, the Liberal Party tended to be more pro-American than the Conservatives. In more recent times, the two parties have switched stances. The NDP, for its part, has always been the most outspoken of the parties in urging Canada to maintain a respectful yet independent position in its relationship with the United States.

A classic example of the shift in the Liberal and Conservative positions on Canada-U.S. relations is free trade, known earlier in this century as "reciprocity". At that time, it was the Liberals who were pushing for closer ties between the two countries. The Laurier government's attempt to negotiate reciprocity with the U.S.A. lost it the 1911 election and ended Laurier's 15 years as Prime Minister. Three-quarters of a century later, the issue was revived when the Conservative government of Brian Mulroney sought a free trade deal with the U.S.A. There were serious objections from the Liberal party, and even more from the NDP.

The ambiguity of Liberal and Conservative foreign policy is also evident in Canada's military ties with the U.S.A. As the governing party throughout World War II and the next 12 years, the Liberals forged a close military relationship between Canada and the United States. Under a Liberal government, but with the support of both the Conservatives and the CCF, Canada became a member of the North Atlantic Treaty Organization (NATO) in 1949. A Liberal government also laid the groundwork for the Canadian role in the North American Air Defence Agreement (NORAD), a Canada-U.S. military alliance which came into existence in the summer of 1957, shortly after the federal election of that year.

In that election, a Conservative minority government under John Diefenbaker came to power. During his six years in office, Diefenbaker had a difficult and at times even hostile relationship with the United States. A major issue of the early 1960's was his extreme reluctance to allow American nuclear weapons to be stored in Canada. (On this issue, which was central to Canada's position in NORAD, not all Conservative Cabinet ministers supported their leader.) The Liberal opposition under Lester Pearson called for Canada to accept the American scheme. The issue was a critical one in the 1963 election, which saw the minority Conservative government displaced by a minority Liberal government.

Later in the decade, the Liberal government of Pierre Trudeau appeared in one respect to be distancing Canada from its military ties to the United States. The number of Canadian troops in NATO was cut by nearly one-half (although it was increased somewhat in the later 1970's). On this occasion, it was the Conservatives who objected to the apparent weakening of Canada's commitment to the western military alliance. Nevertheless, the Trudeau government continued to permit the presence of American nuclear weapons in Canada and even allowed the testing of U.S. cruise missiles in western Canada in the early 1980's.

Supporters of the "Voice of Women" protest nuclear warfare and the cruise missiles.

Meanwhile, the NDP was calling for Canada to withdraw entirely from NATO. By the late 1980's, however, it had softened its stance, agreeing that Canada should play a role in NATO, though a small one. At the same time, the NDP continued to be the most vocal critic of American domination of the Canadian economy.

QUESTIONS

1. Define "party policy".

2. Which party is usually in favour of least government intervention in the economy?

3. (a) What is the difference between a centralist party and a decentralist one?
(b) Which Canadian party is most strongly decentralist?

4. What connection was there between Trudeau's desire to see minority language rights entrenched in the 1982 Constitution, and federal-provincial relations?

5. What was the position of Joe Clark and the Conservatives in the matter of provincial assent to changes in the Constitution?

6. Which party currently tends to be most favourable towards American involvement in Canada?

7. In what way was the Trudeau government's decision to allow the testing of cruise missiles within Canada a reversal of its earlier military policy with regard to the U.S.A. and NATO?

The Structure of Canada's Political Parties

For any political party to be successful, it must be well organized, well financed, and well led. Three critical items to consider about the structure of political parties are, therefore, their manner of organization, their source of funds, and their method of choosing their leaders. You will now examine each of these factors in turn.

Party Organization

While the three major parties do differ in some details of their organization, they all have certain characteristics in common. The most important of these characteristics is the division of each party into a **parliamentary wing** and an **extra-parliamentary wing**.

The parliamentary wing of a party consists of all its Members of Parliament, or party caucus. It is, of course, the most highly visible and publicized section of the party.

Civic Parties in Canada

Civic parties are common throughout Canada. One survey conducted in the 1970's disclosed the existence of over 120 civic parties in all the major cities of Canada. Most are formed by citizens' groups, as names such as Citizens' Committees, Civic Action Leagues, Taxpayers' Associations, and Municipal Reform Associations indicate. Labour unions (United Steelworkers of America—Sudbury, Ontario), business groups (North Hill Businessmen's Association—Calgary, Alberta) and political parties (New Democratic Party, Social Credit Party, Communist Party) have also formed civic parties in many cities to contest municipal elections.

Supporters of civic parties say they are essential to the democratic process, since they allow voters to choose between candidates with different programs. They maintain that this is better than voting for independents with unclear or single-issue campaign positions. Opponents say, on the other hand, that they politicize the local level of government too much, by compelling candidates to support different programs and therefore to take sides on local issues. Such people believe that local government is best run by independents, voting according to their consciences.

Far larger is the extra-parliamentary wing of the party, which consists of all party officers and workers who are not part of the parliamentary wing. This group is organized into three levels, among which are many elaborate links and subgroups that differ from party to party. In short, however, the extra-parliamentary wing of each party takes the form of a pyramid.

At the bottom of the pyramid are the majority of party members, who belong to the **constituency associations**, one for each constituency in the country. The constituency associations are the "grassroots" of the party. Their volunteer workers answer phones, distribute brochures, and nominate candidates.

The next tier of the pyramid is made up of the **provincial associations**, one for each of the provinces. Their main role is to coordinate the activities of the various constituency associations within the province. The provincial associations should not be confused with the provincial version of each party, which is active in provincial politics.

In theory, these two entities are distinct. In practice, however, a provincial political party and the provincial associations of the same party at the federal level may be very closely linked, with many party members active in both groups. In British Columbia, for example, many individuals who worked for the provincial NDP in the provincial elections of 1979, 1983, and 1986 also worked for the federal NDP in the federal elections of 1979, 1980, and 1984.

On the other hand, a provincial association of the federal party and the provincial party may exist separately, in practice as well as in theory, and may sometimes be hostile to each other. An example is the relationship between the Québec branch of the federal Liberal party and the *Parti Libéral du Québec* (PLQ). Since the early 1960's, the two have had no formal links, and any informal links have been greatly strained. Indeed, in the 1984 federal election, many PLQ workers actively campaigned for federal Conservative candidates in Québec!

The third and top level of the extra-parliamentary wing of each party is its **national association**, located in Ottawa. The national association coordinates the activities of the provincial associations. It is typically staffed by a number of full-time, salaried, party officials who act as a link between the parliamentary and extra-parliamentary wings.

In each of the major parties, the national association sponsors **national conventions** roughly every two years. At these conventions, selected party members from both the extra-parliamentary and the parliamentary wing meet to elect party officials and discuss party policy. The various other purposes of party conventions are described in the following excerpt:

> For all three parties, the convention performs similar functions, related more to improving levels of participation, maintaining group solidarity

and garnering free publicity via press and television coverage, than to the establishment of party policy. The national NDP convention may have slightly more influence over party policy than the Liberal and Conservative conventions but, because the NDP has never been in power, and does not have to "deliver" its convention agreements, that might be expected.

The convention functions to create group solidarity. By bringing party members together, it renews acquaintances and rekindles identity with the cause; in doing so, it improves party morale and the chances of success in the next election.

R. J. Van Loon and M.S. Whittington
The Canadian Political System

Party Funding

Political parties require a great deal of money to support their activities. The most obvious expense is the cost of an election campaign. Yet between elections there are other expenses: salaries of full-time party workers, rental of office space, and fees for professional policy research and poll taking, to name just a few.

The *Election Expenses Act* of 1974 regulates the collection and spending of money by the parties and candidates. Under the terms of the *Act*, the names of all donors giving $100 or more to any party must be made public. The *Act* also limits the amount of spending at election time. At the federal level, no party may spend a sum that represents more than 30 cents for each name on the list of all constituencies where it has candidates. The three major parties always nominate candidates in every constituency. Therefore, the limit on their national spending is given by the total number of registered voters in Canada, multiplied by 30 cents. An individual candidate may spend anywhere from 25 cents to $1 per voter, depending on the size of the constituency (see Table 5.4). In a constituency where a candidate stands a good chance of being elected, and where the race is close, the amount spent is usually close to the maximum.

TABLE 5.4 *Spending Limits for Candidates in Federal Constituencies. What would be the maximum that a candidate could spend in a constituency with 30 000 voters?*

• for first 15 000 voters on list:	$1.00 per voter
• for next 10 000 voters on list:	$0.50 per voter
• for any additional voters on list:	$0.25 per voter

Choosing Party Leaders

Some national conventions are leadership conventions at which new leaders are chosen. Next to elections, party leadership conventions are the most newsworthy of all party activities. When the Conservatives or Liberals, in particular, hold such a convention, the whole country watches, because the new leader may or will become Prime Minister. Table 5.5 shows data on the federal party leaders of the past three-and-a-half decades.

The selection of a new leader takes place when a current leader resigns. Sometimes leaders resign simply because they wish to retire from active politics; examples are Liberal leaders Lester Pearson (in 1968) and Pierre Trudeau (in 1984), as well as NDP leaders Tommy Douglas (in 1971) and David Lewis (in 1975). Another reason for resignation is pressure from party members who are unhappy with their leader. A leader who resigns under these circumstances may decide to run in the following leadership convention. John Diefenbaker (in 1967) and Joe Clark (in 1983) are examples of Conservative leaders who tried unsuccessfully to regain party leadership in this way.

Leadership candidates are most often MP's of a given party at the time they run for its leadership. Yet they may come from other backgrounds. Both Tommy Douglas and Robert Stanfield were former provincial premiers. Brian Mulroney was a prominent Québec lawyer

TABLE 5.5 *Federal Party Leaders in Recent Years (to 1988)*

	Leader (Term of Leadership)	*Elections Contested*	*Elections Won*
Liberal:	Lester Pearson (1958–68)	4	2 (M)
	Pierre Trudeau (1968–84)	5	3 (M), 1 (m)
	John Turner (1984–)	1	0
NDP:	Tommy Douglas (1961–71)	4	0
	David Lewis (1971–75)	2	0
	Ed Broadbent (1975–)	3	0
PC:	John Diefenbaker (1956–67)	5	1 (M), 2 (m)
	Robert Stanfield (1967–76)	3	0
	Joe Clark (1976–83)	2	1 (m)
	Brian Mulroney (1983–)	2	2 (M)

Elections Contested = number of elections in which individual was party leader
Elections Won = number of elections in which the leader's party formed a government
(M) = majority government
(m) = minority government

John Turner acknowledges applause from delegates at the 1984 Liberal Leadership Convention in Ottawa.

and businessman who had never run in any election. After more than a decade as a Liberal MP and Cabinet minister, John Turner left active politics in 1976 to become a Toronto-based corporate lawyer. He returned to political life in 1984, to run for the Liberal leadership.

Both the NDP and the Conservatives have had a fairly good regional representation of party leaders. NDP leader Tommy Douglas was a westerner, while Lewis and Broadbent were from Ontario. Lewis was the only major federal party leader who was both an immigrant and of neither British nor French background. Conservative leaders Diefenbaker and Clark were both westerners, Stanfield was from the Maritimes, and Mulroney was from Québec.

The Liberals, on the other hand, have drawn their leaders almost exclusively from Ontario and Québec. An important unwritten rule of Liberal leadership is the "principle of alternation": the party regularly alternates between francophone and anglophone leaders. This rule has held in every change of Liberal leadership since the time of Laurier.

As many as 3000 voting delegates attend a leadership convention. A convention typically opens with a night of speeches which range from pep talks for party members to tributes, if appropriate, to the retiring party leader. The next day is given over to the speeches made by each of the leadership candidates. The leadership vote takes place on the following day.

Voting for the leader lasts for as many ballots as are needed until one candidate gets a majority of delegate votes. The candidate who places highest on the first ballot does not always win, as happened to Joe Clark in 1983. After each ballot, the candidate with the lowest number of votes is automatically eliminated, as indicated in Table 5.6. Other low-ranking candidates may voluntarily drop out and give their support to another candidate.

TABLE 5.6 *Recent Party Leadership Convention Voting Results*

	Ballots			
	1st	*2nd*	*3rd*	*4th*
PC (June 11, 1983)				
* Joe Clark	1,091	1,085	1,058	1,325
Brian Mulroney	874	1,021	1,036	1,584 L
* John Crosbie	639	781	858[e]	
* Michael Wilson	144[w]			
* David Crombie	166	67[e]		
Peter Pocklington	102[w]			
* John Gamble	17[e]			
Neil Fraser				
LIBERAL (June 16, 1984)				
John Turner	1,593	1,862 L		
* Jean Chrétien	1,067	1,368		
* Don Johnston	278	192		
* John Roberts	185[w]			
* Mark MacGuigan	135[w]			
* John Munro	93[w]			
* Eugene Whelan	84[e]			
NDP (July 7, 1985)				
* Ed Broadbent	536	586	694	984 L
Rosemary Brown	413	397	494	658
* Lorne Nystrom	345	342	413[e]	
John Harney	313	299[e]		
Douglas Campbell	11[e]			

L = candidate elected leader
* = candidate was a federal MP at time of leadership convention
[e] = eliminated automatically
[w] = withdrew voluntarily

A great deal of negotiation and persuasion takes place at leadership conventions, right up to and even during the balloting. Front-running candidates and their committed delegates will try to gain the support of lower-ranking candidates and their delegates. A drop-off candidate who directs delegate support to one of the front runners may later find the favour repaid. For example, in the 1983 Conservative leadership race, Michael Wilson dropped out after the first ballot. He then lent his support to Brian Mulroney. After the Conservatives won the election of the following year, Wilson was appointed Minister of Finance in the new government.

A winning leadership candidate who is not an MP at the time is traditionally expected to become one as soon as possible. Such a candidate usually obtains a seat by running in a by-election in a "safe" riding, that is, one where the party is traditionally strong and its victory can be taken for granted. The sitting MP resigns, thus forcing a by-election, which the new party leader contests and (usually) wins. For example, when Brian Mulroney won the Conservative leadership in 1983, he ran in a by-election for a safe Nova Scotia seat which had been held by Elmer Mackay.

QUESTIONS

1. What is the extra parliamentary wing of a political party?
2. Why do political parties hold national conventions?
3. What is the purpose of the *Election Expenses Act*?
4. According to Table 5.5, which recent party leader has been the most successful in terms of elections won compared to elections contested? Who has been least successful?
5. Must a person be an MP to run for the leadership of a party? Explain.
6. Refer to Table 5.6 and examine the statistics for the Liberal Party's leadership convention of June 16, 1984. Did the "principle of alternation" work for or against John Turner? Explain your reasoning.

Brian Mulroney stretches through a bus window to reach potential voters in Wabush, Nfld., on the last stop of his 1984 federal election campaign. Two days later he became Prime Minister.

Elections and Parties: A Look at 1984

So far in this chapter, you have examined the purpose and process of Canada's electoral system. You have also read about the history, regional support, policies, and structure of the major parties. It is now time to unite all these topics in a look at the dynamics of an actual election. Specifically, you will explore the roles of the party leaders, the media, and special interest groups in light of the 1984 election.

Table 5.7 highlights some important events of the seven months before the election.

TABLE 5.7 *Selected Key Dates and Events Before and During the 1984 Election*

February 29	Pierre Trudeau announces his decision to resign as PM as soon as a new Liberal leader is chosen.
March 16	John Turner announces his decision to run for the Liberal leadership.
March 29–31	Gallup poll shows the Liberals ahead of the Conservatives by 6 percent.
June 16	Turner wins the Liberal leadership on the second ballot.
June 21–23	Gallup poll shows the Liberals ahead of the Conservatives by 11 percent.
June 29	Trudeau announces ten patronage appointments.
June 30	Trudeau's resignation takes effect; Turner becomes Prime Minister.
July 5–8	Gallup poll shows the Liberals ahead of the Conservatives by 9 percent.
July 9	Turner calls election for September 4th; announces 17 patronage appointments.
July 24–25	The first two nationally televised leaders' debates take place.
August 9–10	Gallup poll shows the Conservatives ahead of the Liberals by 14 percent.
August 15	The third nationally televised debate (on women's issues) takes place.
August 28–29	Gallup poll shows the Conservatives ahead of the Liberals by 32 percent.
September 4	Election held; Conservatives win majority.

The Role of the Party Leaders

One group of Canadian political scientists has summed up the role of party leaders as follows:

> Party leaders are the superstars of Canadian politics. In their day-to-day coverage of public affairs and political events, television, radio, newspapers and magazines treat party leaders' pronouncements and behaviour as major news items. During election campaigns media coverage of leaders intensifies greatly, with reporters following close at the leaders' heels as parties' campaign tours criss-cross the country...
>
> ...Federal election campaigns frequently become political horseraces in which debates over policies lag behind the emphasis parties place on developing positive images of their leaders in the public mind. Parties

compete for electoral support by attempting to manipulate the mass media to provide favourable coverage of the issues and their leader...

Harold D. Clarke
Absent Mandate: The Politics of Discontent in Canada

Most Canadians would likely agree that this assessment is not far off the mark. "Selling the leader" is an essential feature of an election. The success of a party in an election is in many respects a verdict on the popularity of its leader. The image of the party leader has become increasingly important since the mid-1950's, when television began to play a large role in election coverage. There is, however, a difference between image—how a person appears—and character—what a person is really like. Leaders' clothes or gestures greatly affect their appearance on television, yet these outward appearances reveal nothing about their political ideas.

The Role of the Media

Very few Canadians have direct access to the politicians who represent them. Thus, the images Canadians have of party leaders are those conveyed by the media. It is newspapers, magazines, radio, and especially television that present the information about the party leaders and local candidates on which Canadians base their judgements about their representatives. How reliable and well-balanced is this reporting? How much of the media's election coverage concerns substance, and how much concerns image?

In this connection, consider a leading policy issue of the 1984 campaign: the national deficit. Throughout the previous decade, the federal government had borrowed enormous sums of money. The borrowing had reached the point where nearly 30 cents of every tax dollar was needed just to pay the interest on the debt. Leaders of all three parties pledged to curb the deficit, but without making severe cutbacks in major social programs. However, the NDP was the only party to assert that social programs took priority over the deficit.

John Turner laughs with former provincial NDP leader Dave Barrett while being interviewed by the politician-turned-broadcaster at a Vancouver radio station.

Managing the deficit is an extremely complex and difficult task. For most Canadians, it lies in the dull, remote world of accountants' figures and balance sheets. As important as it is, the deficit is not a colourful issue. It does not readily make exciting news clips on the evening news, nor lend itself to eye-catching newspaper photographs. Voters tend to relate more easily to matters with a "human-touch" appeal, and it is this sort of coverage that the media often gives. Therefore, in the 1984 campaign, much media time was devoted to items which, in retrospect, seem trivial. Throughout the campaign, for instance, John Turner's speech mannerisms were a matter of media concern, as was the wardrobe of Mila Mulroney.

Another factor in the campaign that received extensive coverage was the patronage issue. In the long run it, too, was a far less serious issue than the deficit. However, patronage has highly symbolic overtones and raises much emotion. The issue helped Mulroney's cause as much as it hurt Turner's.

In a nutshell, patronage occurs when the government party appoints its own party people to government jobs, many of which pay high salaries. An appointment to the Senate, a position worth $65 000 a year in the mid-1980's, is one prominent patronage "plum". Others include diplomatic appointments, or appointments to various Crown corporations or other government agencies. Patronage has long been an accepted, if controversial, feature of political life in Canada and elsewhere.

A series of Liberal patronage appointments in the summer of 1984 therefore caused a considerable outcry. The circumstances of the appointments were complex and confusing, but their net result was that John Turner found himself accused of behaving like an "old-guard" Liberal. As journalist Charles Lynch observed, "Turner, the darling of the media during the Liberal leadership campaign, quickly became the goat."

By the fourth week of the campaign, the patronage issue was still a hot item. In that week, the leaders met for nationally televised debates, the first in French and the second in English. For many Canadians, these debates were the highlight of the campaign; they presented an opportunity to see the leaders confront one another. An exchange in the second debate marked what was, according to Charles Lynch, the turning point in the campaign. The incident amply demonstrated that a single moment on national television can drastically influence public impressions of the leaders. In the course of the debate, Mulroney attacked Turner's role in the patronage appointments. Here, in part, is what the two men said:

> *Mulroney:* . . . You, sir, owe the Canadian people a deep apology for having indulged in that kind of practice with those kinds of appointments.
>
> *Turner:* Well, I have told you and told the Canadian people, Mr. Mulroney, that I had no option.
>
> *Mulroney:* You had an option, sir. You could have said, "I am not going to do it. This is wrong for Canada, and I am not going to ask Canadians to pay the price." You had an option, sir, to say no, and you chose to say yes to the old attitudes and the old stories of the Liberal Party. That, sir, if I may say respectfully, that is not good enough for Canadians.
>
> *Turner:* I had no option. I was—
>
> *Mulroney:* That is an avowal of failure. That is a confession of non-leadership and this country needs leadership. You had an option sir. You could have done better.
>
> C. Lynch
> *Race for the Rose*

During this exchange, Turner was clearly on the defensive, looking nervous and fidgety. Meanwhile, Mulroney sounded forceful and determined, pointing an accusatory finger at Turner as he insisted that his opponent did "have an option" in the patronage affair. The episode lingered in the minds of many voters right until election day.

CLOSE-UP

How Significant Are Polls?

Poll-taking is a feature of Canadian political life. Various agencies are forever attempting to determine the public's opinion on every subject imaginable, from capital punishment to abortion. The most common kind of poll tries to assess the popularity of political parties. Such polls often appear at the rate of once a month or more between election campaigns, and even more often during campaigns. The year 1984 saw a flood of poll taking, unparalleled in Canadian history, on the subject of electoral preferences. In fact, the polls themselves made headlines on several occasions.

While many agencies do polling in Canada, there are perhaps five that stand out. Three of them might be called "neutral", in that they have no ties to any political party. The other two might be called "contracted": although privately owned, each consistently has its services contracted out by one of the major parties, and its data on the voters' current opinions are taken seriously by that party.

The oldest and most famous neutral poll is the Gallup Report, put out by the Toronto-based Canadian Institute of Public Opinion. In recent years, two other important neutral polls have been the Globe-CROP and the Carleton-Southam. The former is a joint operation of the *Globe and Mail*, a Toronto newspaper, and the Montréal-based *Centre de recherche d'opinion publique*. The latter is a joint operation of the School of Journalism of Carleton University in Ottawa and the Southam newspaper chain. The main contracted pollsters are Martin Goldfarb Associates, traditionally hired by the Liberal Party, and Decima Research, a newer organization whose services are used extensively by the Conservatives.

Pollsters usually obtain their data by computer-selecting a sample of 1000 to 2000 citizens whom they then contact by telephone. This sample is assumed to be representative of the

Ed Broadbent, leader of the New Democratic Party, takes a bow in the House of Commons for leading his party to the top of an opinion poll for the first time in the NDP's 16-year history.

regional, ethnic, and occupational make-up of the country. An opinion taken from this cross-section of Canadians should, therefore, indicate the views of the country at large. Depending on the size of the poll and the agency involved, it takes from a few days to a few weeks to complete all the interviews and compile the results, which are then released and published in the newspapers (see Table 5.8).

TABLE 5.8 *Selected Gallup Poll Results, 1983–84*

From the time of Brian Mulroney's winning of the Progressive Conservative leadership in June, 1983 until the federal election of September, 1984, the Gallup organization took a total of 16 polls asking the question, "If a federal election were held today, which party's candidate do you think you would favour?" The results of some of these polls are shown below. The figures represent their percentage of the total of the "decided" vote and the "undecided" vote. (The percentage of the undecided vote is shown in parentheses.)

Poll Taken	*Results Released*	*PC*	*Liberal*	*NDP*	*Other*	*Undecided/ Refused*
July 7–9, 1983	Aug. 4, 1983	55	27	16	2	(23)
Dec. 1–3, 1983	Jan. 5, 1984	53	30	15	2	(27)
Mar. 29–31, 1984	May 1, 1984	40	46	13	2	(26)
June 21–23, 1984	July 6, 1984	38	49	11	1	(28)
July 5–8, 1984	July 27, 1984	39	48	11	2	(38)
Aug. 9–10, 1984	Aug. 18, 1984	46	32	18	4	(11)
Aug. 28–29, 1984	Sept. 1, 1984	50	28	19	3	(10)

Polls show results in two ways: decided vote and total vote. The former is generally considered the more significant figure. For example, look at the figures for the poll of August 9–10 in Table 5.8. The "11" under "Undecided/Refused" means that 11 of every 100 people interviewed did not say or refused to say which party they favoured. The "46" under "PC" means that, of the remaining 89, who did indicate a preference, 46 percent (41 out of the 89) preferred the Conservative Party.

The larger the "undecided" factor in a poll, the more carefully the results must be interpreted. Yet keep in mind that in any federal election, 20 to 25 percent of eligible voters usually do not cast ballots. The popular vote in elections is therefore also a measure of the decided vote, not of the total vote.

Polls exercise a degree of influence—though it is difficult to say how great—over both the parties and the voters, especially just before and during an election campaign. A Prime Minister will generally set an election date "when the polls are right". In other words, if the polls show the government party well ahead of its opponents, the PM will try to take advantage of the tide of opinion. He will call an election, hoping that its results will match what the polls are saying.

Interpreting the polls can, however, be a dangerous business, as it proved to be for the Liberals in the summer of 1984. Polls taken a year earlier had shown enormous support for the Conservatives. This support was not surprising: Brian Mulroney had become the new Conservative leader in June 1983, and a party's popularity always soars in the polls when it gets a new leader. The mere novelty of a leadership change, with all the accompanying publicity from the media, seems to account for this surge in popularity. As the novelty wore off, however, PC support gradually dropped in the polls, and Liberal support rose accordingly. In polls taken in early 1984, the Liberals and Conservatives were running neck-and-neck. Then, in March, the Liberals pulled ahead. Pierre Trudeau had announced his intention to resign at the end of February, and two weeks later John Turner announced his leadership bid. Liberal support, as measured by the Gallup poll, ranged a few points ahead of PC support from March to the end of May 1984, and then took a big leap in June, after Turner's leadership victory.

It was partly on the basis of this late June Gallup poll and of similar polls taken by other agencies, that Turner decided the time was ripe for an election. For whatever reason, however, Liberal support appears to have peaked by that time. In the Gallup poll of early July, the Liberals lost one percentage point to the Conservatives. A month later, the Gallup had the Conservatives 14 percent ahead, and in the week before the election, 22 percent ahead. Other polls gave figures similar to those of the Gallup. As it turned out, the Gallup figures of late August for the three parties were exactly the same as the popular vote each party received on election day!

There were complaints that the polls were occupying too much of the public's attention. Jean Chrétien, a prominent Liberal and the runner-up to Turner in the leadership race, declared during the 1984 campaign that the flurry of polling "puts aside all the issues. It seems to be distorting the political debate." Perhaps there was, in fact, a "bandwagon" effect: it may be that as each successive poll in July and August showed a growing Conservative lead, more and more voters decided to get on the bandwagon and go along with what the polls were predicting.

Some critics have even argued that polls should be banned during the last few weeks of an election campaign (as they are in

France, for example). The ban would reduce the chance of the polls unduly influencing voters. Yet the provisions for freedom of expression in the *Charter of Rights and Freedoms* make it likely that any measures to restrict polling would be ruled unconstitutional.

QUESTIONS

1. Why are polling agencies careful to select a good cross-section of Canadians to interview?
2. According to Table 5.8, did the Liberals choose a good or poor moment to call an election for September 4, 1984? Explain.
3. Why does a political party's popularity often rise when a new leader is named?
4. **(a)** Do you think that polls should be banned during the last weeks of a campaign? Give your reason.
   (b) Why is it that such a ban would be unlikely?

The Role of Special Interest Groups

Groups of concerned citizens have a special opportunity to make their views known during election campaigns. In 1984, one such group was the National Action Committee on the Status of Women (NACSW), which helped to organize the third of the national television debates among party leaders. This debate was concerned exclusively with women's issues.

In this debate, the NDP's Ed Broadbent emerged as the clear winner. Among other statements, Broadbent declared that nationally subsidized day care should be made available. Unlike the other two leaders, he had no reservations about granting women's request for equal pay for work of equal value.

The NACSW is only one of a vast and ever-growing number of **special interest groups**, or **pressure groups** as they are sometimes called. Special interest groups are concerned about economic, professional, social, or other specific issues, such as the environment.

Among the special interest groups concerned primarily with economic issues are the Canadian Manufacturers' Association, the Canadian Federation of Small Business, the Canadian Labour Congress (CLC), and the Consumers' Association of Canada. The first two groups are constantly urging governments to take measures that will improve opportunities for Canadian business people. The CLC represents unionized labour. The Consumers' Association of Canada is a "watchdog" group which attempts to ensure the fair treatment of Canadian consumers by government, business and unions.

Professionally based special interest groups include the Canadian Bar Association, the Canadian Medical Association, the Canadian Dental Association, and the Canadian Council of Professional Engineers. Such groups usually have sub-associations at the provincial level.

Special interest groups concerned with social issues often have mainly religious or ethnic concerns. The Canadian Council of Churches, the Canadian Conference of Catholic Bishops, the Canadian Jewish Congress, the Ukrainian National Association, the Native Council of Canada (speaking for Métis and non-status Indians), and the Assembly of First Nations (speaking for status Indians) are examples of this type of group.

Groups which do not have a particular economic, professional, or social base are made up of individuals who are concerned about a specific social or political problem. Greenpeace concentrates on environmental issues. Amnesty International tries to help political prisoners around the world. Energy Probe keeps a watchful eye on both government and corporate handling and pricing of Canada's oil and gas resources.

All these groups convey their message to the government in a number of ways. One way is to make direct representations to MP's or Cabinet ministers. Another way is to buy advertising in the media. Still another method is to publish newsletters or hold public demonstrations.

The role of special interest groups in elections has so far been the subject of comparatively little study by Canadian political scientists. There are many groups, representing diverse interests and working in different ways. These differences make it very difficult to analyze what kind and degree of influence these groups have on the government. In the past two decades, the number of special interest groups in Canadian society has grown enormously. Their influence is likely to grow as well.

QUESTIONS

1. Why is the image of a party leader so important in an election campaign and at other times?

2. Why are trivial issues often highlighted during election campaigns, rather than important issues such as the deficit?

3. **(a)** What single event during the 1984 election campaign may have brought about the defeat of the Liberals?
(b) Why do you think its effect was so serious?

4. **(a)** What are special interest groups?
(b) What is the special interest of the CLC?

Chapter Summary

Elections are the means by which the idea of representative democracy is put into practice. Canada's federal representatives, the Members of Parliament, are elected through a process that has six stages: dissolution, enumeration, nomination, campaigning, balloting, and tabulation.

In Canada today, there are three major parties at the federal level: the Liberals, the Progressive Conservatives, and the New Democratic Party. In this century, the Liberals have most often formed the government, with the Conservatives as the Official Opposition. Support for the three parties has often shown regional trends. Québec has traditionally been a Liberal stronghold, while the West has consistently backed the Conservatives. Atlantic Canada has supported both Liberals and Conservatives in varying degrees. The NDP has drawn its support from Ontario and the West. Differences among the parties can be seen in party policy as well. However, parties have quite often switched positions on a policy issue. This has occurred in the areas of militarism, free trade, and Canada's relations with the United States. Where party structure is concerned, however, the three major parties show more similarities than differences.

The 1984 election serves to demonstrate the important contribution of both the party leaders and the media to a successful campaign. Often the image conveyed by the leaders and the media influences voters more than the substance of the parties' policies.

IN REVIEW

1. What two Prime Ministers held office for the greatest number of years?
2. Why can it now be seen as ironic that the Conservatives won the 1911 election by opposing reciprocity?
3. What political party has been most consistent in its U.S. policies?
4. What did the media focus on during the 1984 campaign?

APPLYING YOUR KNOWLEDGE

1. Why is it extremely unlikely that a majority government would be defeated on a non-confidence motion?
2. The Liberals were in office for the 22 years between 1935 and 1957. Given what you have learned about public appointments, what effects on the Senate and on the federal bureaucracy would you predict from such a long period in power?
3. Regional imbalance in representation within the federal government is considered undesirable. Why?

4. What might cause one political party to adopt certain policies of another party?

5. Suppose that you are a delegate to a party leadership conference. Name three personal qualities you would look for in a leadership candidate.

6. If you were a member of a special interest group, how would you use the calling of an election to promote your views?

FURTHER INVESTIGATION

1. Because of the time difference between eastern and western Canada, the ballots in eastern Canada may be counted hours before the voting is completed in British Columbia. What is your opinion of the suggestion that all Canadians should vote at the same time? Suggest a suitable time for nation-wide voting, and explain the merits and drawbacks of the idea.

2. Study Table 5.2, and review the information in it about the popular vote. Do you think the present method of allocating seats is fair, or would you favour the assignment of seats on the basis of the popular vote? Give reasons for your opinion.

3. Do you think that a province should control its own natural resources (and thus receive all the benefits from them), or that natural resources should be controlled by the federal government? Defend your answer.

4. Why are there regulations covering the spending permitted on election campaigns? Do you think this regulation is a good idea?

5. Some Canadians believe that polls can unduly and unfairly influence the outcome of elections (or of proposed legislation) and should therefore be banned. Do you agree or disagree? Explain your position.

6. Undertake further research on one or more of the following topics:
   (a) a Prime Minister who interests you;
   (b) a comparison of reciprocity in 1911 and free trade in 1988;
   (c) the Gallup poll;
   (d) political party fund raising;
   (e) a special interest group.

7. Do you support or oppose Pierre Trudeau's position that the federal government must lead and the provinces follow? Give reasons to support your opinion.

8. Do you think that the media focus on appropriate issues during election campaigns? Give reasons for your answer.

CHAPTER 6

The Canadian Constitution

□ *The government of British Columbia controls the amount of timber that may be cut in the province's forests. However, the government of Canada controls the number of fish that may be harvested from British Columbia's coastal waters. Why does the provincial government have control in the first case, while the federal government has control in the second?*

□ *A female student in your community is an excellent hockey player. She is eager to join the high school team. The league management argues that it would be improper to have girls playing in the league. With the help of a lawyer, the girl takes her case to court. The court rules that she must be allowed to play on the team. Why did the court make this ruling?*

□ *A francophone living in a small B.C. community tries to obtain a French-language income tax form from the local Revenue Canada office. The office has only English forms in stock. The man insists that a French form be obtained for him, and the tax office must comply with his request. Why must it do so?*

At first glance, these three situations and the questions they raise seem to have nothing in common. Yet the answers to all the questions can be found in the same place: Canada's Constitution. In the first instance, the Constitution divides responsibilities between Ottawa and the provinces, and makes the provinces responsible for forest resources and Ottawa for fisheries. The Constitution also disallows discrimination on the basis of sex. As for the third situation, the Constitution guarantees that communications with any federal government agency, such as Revenue Canada, may be in either French or English as the user chooses.

In this chapter, you will learn about Canada's Constitution. You will begin by considering briefly what the Constitution does. Then you will look at constitutional documents in Canada prior to Confederation in 1867. Next you will examine the British North America Act, *the British statute which created Confederation. Following Confederation, a number of documents were added to Canada's Constitution. Then, in 1982, the Constitution was patriated. The passage of the* Canada Act, 1982 *brought about significant constitutional changes. As you read the chapter, you will discover answers to the following questions:*

- *How does the Constitution fit into Canada's political structure?*
- *What were the major constitutional documents in Canada prior to Confederation?*
- *What were the major provisions of the* British North America Act *of 1867?*
- *Between 1867 and 1982, what documents were added to Canada's Constitution?*
- *What were the key events leading to the adoption of the* Canada Act, 1982?
- *What are the components of the* Canada Act, 1982?

Under a provincial reforestation program, these workers (left) are planting seedlings in the Rockies. The crop will be ready to harvest in about 80 to 100 years.

This student (top right) is pleased with the ruling of the Ontario Human Rights Commission that her constitutional rights had been violated when the Metropolitan Toronto Hockey League refused to allow her to play with the Etobicoke Canucks, a suburban boys' team. The ruling allowed her to play on the team.

The B.C. Baron *(bottom right) fishes for salmon off the western coast of Canada, under the rules and regulations of the federal government.*

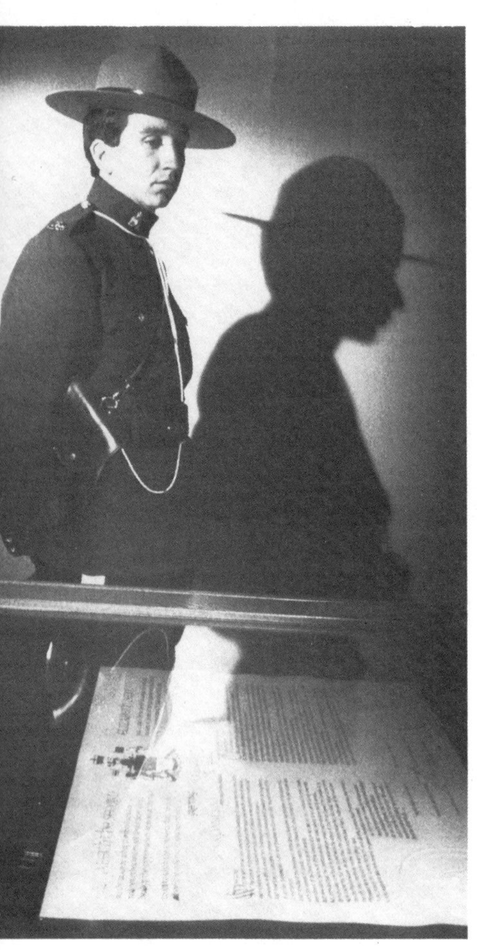

The original of Canada's Constitution was signed in 1982 by Queen Elizabeth II. It is guarded here by RCMP Constable Yvon Brault.

Canada's Constitution: The Background

Our Constitution is, in essence, a set of rules and practices relating to the composition, powers, and methods of operation of governments in Canada. In short, the Constitution defines the political structure of the country. It also outlines the relationship between the government and the people.

How does the Constitution accomplish these things? Consider, first of all, the relationship between the Constitution and the powers of government. You read earlier in this book that Canada's system of government is founded on the principle known as the "rule of law". This fundamental principle is enshrined in the Canadian Constitution. The rule of law guarantees all Canadians both justice and equality before the law. A central tenet of the rule of law is that no one—not even those who govern—is above the laws of the land. The Constitution is the framework within which those laws can be developed. The framework adheres to the rule of law, as do the laws themselves. Therefore, through the principle of the rule of law, the Constitution defines the extent of the government's power: that power is limited by the laws of the land.

The Constitution also sets forth the composition of Canada's governments. As you know, Canada is a monarchy. The monarch's representative in Canada is the Governor General. The Constitution provides for a Parliament and makes the House of Commons that body's most important component. The concept of the Cabinet is also included in the Constitution. In addition, the Constitution sets up two main levels of government, federal and provincial, and divides between them the power to make laws in certain areas. You saw an example of this division of powers at the beginning of this chapter. Finally, the Constitution makes provision for the three branches of government: legislative, executive, and judicial.

You read above that the Constitution defines the relationship between Canadians and their government by making those who are governed equal to those who govern, through the rule of law. The Constitution also makes Canada a democracy, in that political power comes from the people. Since Canada has a monarch under the Constitution, it can be called both a democracy and a monarchy. In practice, the country is a representative democracy, since Canadians elect their representatives.

So far you have seen, in broad terms, what the Constitution does. But what *is* the Constitution? Perhaps, when you ponder this question, you see in your mind's eye a huge sheaf of papers covered with lengthy rules written in difficult legal language. This view is not quite accurate. Like the constitutions of all western democracies, Canada's Constitution has various components. It consists partly of written documents, and partly of unwritten traditions, or **conventions**. The Constitution of the United States is mostly document; that of Great Britain is mainly convention. The Canadian Constitution falls midway between the two; it consists of less document and more convention than that of the U.S.A., but of more document and less convention than that of Great Britain.

The major components of Canada's written Constitution today are the *British North America Act* (renamed in 1982 the *Constitution Act, 1867*) and the *Constitution Act, 1982*. Certain other more minor documents also form part of the Constitution of Canada.

The unwritten part of the Constitution comes largely from the conventions of the British Constitution and from conventions which have developed in Canada. For example, in Canada (as in Britain), the Prime Minister is traditionally the leader of the party holding the most seats in the House of Commons. But nowhere is this rule formally written down. Because it is a time-honoured convention, however, the rule has constitutional force.

CLOSE-UP

The Canadian and American Political Systems

Former senator Eugene Forsey has been widely acknowledged as one of Canada's leading constitutional experts. Born in Newfoundland, he spent virtually his whole childhood in Ottawa. In the 1920's, he attended both McGill University in Montréal and Oxford University in Britain, later becoming a professor of political science at McGill. He remained there for a dozen years, after which he went to work for the Canadian Labour Congress, and also became involved with the CCF Party and its successor, the NDP. He continued to teach part time at various universities, all the while producing a vast and impressive collection of learned and lucidly written articles on the Constitution and related matters. In 1970, he was appointed to the Senate, where he stayed for eight years. Although now officially retired, he has continued to write and speak on a wide variety of public issues.

The passage which follows is taken from Forsey's book *How Canadians Govern Themselves*. It compares the contrast between Canada's Constitution and political system with those of the United States. Forsey considers four main areas of difference: language and culture, forms of government, constitutional convention, and types of federalism.

Senator Eugene Forsey in 1978.

Canada and the United States are both democracies. They are also both federal states. But there are important differences in the way Canadians and Americans govern themselves.

Language and Culture

One basic difference is that the United States is a country of one basic language and culture. It has just one official language for its federal government and for every state. Canada is a country of two basic languages. The Fathers of Confederation deliberately chose to make it so.

Our official recognition of bilingualism is limited, but expanding. For example, it was at the specific request of the New Brunswick government that the adoption of French and English as the official languages of that province was enshrined in the Constitution . . .

Ontario, which has the largest number of French-speaking people outside Québec, has provided French schools and an increasing range of services in French for Franco-Ontarians. Several other provinces have taken steps in the same direction . . .

Forms of Government

A second basic difference between our Constitution and the American is, of course, that we are a constitutional monarchy and they are a republic. That looks like only a formal difference. It is very much more, for we have a parliamentary-cabinet government, while the Americans have a presidential-congressional government.

What does that mean? What difference does it make?

First, in the United States the head of state and the head of the government are one and the same. The president is both at once. Here, the Queen, ordinarily represented by the Governor General, is the head of state, and the prime minister is the head of the government. Does that make any real difference? Yes: in Canada, the head of state can, in exceptional circumstances, protect Parliament and the people against a prime minister and ministers who may forget that "minister" means "servant," and may try to make themselves masters. For example, the head of state could refuse to let a cabinet dissolve a newly-elected House of Commons before it could even meet, or could refuse to let ministers bludgeon the people into submission by a continuous series of general elections. The American head of state cannot restrain the American head of government because they are the same person.

For another thing, presidential-congressional government is based on a separation of powers. The American president cannot be a member of either house of Congress. Neither can any of the members of his cabinet. Neither he nor any member of his cabinet can appear in Congress to introduce a bill, or defend it, or answer questions, or rebut attacks on policies. No member of either house can be president or a member of the cabinet.

Parliamentary cabinet government is based on concentration of powers. The prime minister, and every other minister, must, by custom (though not by law) be a member of one house or the other, or get a seat in one house or the other within a short time of appointment. All government bills must be introduced by a minister or someone speaking on his or her behalf, and ministers must appear in Parliament to defend government bills, answer daily questions on government actions or policies, and rebut attacks on such actions or policies.

In the United States, the president and every member of both houses are elected for a fixed term: the president for four years, the senators for six, the members of the House of Representatives for two. The only way to get rid of a president before the end of his four-year term is to impeach him, which is very hard to do, and has never been done and only twice attempted.

As the president, the senators and the representatives are elected for different periods, it can happen, and often does, that the president belongs to one party while the opposing party has a majority in either the Senate or the House of Representatives or both. So for years on end, the president may find his legislation and his policies blocked by an adverse majority in one or both houses. He cannot appeal to the people by dissolving either house, or both: he has no such power, and the two houses are there for their fixed terms, come what may, till the constitutionally fixed hour strikes . . .

Constitutional Convention

A third basic difference between our system and the Americans' is that custom, usage, practice, and "convention" play a far larger part in our Constitution than in theirs. For example, the president of the United States is right there in the written Constitution; his qualifications, how he is elected, how he can be removed, all the essential powers of his office, in black and white, unchangeable except by formal constitutional amendment . . .

. . . There is nothing in any law requiring the prime minister or any other minister to have a seat in Parliament; there is just a custom that he or she must have a seat, or get one within a reasonable time. There is nothing in any law to say that a government that loses its majority in the House of Commons on a matter of confidence must either resign (making way for a different government in the same House) or ask for a fresh election.

Type of Federalism

A fourth basic difference between the American and Canadian systems is the type of federalism they embody. The American system was originally highly decentralized. The federal Congress was given a short list of specific powers; everything not mentioned in that list belonged to the states "or to the people" (that is, was not within the power of either Congress or any state legislature).

"States' rights" were fundamental. The Fathers of Confederation, gazing with horror at the American Civil War [1861–1865], decided that "states' rights" were precisely what had caused it, and acted accordingly...

The Fathers... also gave a long list of specific examples of exclusive national powers. They further provided that the members of the Senate... should be appointed by the national government, and that all lieutenant-governors of the provinces should be appointed, instructed and removable by the national government. They gave the national government and Parliament certain specific powers to protect the educational rights of the Protestant and Roman Catholic minorities of the Queen's subjects. They gave the national government power to disallow (wipe off the statute book) within one year of their passage, any acts of provincial legislatures.

In both the United States and Canada, however, the precise meaning of the written Constitution is settled by the courts. In the United States the courts have, in general, so interpreted the Constitution as to widen federal and narrow state power. In Canada, the courts... have in general so interpreted the *Constitution Act, 1867* as to narrow federal power and widen provincial power. The result is that the United States is, in actual fact, now a much more highly centralized federation than Canada, and Canada has become perhaps the most decentralized federation in the world. Nonetheless, the fact that under our Constitution the powers not specifically mentioned come under the national Parliament gives the central authority enough strength and leeway to meet many of the changed and changing conditions the years have brought.

Eugene A. Forsey
How Canadians Govern Themselves

QUESTIONS

1. Prepare a table in which you compare the Canadian and American systems of government. You might include the following headings: head of state, head of government, distribution of power, term of office and unwritten practices. Try to add other headings.
2. How does American federalism differ from Canadian federalism?
3. Name two advantages and two disadvantages of the political system of each country.

Constitutional Documents before Confederation

The first important documents in Canada's constitutional history were the *Royal Proclamation* of 1763, the *Quebec Act* of 1774, the *Constitutional Act* of 1791, and the *Act of Union* of 1840. Each statute changed or

The Battle of the Plains of Abraham, fought at Québec in 1759, was an event that helped shape the structure of Canada's government. British ownership of French territories, including those in the St. Lawrence area, was confirmed by the Royal Proclamation of 1763.

modified provisions of the earlier one(s). These documents had virtually nothing to say about the rights of individuals. Rather, they were concerned with establishing the general structures of government for Britain's North American colonies.

The *Royal Proclamation* of 1763 marked the end of a century-and-a-half of intermittent wars between Britain and France for control of North America. It confirmed British ownership of the French territories of the Great Lakes/St. Lawrence area and the lands bordering the Gulf of St. Lawrence. The *Royal Proclamation* declared that English laws and institutions, as well as the English language and the Church of England (the Anglican Church), would prevail in the political life of the Québec colony. In practice, however, French became the working language at most levels of the new colonial government, and Catholicism was tolerated (even if Catholics were forbidden to hold senior public office). Such practices recognized the fact that, in 1763, the Québec colony had about 70 000 Roman Catholic francophones, but only a few hundred Protestant anglophones.

The *Quebec Act* of 1774 repeated the provision of the *Royal Proclamation* that English criminal law would be in force in the colony. However, it restored the use of the French Civil Code, the system of codified law which is still used in Québec. The *Quebec Act* said nothing about the official use of French in the colony, but it did make some allowances for Catholics to hold public office. This *Act* was one of several British statutes that led to the American War of Independence (1775–83) and the founding of the United States.

Following the War of Independence, the influx of Loyalists to the Québec colony and to the present-day Maritimes greatly increased the English-speaking population of British North America. In 1784, the colony of Nova Scotia was divided into two colonies: New Brunswick and Nova Scotia. In 1791, the *Constitutional Act* divided the colony of Québec into two parts: Upper Canada and Lower Canada. Under the terms of this *Act*, Lower Canada retained English criminal law and the

A re-enactment of the Rebellion of 1837 shows victorious militiamen, as played by the Queen's York Rangers, marching away from a burning model of Montgomery's Tavern, where rebels had met to plan their occupation of Toronto, then a few miles to the southeast.

French Civil Code, while Upper Canada was to have both English criminal law and English common law. In addition, all the colonies of British North America were granted a degree of representative government. At the time, this provision meant only that male property owners in the colony could elect representatives to a colonial legislature. However, the British-appointed governor and his appointed councils held the real power, and could disallow laws passed by the elected legislature.

During the following decades, frustration grew in the colonies over the lack of power of the elected assemblies. This feeling was one of the major causes of the rebellions of 1837–38 in both the Canadas. The 1838 report of Lord Durham about the causes of the rebellions recommended, among other things, that the two Canadas be reunited into one. This reunion took place with the 1840 *Act of Union*. Under the *Act of Union*, the two halves of the colony, Canada East (Lower Canada) and Canada West (Upper Canada), were equally represented in a single elected assembly. Although not authorized by the *Act*, French was widely used in the legislature.

Not until the late 1840's, however, did the elected assembly of the colony of Canada (or any of the Atlantic colonies) come to exercise real power. In other words, it was only then that **responsible government** came into being. Responsible government means, in essence, that the executive branch of government is answerable to, and must act on the decisions of, the legislative branch. Responsible government began in Canada when laws passed by the elected assembly were acted upon by the appointed officials. Nova Scotia, in 1848, was the first British North American colony to achieve responsible government.

Nowhere, even today, is it written down that the Governor General in his legislative role *must* accept laws made by Parliament. But no Governor General would disallow a law passed by Parliament. The convention of responsible government is central to Canada's unwritten Constitution.

QUESTIONS

1. The two main functions of Canada's Constitution are to define the country's political structure, and to outline the relationship between the government and the people. Describe how the Constitution accomplishes each of these purposes.

2. **(a)** What does the rule of law guarantee to all Canadians?
(b) Where is this enshrined?

3. How does Canada's constitution incorporate the major components of the United States' and Britain's constitutions?

4. **(a)** Name the four principal constitutional documents in Canada prior to 1867.
(b) Outline the provisions of each.

5. **(a)** What is responsible government?
   (b) How did responsible government develop in Canada?
   (c) How does it fit into the Constitution of Canada?

Confederation: The *British North America Act*

By the early 1860's, both the British North American colonies and Britain itself had become dissatisfied with the colonies' political structure. Discussions on the status of the colonies were held at a series of conferences involving representatives of Canada and the Atlantic colonies. In 1867, the conferences led to the union or confederation of three of the colonies: Canada, New Brunswick, and Nova Scotia. The statute that created Confederation was the *British North America* (*BNA*) *Act*.

The *BNA Act* remained the central component of Canada's Constitution for over a century. The introduction to the *Act* stated that the Constitution was to be "similar in principle to that of the United Kingdom". In other words, it would adhere to the British conventions of free speech, parliamentary democracy, Cabinet government, and the rule of law. Because they were part of British constitutional traditions, centuries-old documents such as the *Magna Carta* (1215) and the *Bill of Rights* (1689) would also, indirectly, become part of Canada's Constitution.

Most of the *BNA Act*'s 147 sections fall into one of eight categories: the terms of union, executive power, legislative power, provincial institutions, distribution of legislative power, judicial power, revenue and taxation, and the admission of other colonies into Confederation.

The terms of union provided that the former colony of Canada be divided into the provinces of Ontario and Québec. The colonies of New Brunswick and Nova Scotia would become the other two provinces of the new Dominion of Canada.

The sections dealing with executive power stated that "authority over Canada is hereby declared to continue and be vested in the Queen" (s. 9). In other words, Canada was to be—and remains—a monarchy. This royal authority, the *Act* noted, was to be "exercisable by the Governor General" (s. 14), meaning that the Governor General would represent the Crown.

The sections treating legislative power stipulated that "there shall be One Parliament for Canada, consisting of the Queen, an Upper House styled the Senate, and the House of Commons" (s. 17). The *Act* also noted that "there shall be a session of the Parliament of Canada at least once in every year" (s. 20), and that federal elections were to be held at least once every five years.

The part of the *BNA Act* dealing with provincial institutions noted

The British North America Act *was passed by Britain's Parliament at Westminster, London, on March 29, 1867. Under this* Act, *provision was made for Confederation, which established the Dominion of Canada.*

Hospitals, the administration of justice, municipal government, and local business fall under the administration of provincial governments, under the terms of the BNA Act.

The Children's Hospital, Vancouver (top)

A judge sitting on his bench, considers evidence (bottom left)

Testing an elevated street-railway car in Vancouver (bottom centre)

Maple-syrup farmer, Springhill, Nova Scotia (bottom right)

that "for each province, there shall be an Officer, styled the Lieutenant Governor" (s. 58), to be appointed by the federal Cabinet. The *Act* also established that the provincial assemblies would meet at least once a year.

Sections 91 to 95 of the *BNA Act* dealt with the division of legislative powers between the federal and provincial governments. Section 91 listed certain areas in which the federal government would have exclusive power, including defence, the postal system, the fisheries, and currency. In many respects, s. 91 has been the most controversial section of the document. The section stated in part:

> It shall be lawful for the Queen, by and with the Advice and Consent of the Senate and House of Commons, to make Laws for the Peace, Order and Good Government of Canada, in relation to all matters not . . . assigned exclusively to the Legislatures of the Provinces.

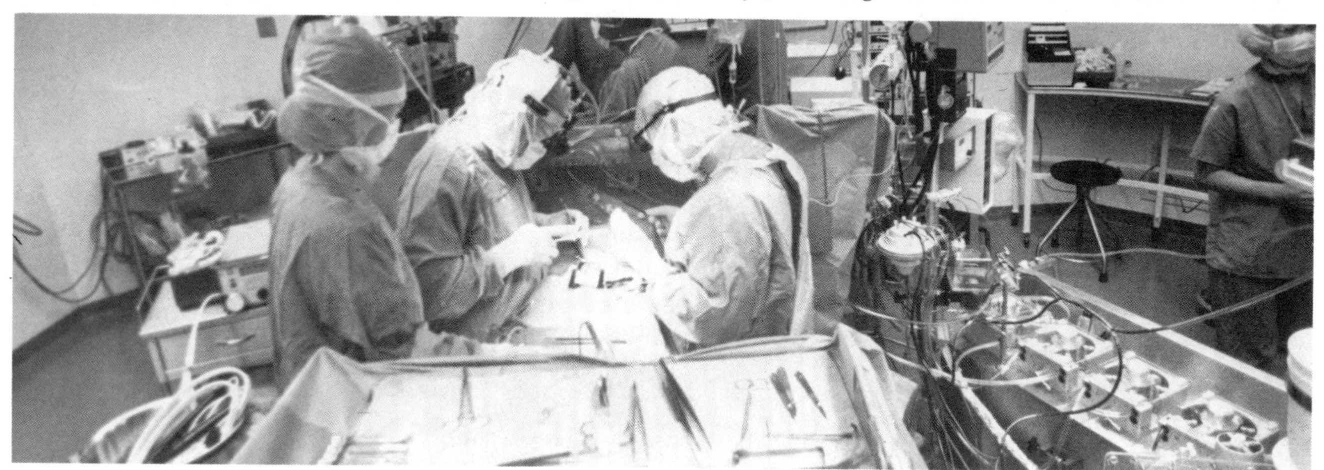

In short, this passage meant that anything not listed specifically as a provincial power was constitutionally a federal power.

Section 92 named areas in which the provinces held exclusive authority. The list included hospitals, forested lands, and the administration of justice, municipal government, and local business.

Section 93 was devoted entirely to the subject of education. It noted that "in and for each Province, the Legislature may exclusively make Laws in relation to Education." This section also established that the Catholic schools of Ontario and both the Protestant and the Catholic schools of Québec would retain their legal status.

Students using their school resource centre in Gatineau, Québec.

The sections of the *BNA Act* dealing with judicial power essentially confirmed the legal system already existing in the colonies before Confederation. They did, however, provide that "the Parliament of Canada may... from time to time provide for... the establishment of any additional Courts for the better Administration of the Laws of Canada" (s. 101). That is to say, the federal government was empowered to create a special court system alongside the existing court system if the need arose. These provisions also empowered Parliament to create a "General Court of Appeal" for the country.

On the subject of revenue and taxation, the *BNA Act* ruled that all publicly owned lands, whether federal or provincial, would be free from taxation. Section 121 noted that "all Articles of the Growth, Produce or Manufacture of any one of the Provinces shall, from and after the Union, be admitted free into each of the other Provinces."

Sections 146 and 147 of the *BNA Act* made provision for the entry of other colonies into the new dominion, as either territories or provinces. The entry of Prince Edward Island, Newfoundland, and British Columbia was fully anticipated in these sections of the *Act*.

The subject of language, a topic which is central to Canada's political development, received only a couple of paragraphs in the *BNA Act*. Section 133 stated in part:

> Either the English or French Language may be used by any Person in the Debates of the Houses of Parliament of Canada and the House of the Legislature of Quebec... The Acts of the Parliament of Canada and of the Legislature of Quebec shall be printed and published in both those Languages.

QUESTIONS

1. What relationship was there between the *BNA Act* and the British Constitution, as stated in the introduction to the *Act*?
2. Why is s. 91 of the *BNA Act* controversial?
3. Summarize the provisions of the *British North America Act* for each of the following areas:
   (a) judicial power; **(b)** revenue and taxation.

The Constitution from the *BNA Act* to 1960

The *BNA Act* remained the centrepiece of the Canadian Constitution for over a century. But its provisions were supplemented and modified by a number of developments: **amendments** (changes) to the *BNA Act* itself, other statutes, and conventional practices.

Amendments to the *BNA Act*

One significant omission from the *BNA Act* was an **amending formula**, that is, a method by which changes could be made to the *Act*. Since the *BNA Act* was a statute of the British Parliament, the Parliament of Canada had to send any proposed changes to Britain for enactment by the British Parliament, and ultimately, the monarch's assent.

A major difficulty with the process of amendment was the question of who had the right to suggest such changes. Was it the federal government alone? Or both the federal government and the provinces? And if the provinces were to be involved, how many, and which ones? Proposed changes to the *BNA Act* therefore had to be thrashed out between the federal government and some or all of the provinces, on an ever-shifting, give-and-take basis. In cases where the federal government could not obtain significant provincial support, it sometimes acted on its own.

While there were almost two dozen amendments to the *BNA Act*, a few stand out. In 1930, an amendment transferred power over natural resources from the federal government to the prairie provinces. An amendment in 1940 allowed for the creation of a national system of unemployment insurance. In 1951, an amendment gave the federal government some authority over old age pensions. This amendment was extended and clarified in 1964. From time to time, various other amendments redistributed seats in the House of Commons according to changes in provincial populations. In addition, a 1949 amendment made some provision for the Parliament of Canada to make changes in the *BNA Act* independently of British approval. However, major sections of the *BNA Act* dealing with language and the federal-provincial division of powers were excluded from this amendment.

Other Statutes

After 1867, both the British and the Canadian Parliaments enacted a number of statutes which became part of the political framework of Canada. The *Constitution Act, 1982* formally recognized many of these enactments as part of Canada's written Constitution.

Some of the statutes created new provinces or territories, or changed provincial boundaries. The *Rupert's Land and North Western Territory*

Order of 1870, for instance, transferred ownership of the vast Hudson's Bay Company lands from Britain to the Dominion of Canada. Other statutes created the provinces of Manitoba (1870), British Columbia (1871), and Prince Edward Island (1873). The *Adjacent Territories Act* of 1880 transferred ownership of the Arctic Islands from Britain to Canada. Under the *Alberta Act* and the *Saskatchewan Act*, both passed in 1905, two new provinces were created from parts of what had been Rupert's Land. In 1912, the borders of Manitoba, Ontario, and Québec were extended northward to include other portions of the former Rupert's Land. With the *Newfoundland Act* of 1949, the map of Canada became what it is today.

Other enactments of a constitutional character included the *Dominion Act* of 1875 and the *Statute of Westminster* of 1931. The *Dominion Act* established the Supreme Court of Canada. Not until three-quarters of a century later, however, did the Supreme Court of Canada become the court of last appeal for Canadians. Until 1949, the Judicial Committee of the Privy Council in Britain served this function. The *Statute of Westminster* was also extremely significant in furthering Canada's independence from Britain. It stipulated that Britain could no longer legislate for Canada unless Canada asked Britain to do so.

When Newfoundland joined Confederation in 1949, some opponents to the Newfoundland Act *flew flags at half-mast, drew their blinds, and placed black crepe on their doors. Here a St. John's youth protests the* Act.

Conventional Practices

Neither the Prime Minister nor the Cabinet is mentioned in the *BNA Act*. Yet Prime Minister and Cabinet are the very centre of the executive branch of government in Canada. Their existence is, by convention, an integral part of the Constitution.

The practice that legislation passed by the House of Commons and the Senate becomes the law of the land is likewise an established convention, even if the assent of the monarch is formally required by the Constitution. Strictly speaking, s. 55 of the *BNA Act* allows the Governor General to "withhold the Queen's assent". Since the late 1870's, however, this power has never been exercised. The convention of the legislative supremacy of the Houses of Parliament has gained such constitutional force that the Governor General's role is now a purely ceremonial one.

Another vital constitutional convention which is nowhere even indirectly suggested in the *BNA Act* is that a government will resign when it loses support on an issue of confidence in the House of Commons. Yet this is a practice which Canadians have long taken for granted.

The guarantees of rights and freedoms now entrenched in the *Canadian Charter of Rights and Freedoms* portion of the *Constitution Act, 1982* were, until 1982, little more than matters of convention. As you have already seen, the introduction to the *BNA Act* stated that Canada's Constitution was to be "similar in principle to that of the United Kingdom". The British Constitution itself is composed almost wholly of conventions. In Britain, civil liberties have always been protected, not by documentary guarantees, but by an unwritten, vaguely-defined and centuries-old sense of "fair play" and "what is right". Fundamental to this sense are the concepts of free speech and free debate.

Two examples, one from Alberta and the other from Québec, illustrate how provincial governments have tried to use legislation to curtail these freedoms. In 1937, the provincial government of Alberta passed a piece of legislation known as the *Accurate News and Information Act*. Under the terms of the *Act*, the provincial government would, in effect, have had the power to censor newspapers in the province, allowing them to print only news that government officials deemed to be "accurate". In the same year, the Québec government passed the so-called "Padlock Law", which prohibited the use of buildings for "communistic" purposes. In 1938, a majority of Supreme Court judges ruled that the government of Alberta lacked the power to enact such legislation. In 1957, the Supreme Court finally made the same ruling on Québec's Padlock Law. In both cases, the judges' decision was influenced by the restrictions these enactments imposed on freedom of speech.

QUESTIONS

1. Why was it difficult to make amendments to the *BNA Act*?
2. Name three statutes passed after 1867 which had to do with the admission of new territories into Confederation.
3. What were the effects of the *Dominion Act* of 1875 and the *Statute of Westminster* of 1931?
4. Give three examples of government practices in Canada which are based on convention rather than on any document.

Towards Patriation: Constitutional Issues from 1960 to 1982

The federal-provincial quarrels that marked Canadian political life during the 1960's and 1970's centred upon the sometimes vague division of federal and provincial powers set forth in the *BNA Act*. To be sure, such quarrels had occurred since 1867. But by the 1960's, a number of issues had made the debates livelier than ever. Chief among the issues were Québec's concern over language and social policy, and the concern of the western provinces over natural resources. The 1960 Québec election and the ensuing Quiet Revolution can be taken as marking the beginning of this phase of Canada's constitutional development.

Delegates attending a series of constitutional conferences held during the 1960's and 1970's sought to resolve the issues behind federal-provincial disagreement. The participants in these conferences also tried to find an acceptable amending formula for the *BNA Act*. In 1964 and again in 1971, unanimous agreement was almost reached, but Québec's rejection of the proposed amending formula on both occasions was a stumbling-block. Until a formula could be agreed on, it seemed that the authority to amend the *BNA Act* would remain with Britain. Canada would continue to be a supposedly sovereign nation but remain unable to change its own Constitution without the formal approval of Britain. As the political scientist D. Milne summed up the situation, most provinces "preferred the safety of the British connection to the uncertain dangers of a final Canadian constitutional marriage."

The issue that sparked a renewed effort for constitutional change was the Québec referendum on sovereignty-association, held in May 1980. To persuade *Québécois* to remain within Confederation, Prime Minister Pierre Trudeau and his government pledged that Québec's interests would be protected in a new constitutional arrangement. At the same time, a host of other issues was up for negotiation: provincial control of the economy, women's and Native peoples' rights, minority language rights, and reform of the Senate, among others.

In October of the same year, then Prime Minister Trudeau, frustrated by lack of agreement, decided to proceed without the provinces. His government moved to request the British government to amend the *BNA Act* by adding an amending formula and a *Charter of Rights and Freedoms*. The British government would then give the necessary approval to the transfer of control over the Constitution to Canada. This proposal for **patriation** of the Constitution was made despite the objections of eight of the provinces.

Trudeau's proposal had limited success. Within a year, the Supreme Court of Canada ruled that the proposal, while inconsistent with

The Québec referendum on sovereignty-association was supported actively by both sides as the signs on this apartment building in Québec City show.

This cartoon appeared in the Saint John Telegraph-Journal *on November 7, 1981 as a comment on the provincial negotiations on a new constitutional package for Canada. Which province did not agree on the terms?*

constitutional convention, was not inconsistent with constitutional law. In other words, constitutional convention required the Prime Minister to obtain the consent of more than two provinces, but constitutional law did not.

After the judgment, Trudeau decided to make one last attempt to persuade the provinces to agree on the amendments to be made to the Constitution. These constitutional changes would take the form of both amendments to the *BNA Act* and a set of new documents. As noted above, a *Charter of Rights and Freedoms* was to be among the new documents. It would entrench rights and freedoms which had previously been protected only by convention, the common law, and ordinary statutes.

The last round of negotiations was carried on during the first week of November, 1981. As a result of the negotiations, nine provinces and the federal government agreed on the terms of a new constitutional package. (Unhappy with the powers that it would hold under the proposed changes, Québec held out.) Five months later, on April 17, 1982, Queen Elizabeth II gave Royal Assent, in Ottawa, to the amendments as part of the *Canada Act, 1982*. Together with the existing constitutional documents, the amendments were officially titled the *Constitution of Canada*.

QUESTIONS

1. Name the two main issues which fuelled constitutional debate in the 1960's and 1970's.
2. Why could an amending formula for the *BNA Act* not be found during these two decades?
3. (a) What historic event led to renewed efforts for constitutional change during the 1980's?
   (b) Briefly describe the course of these efforts. What was their result?

Canada's Constitution Today

The *Constitution of Canada* contains the *Canada Act, 1982*, which has two major components: the *Constitution Act, 1982* and the *BNA Act*, which was renamed the *Constitution Act, 1867*. The *Canada Act* also

In September 1864, delegates to the Charlottetown Conference posed for the top photograph during discussions on the political union of the Maritimes and Upper and Lower Canada. This and subsequent conferences led to Confederation.

In October 1978, Prime Minister Trudeau met with the provincial premiers to discuss the drafting of a new Canadian constitution.

contains provisions which ended the power of the British parliament to legislate for Canada.

The *Constitution Act, 1982* itself has several parts. The first and longest, making up over half of the text, is the *Canadian Charter of Rights and Freedoms*. You will examine the Charter in detail in the next chapter. For the moment, it is worth stating that the Charter sets forth various rights and freedoms which, while recognized in Canadian law prior to 1982, were not constitutionally entrenched. For example, the 1960 *Bill of Rights* and the 1969 *Official Languages Act* both contained provisions similar to those in the Charter. However, these statutes were, in effect, only pieces of ordinary legislation which could be applied only in areas of federal jurisdiction. In addition, they could have been changed at any time by the federal government. The rights and freedoms set forth in the two documents have been reinforced by the Charter. Because the Charter is part of the Constitution, it has primacy over all federal and provincial legislation, and may not be changed except by constitutional amendment.

Other parts of the *Constitution Act, 1982* deal with aboriginal rights, equalization payments, constitutional conferences and amendment procedures, and changes to the division of powers between Parliament and the provincial legislatures.

The section dealing with aboriginal rights is only a few sentences long. It states in part that "the existing aboriginal and treaty rights of the aboriginal peoples of Canada are hereby recognized and affirmed" (s. 35(1)). Despite its brevity, the section is significant. Partly on the basis of the provision, the Haida people of the Queen Charlotte Islands launched a court action in the mid-1980's to prevent logging on their ancestral lands. The Haida argued that title to the forested lands was one of their aboriginal rights.

Haida Indians form a blockade to stop logging operations on Lyell Island in 1985.

Equalization payments are funds transferred by the federal government from the richer provinces to the poorer ones. Their purpose is to minimize regional disparities. Such payments, in one form or another, have been a fact of Canadian political life since 1867. The *Constitution Act, 1982* entrenches the commitment "to ensure that provincial governments have sufficient revenues to provide reasonably comparable levels of public services at reasonably comparable levels of taxation" (s. 36(2)).

The sections of the *Constitution Act, 1982* which address constitutional amendment make up its second-longest part. Several general rules, each one applicable under certain circumstances, are spelled out. One important rule is that changes to the *Constitution of Canada* require the approval of two-thirds of the provinces (that is, at least seven of the ten), as well as of the House of Commons and the Senate. A further provision is that the seven provinces must represent at least 50 percent of the population of Canada.

Part VI of the *Constitution Act, 1982* amends s. 92 of the *BNA Act*, which deals with provincial powers. Under the amended s. 92, the provinces now have broader and more specific powers over their natural resources.

A special schedule attached to the *Constitution Act, 1982* renames the *BNA Act*. In addition, it makes the various constitutional statutes discussed earlier—the *Royal Proclamation*, the *Quebec Act*, the *Constitutional Act*, the *Act of Union*, the *Dominion Act*, the *Statute of Westminster*, and the rest—part of the Constitution of Canada.

A final, general section of the *Constitution Act, 1982* stipulates that "the English and French versions of the *Act* are equally authoritative." This provision reflects the policy of official bilingualism for Canada.

How significant are the additions and amendments to the Constitution? What changes have they made to the political life of the nation, and what changes will they bring in the future? Will the changes have positive or negative effects? Political scientists who have studied the Constitution give different answers to these questions. Below are three such answers.

> Even though the new Constitution does not repeal the substance of the old Constitution . . . it has permanently altered the nature of the Canadian federal state . . . The amending formula declared a new federal order where even the weakest and smallest province . . . can look for a fairer set of relationships . . . The new Constitution also attempted to restructure Canadian federalism in the light of separatism in Quebec and regionalism elsewhere. The French-English conflict was addressed in terms of guaranteed linguistic equality and access to schooling in either official tongue, while the burden of defending these rights was shifted to the courts . . . By entrenching these rights, Parliament has tacitly admitted that this role as defender of linguistic minorities should be assumed by an independent judiciary.

As with language rights, so too with human rights. In large part these were entrusted to the care of the courts who will help check governmental abuses of the individual rights of citizens . . . The strength of the strategy finally depends on Canadians' commitment to the Charter of Rights as a new compact between English- and French-speaking federalists, as well as a compact over the rights of individual citizens and the powers of government. In that sense, the Constitution will be a document of extraordinary national significance.

D. Milne
The New Canadian Constitution

There is little cause for national self-congratulation in the *Constitution Act, 1982*, and the procedures by which it became part of the Constitution . . . On balance, the damage done to our legal, political and constitutional order outweighs the gains. The act of changing the elements of the Constitution embodying the powers of the provinces was a betrayal of the commitments made to the Quebec electorate in 1980 and created new hazards in the relations between Quebec and the wider Canadian community. The Charter imposes on the judiciary a set of responsibilities the courts are ill-equipped to deal with. And by embodying in the Constitution important provisions which were hastily drafted, we have done what has been done in an inexpert and unsophisticated way.

Donald Smiley
"A Dangerous Deed: the Constitution Act, 1982".
In K. Banting and R. Simeon, ed.,
And No One Cheered: Federalism,
Democracy and the Constitution Act

The November [1981] accord and the ensuing political manoeuvering to obtain revisions and additions to it produced a constitutional text which effected four significant changes in Canada's constitutional arrangements. First, individual and language rights were entrenched; second, aboriginal rights were recognized; third, rules for amending the Constitution were created; and, finally, new authority was allocated to the provinces in respect of non-renewable natural resources. In all cases the text which was arrived at was the product of compromises made in order to obtain agreement . . . The extent of political accommodation at work in the making of a new Constitution was impressive . . .

One government, however, did not adjust its demands and did not concur in the political bargain which was reached. Formal implementation of the Constitution was proceeded with notwithstanding Quebec's objection . . .

But as Canada's history demonstrates, no single constitutional pact is adequate to meet all of the country's challenges; constitutional arrangements require constant re-evaluation and re-wording. Quebec, with its special linguistic and cultural place in Canada, presents a constitutional challenge that has not been met, and this is the major part of Canada's unfinished constitutional business.

Roy Romanow *et al.*
Canada . . . Notwithstanding: The Making
of the Constitution 1976–1982.

A spectator holds up a sign welcoming home Canada's Constitution during the proclamation ceremonies on Parliament Hill in 1982.

QUESTIONS

1. Name the two main components of the *Canada Act, 1982*.

2. Why were rights and freedoms, as detailed in the Charter, made an integral part of Canada's Constitution?

3. (a) If eight provinces proposed an amendment to the *Constitution Act, 1982*, the proposal would fail if Ontario and Québec were not included among the eight? Why?
(b) Do you think this is fair? Explain your answer.

4. What is Smiley's view concerning the ability of the courts to defend the rights contained in the Charter?

5. According to Romanow, what unfinished constitutional business has yet to be completed?

6. Romanow states that "constitutional arrangements require constant re-evaluation and re-wording." How might federal-provincial relations be affected if Romanow's view were put into practice?

Chapter Summary

Canada's Constitution is in many respects a reflection of the most important features and values of our political system. The first and most vital of these is the concept of the rule of law. Other important features of our political system are monarchy, democracy, parliamentary government, Cabinet government, federalism, and separation of powers.

Canada's Constitution is in part written (documents) and in part unwritten (conventions). In the pre-Confederation period, the significant constitutional documents were the Royal Proclamation *of 1763, the* Quebec Act *of 1774, the* Constitutional Act *of 1791, and the* Act of Union *of 1840. Responsible government, achieved after 1840, became and has remained a vital part of Canada's unwritten Constitution.*

From 1867 to 1982, the BNA Act *was the central document of Canada's Constitution. It addressed a number of topics, including the structure of the three branches of government in the new Dominion and the sharing of powers between the federal and provincial governments. Supplementing and modifying the* BNA Act *were amendments to the* Act *itself, other statutes, and a number of conventional practices. Civil liberties, which are now protected in the written Constitution, were until 1982 largely a matter of constitutional convention and the common law.*

The Canada Act, 1982 *was achieved after a long and quarrelsome series of federal-provincial negotiations. The Constitution of Canada includes both the* BNA Act *(renamed the* Constitution Act, 1867*) and a new document, the* Constitution Act, 1982. *This new document's longest part is the* Canadian Charter of Rights and Freedoms. *The* Constitution Act, 1982 *also contains sections dealing with aboriginal rights and amending procedures, among other matters. The significance and effects of the new constitutional provisions are still unfolding.*

IN REVIEW

1. Why is Canada both a monarchy and a representative democracy?

2. List six statutes which were included in the document titled the *Constitution of Canada*, 1982.

3. (a) To which level of government does the Constitution give jurisdiction over matters concerning Native peoples?

(b) The section on aboriginal rights in the *Charter of Rights and Freedoms* is brief but significant. Why?

APPLYING YOUR KNOWLEDGE

1. Why has the 1930 amendment to the *BNA Act*, which gave the prairie provinces control over their natural resources, proved expensive for the federal government?
2. In 1981, Prime Minister Trudeau wanted to proceed with asking the British government for an amending formula to the *BNA Act*. Why was this action so controversial?
3. How might a proposal to undertake logging in an area of salmon spawning lead to a federal-provincial disagreement?
4. Historically, Canada has been closely associated with Britain, yet Eugene Forsey chose to compare Canada's Constitution and government with those of the United States. Why do you think he did so?
5. When the Supreme Court disallowed the Padlock Law and the *Accurate News and Information Act*, it demonstrated that the federal government can overrule a provincial government. Do you think this is desirable or undesirable? Give reasons for your answer.
6. Into what two broad categories can the Constitution be divided? Comment briefly on each.

FURTHER INVESTIGATION

1. Can it be said with any justification that the *Royal Proclamation of 1763* could have avoided the present division of this country into "French Canada" and "English Canada" if it had been differently worded? Explain your answer.
2. Can you think of any reason(s) why the British, in 1774, restored the French Civil Code in Québec, which was a British colony?
3. What is **(a)** one advantage and **(b)** one disadvantage of a written constitution, as compared to a constitution largely made up of conventional practices?
4. Undertake research on one of the following topics:
   (a) the origins of Canada's bilingual policy;
   (b) the rebellions of 1837–38;
   (c) Pierre Trudeau's role in the creation of the *Constitution Act, 1982*;
   (d) the role of Québec in the patriation of the Constitution.
5. Why is the rule of law said to be fundamental to Canadian society, particularly to the system of government?

CHAPTER 7

The Canadian Charter of Rights and Freedoms

In the previous chapter, you examined Canada's Constitution and its vital role in government and society. Now you will focus on a highly significant part of the Constitution: the sections which set out the basic rights and freedoms of all Canadians.

All the diverse headlines shown refer in some way to changes, conflicts, or concerns which have resulted from the enactment of the Canadian Charter of Rights and Freedoms. *They are just a small sampling of the thousands of articles that have been written on the Charter since it was enacted in 1982.*

You will first consider the seven categories of rights and freedoms which are set out in the Charter, as well as some other important sections. Next you will look briefly at the effect of the Charter on the lives of Canadians. In the third section of the chapter, you will learn about some of the considerations which judges must take into account when applying the Charter to legal issues. In the final section you will review some concerns about the expanded legal scope given to judges by the passage of the Charter. As you read this chapter, consider the following key questions:

- *How important is the Charter to Canada's government?*
- *What are the major sections of the Charter?*
- *How can Canadians' rights and freedoms be limited? How are they enforced?*
- *What two major social changes have resulted from the Charter?*
- *Why is it important always to balance the rights of all groups within society?*
- *Does the Charter give Canadian judges too much legal scope? If so, should changes be made to the Charter or to the way in which judges are chosen?*

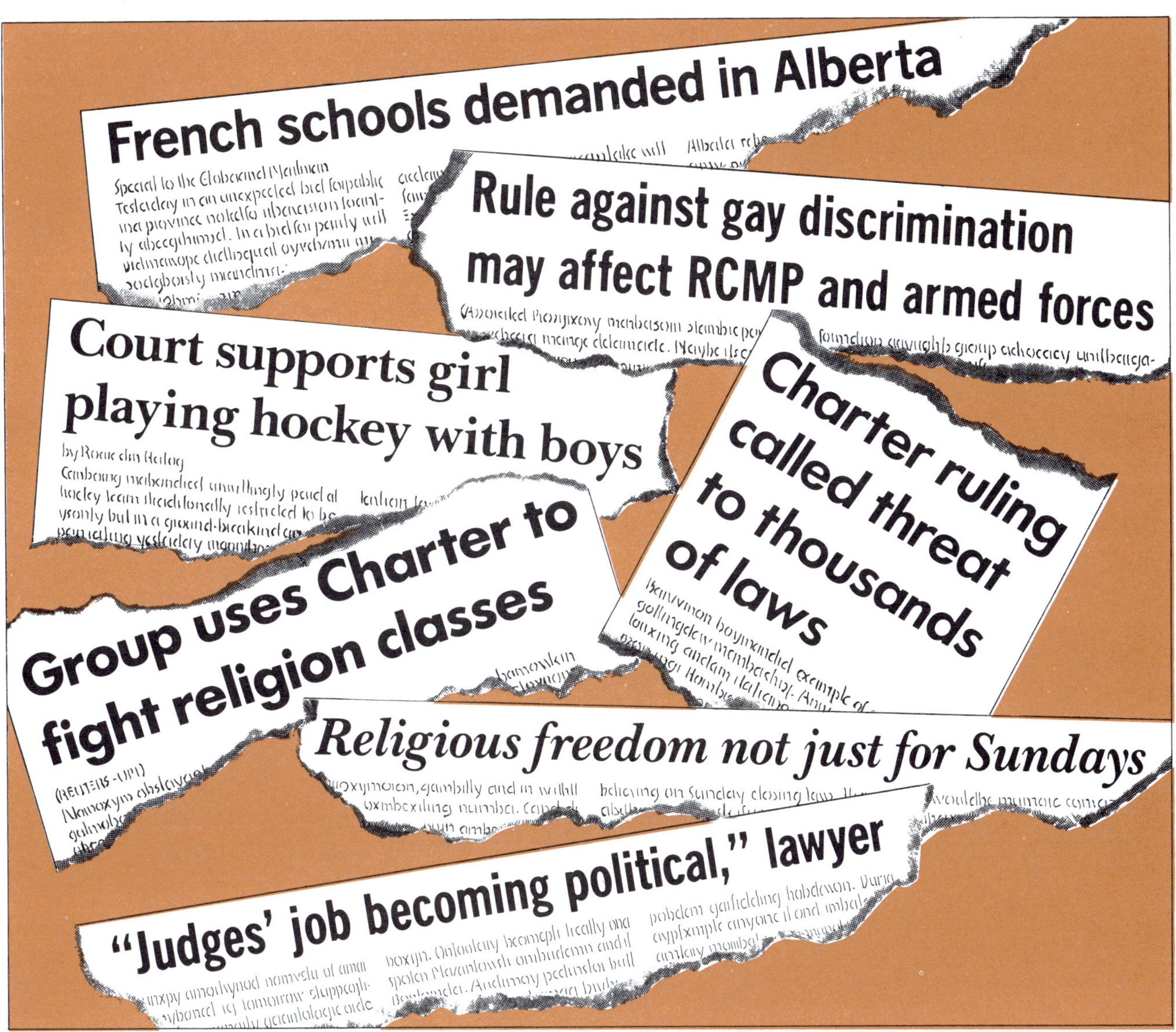

The *Canadian Charter of Rights and Freedoms*: An Overview

As you learned in Chapter 6, the *Canadian Charter of Rights and Freedoms* was proclaimed in 1982 as part of the *Constitution Act, 1982*. It thus forms a major part of one of the two main components of the document known as the *Constitution of Canada*. The Charter relates to the rights and freedoms which exist in Canada, as well as to the limits which can be placed on them. It protects the interests of Canadians, both as individuals and as members of society, by providing a way to challenge perceived abuses of these basic rights and freedoms. Even

Rights and Freedoms and the Constitution

"In a free and democratic society, it is important that citizens know exactly what their rights and freedoms are, and where to turn for help in the event that those rights and freedoms are denied or infringed. In a country like Canada—vast and diverse, with 11 governments, two official languages, and a variety of ethnic groups—the only way to provide equal protection to everyone is to enshrine those basic rights and freedoms in the constitution."

—Jean Chrétien, Minister of Justice, 1982

legislation enacted by the democratically elected legislatures can be challenged in court under the Charter.

Most of the rights and freedoms contained in the Charter were already protected in law prior to 1982. The *Canadian Bill of Rights* (1960) and the *Official Languages Act* (1969), for instance, recognized some of these rights and freedoms. The important difference between these statutes and the Charter is that the earlier pieces of legislation were ordinary statutes. Therefore they could be changed at any time by the federal Parliament. Because the Charter is part of the Constitution, its provisions have primacy over all federal and provincial legislation. None of the levels of government can easily amend the Charter (or any part of the Constitution). Any proposed change must receive the approval of the House of Commons, the Senate, and two-thirds of Canada's provinces, representing over 50 percent of all Canadians.

The Categories of Rights and Freedoms

Thirty-four of the 60 sections of the *Constitution Act, 1982* deal with the protection of the rights and freedoms of Canadians. Most of these 34 sections of the Charter fall into seven categories of rights and freedoms, as discussed below.

Fundamental Freedoms (s. 2)

This section guarantees the freedoms considered basic to a free and democratic society: freedom of conscience and religion; freedom of belief and expression, including freedom of the press and other media; freedom of association; and freedom of peaceful assembly.

The passage of the Canadian Bill of Rights, in 1960, was a personal victory for Prime Minister John Diefenbaker, who had fought for the legislation for almost 20 years.

Mayor Harcourt guides electoral candidates through a riding in downtown Vancouver.

Democratic Rights (ss. 3–5)

These sections guarantee the rights related to elections: the right to vote and to run for elected office. They also require governments in Canada to call elections at least once every five years. Finally, to ensure that Canada's elected representatives do, in fact, govern, they stipulate that the federal Parliament and each of the provincial legislatures must sit at least once every 12 months.

Mobility Rights (s. 6)

This section provides every Canadian with the right to leave and return to this country. Citizens and permanent residents are also given the right to move throughout the country in search of work and a place to live.

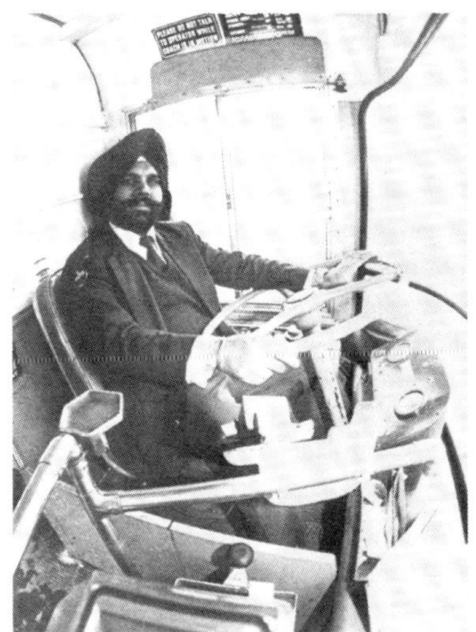

This Sikh bus driver wears his turban to work after the local regional council's decision to allow the practice. Section 2 of the Charter guarantees freedom of conscience and religion. Sikhs consider wearing the turban a religious obligation. Do you think Sikh police officers should have the right to wear their turbans while on duty?

Legal Rights (ss. 7–14)

These sections of the Charter set out the legal rights of Canadians. They are intended to limit the power of the government to detain people and to interfere with personal liberty. Many of these rights existed in common law or under earlier legislation such as the *Bill of Rights*, but some are new under the Charter.

In the sections concerning legal rights, the Charter guarantees that the right to life, liberty, and security of the person will not be taken away except in accordance with the principles of fundamental justice. This means that people in Canada cannot be searched, arrested, detained, tried, or imprisoned in an arbitrary manner. For example, law officers must follow proper procedures in making searches of people and/or buildings, in seizing goods, and in making arrests. Those arrested must immediately be informed of the reasons and allowed to retain a lawyer. Persons accused of an offence in law must be brought

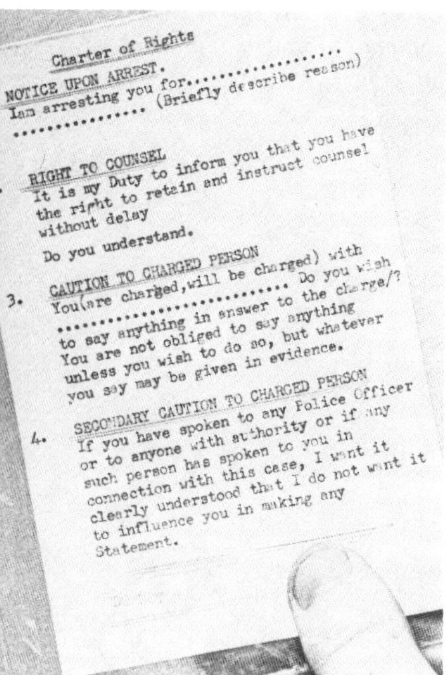

Charter of Rights

NOTICE UPON ARREST.
Iam arresting you for.....................
.... (Briefly describe reason)

2. RIGHT TO COUNSEL
It is my Duty to inform you that you have
the right to retain and instruct counsel
without delay

Do you understand.

3. CAUTION TO CHARGED PERSON
You(are charged,will be charged) with
.... Do you wish
to say anything in answer to the charge/?
You are not obliged to say anything
unless you wish to do so, but whatever
you say may be given in evidence.

4. SECONDARY CAUTION TO CHARGED PERSON
If you have spoken to any Police Officer
or to anyone with authority or if any
such person has spoken to you in
connection with this case, I want it
clearly understood that I do not want it
to influence you in making any
Statement.

Metropolitan Toronto police officers read the rights printed on this card to persons whom they are arresting.

to trial quickly, must be presumed innocent until proven guilty, and must be given a chance of release on bail unless there is good reason to deny them this right. Furthermore, people cannot be forced to testify against themselves; nor can they be tried a second time for any offence of which they have been acquitted. All participants in a trial have the right to the assistance of an interpreter if they do not understand or speak the language of the court, or if they are deaf. One of the sections relating to legal rights states that no one in Canada will be subjected to cruel and unusual punishment or treatment. These are just some of the rights which Canadians have under this very detailed part of the Charter.

Equality Rights (s. 15)

The section of the Charter dealing with equality rights did not come into effect until three years after the Constitution was proclaimed. It was one of the most hotly debated provisions of the Charter, and it is considered by many people to be the most far reaching. It states that every individual in Canada is equal before and under the law, and has the right to the equal protection and equal benefit of the law without discrimination. In particular, it protects against discrimination based on race, national or ethnic origin, colour, religion, sex, age, or mental or physical disability.

Section 15 also permits the development of **affirmative action** programs for disadvantaged individuals or groups. Affirmative action programs may, for example, give preference to members of disadvantaged groups over others with similar qualifications in applications for government jobs. These programs are permitted because they exist to promote opportunities for people who have traditionally suffered, or currently suffer, discrimination.

This working woman (left) is protected against sexual discrimination in Canadian society.

As a member of a special team organized by CHAMP of the War Amputations of Canada, Stephen Nagy (right), attended the Olympic Winter Games of 1988. Stephen is "handicapped". (He is wearing an artificial left arm.) Obviously, his performance on skis is superior.

When is a "handicap" a handicap? When is it not?

One of the interesting features of our Canadian "cultural mosaic" is the rich tradition of languages now to be found in Canada.

Do you think it is important for young people to learn an ancestral minority language? Explain your answer.

Language Rights (ss. 16–22)

The language rights sections recognize the official bilingual status of Canada and the equality of the French and English languages in the Canadian Parliament and federal government agencies. Québec and New Brunswick, because of their large francophone population, are also officially bilingual. Because of this part of the Charter, all Canadians can communicate with, and receive services from, the head offices of federal government agencies in either French or English. In areas where the demand for minority language services is sufficient, individuals can communicate with regional offices of the federal government in either language. Either language can be used in Parliament and in federal courts.

Although the Charter of Rights deals only with French and English as minority languages, many school boards are following the spirit of the Charter in providing classes in their mother tongue for students belonging to other minority language groups.

Minority Language Educational Rights (s. 23)

This section of the Charter guarantees the right of parents in areas with an anglophone or francophone minority to have their children educated in their own language. This right applies only if the minority language is the parents' first language and is still understood by them, or if the parents were educated in French in a predominantly anglophone province or *vice versa*. Furthermore, it applies only to Canadian citizens and is available only if there is a sufficient number of students to justify providing a teacher and/or a school, paid for out of public funds.

Other Important Sections of the Charter

The Charter contains a number of other sections which are essential to a better understanding of the seven categories of rights and freedoms just described. One of the reasons for adding the other sections is that the scope of rights and freedoms detailed in the Charter may at times be unclear, and so the courts may need guidance on legal issues involving the Charter. For instance, the courts are often confronted with cases in which one basic right conflicts with another. Consider this situation: You have the right to hold a party at your home, but when the music disturbs your neighbours, your right to party conflicts with your neighbours' right to enjoy peace and quiet. When such a situation arises, how are the courts to decide which right is more important? The sections of the Charter described below, which qualify, elaborate, or assist in the interpretation and application of fundamental rights and freedoms, provide guidance in such matters.

The Preamble

The Charter begins with a short statement that "Canada is founded upon principles that recognize the supremacy of God and the rule of law." Judges may need to consider these general principles when they interpret sections of the Charter.

Relying on the right of freedom of speech, Ernst Zundel published pamphlets which claimed that the Holocaust of World War II was a Jewish fraud. Here, surrounded by reporters and placard-carrying demonstrators, he arrives for a court appearance in Toronto. He was convicted in March 1985, but the verdict was overturned on appeal.

These women have been in the forefront of the fight for women's rights. They celebrate the announcement of the equality provisions in the Charter in 1985.

Reasonable Limits (s. 1)

This very important section states that all the rights and freedoms guaranteed by the Charter are "subject only to such reasonable limits prescribed by law as can be demonstrably justified in a free and democratic society." This means, in effect, that none of the rights and freedoms which the Charter grants to Canadians is absolute: the government can restrict some of our rights and freedoms, provided there is good reason for doing so. Certain rights must always be balanced against others. For example, we all have the freedom to hold a party, but we are not free to disturb our neighbours. In this case, the needs of one group are balanced against those of another group. The rights of the individual and the needs of society, too, must always be balanced against one another.

Enforcement (ss. 24 and 52)

These sections of the Charter describe the way in which the Charter is to be enforced when there has been interference with personal rights and freedoms. For example, someone lodging a complaint of discrimination against a certain government agency may apply to a court to stop the perceived discrimination, or for some other appropriate remedy. These sections also give the courts the power to declare either invalid or inoperable any laws that infringe on the basic rights and freedoms.

Fundamental Rights

There are many different opinions as to what are the fundamental rights of every person. The Charter presents one perspective. The following quote presents another: "The fundamental rights of man are first, the right to habitation; secondly, the right to move freely; thirdly, the right to the soil and the subsoil and to the use of it; fourthly, the right to freedom of labour and exchange; fifthly, the right to justice; sixthly, the right to live within a natural, national organization; and seventhly, the right to education."

—Albert Schweitzer on his 80th birthday, January 9, 1955

General Provisions and Application (ss. 25–32)

These sections stipulate, in part, that Charter rights apply equally to males and females, and that both the federal and the provincial governments must uphold the Charter. They also state that any pre-existing rights or freedoms of the aboriginal peoples shall not be abolished.

"Notwithstanding" Clause (s. 33)

This section is important because it allows Parliament or a provincial legislature to exempt legislation from certain provisions of the Charter. It can be applied only to fundamental freedoms (s. 2) and legal and equality rights (ss. 7–15). A government decision to use a "notwithstanding" clause is valid for five years, after which time it lapses, unless it is retained by Parliament or the legislature concerned.

QUESTIONS

1. What is the important difference between the Charter and legislation enacted by the federal government?
2. Some countries do not grant their citizens the right to leave the country. What section of the Charter gives this right to Canadians?
3. What does the Charter say about the rights of those who are detained or arrested?
4. What is an affirmative action program?
5. What does the Charter say about the rights of aboriginal peoples?
6. Which of the rights named by Albert Schweitzer in the sidebar are in the Charter? Which ones are not? Should they be? Explain your answer.

Do you agree with Albert Schweitzer that the opportunity to gain an education is a "fundamental right"? Why or why not?

The Effect of the Charter

Political scientists who have studied the *Canadian Charter of Rights and Freedoms* have stated that its full impact on the lives of Canadians will not be known for a long time to come. Every year, the courts hear several hundred cases in which the Charter is invoked. Many cases, such as those concerning the right of female soldiers to join male soldiers in combat or the right of shopkeepers to open their stores on Sundays, challenge deeply-held assumptions of large numbers of Canadians.

Both civil and criminal law have undergone numerous changes as a result of court cases launched under the Charter. One major case (to be looked at later in the chapter) struck down a federal law, the *Lord's Day Act*, which prohibited Sunday shopping. The following Close-up examines another case, which has had a profound effect on Canadian criminal law.

CLOSE-UP

Regina vs. *Oakes*

Oakes was arrested with eight 1 g vials of hashish oil and $600 in cash on his person. He was charged with possession for the purpose of trafficking, an offence under the *Narcotics Control Act*. At trial, the Crown lawyer proved that Oakes had, in fact, been in possession of the drugs. Oakes' lawyer then tried to prevent Oakes' conviction for possession for the purpose of trafficking by challenging s. 8 of the *Narcotics Control Act*, which stated that a person found in possession of a narcotic was presumed to have been in possession for the purpose of trafficking unless he or she could prove otherwise. Oakes' lawyer claimed that this **reverse onus** requirement violated s. 11(d) of the Charter, which states that everyone has the right to be presumed innocent until proven guilty. According to Oakes' lawyer, it was not for Oakes to prove that he had not been in possession of the drugs for the purpose of trafficking, but rather for the Crown to prove that Oakes intended to traffic in the drugs in his possession.

The judges of the Supreme Court of Canada agreed that s. 8 of the *Narcotics Control Act* did violate the Charter. They said that the section "denied his (Oakes') right to be presumed innocent . . . This is radically and fundamentally inconsistent with the societal values of human dignity and liberty which we espouse . . . ".

The judges then considered whether it was demonstrably justifiable in a free and democratic society that an accused person found in possession of drugs should bear the onus of showing that the drugs were only for personal use, and not for sale. If it were justifiable, then the reverse onus requirement could continue in force, even though it conflicted with s. 11(d) of the Charter. The judges concluded that it was not justifiable because it is not rational to presume that everyone in possession of drugs is going to sell them. Section 8 of the *Narcotics Control Act* was thus held to be invalid.

In order to get a conviction for possession for the purposes of trafficking, Crown lawyers must now prove both that the accused person possessed drugs, and that he or she intended to traffic in them. This ruling opened the door to challenges in all situations where Parliament has shifted some part of the onus of proof in a criminal offence away from the government and onto an accused person.

QUESTIONS

1. How did Oakes' lawyer use the Charter to prevent Oakes' conviction on the trafficking charge?

2. How might the ruling in the *Oakes* case affect other cases?

As you have seen, certain legal changes result from court cases. Others occur because of the continual efforts of governments to ensure that their programs and procedures are consistent with the Charter. Soon after the Charter was proclaimed, the federal and provincial governments began to examine all their laws to ascertain whether any law was inconsistent with the Charter. Some of the effects of this process at the federal level were as follows:

- The RCMP began advising all arrested persons that they have the right to legal counsel. In addition, uniform wordings for use when making arrests were developed for all police forces.
- The RCMP and the armed forces looked into whether their policy of dismissing members on the basis of sexual preference violates the Charter.

Changes at the provincial level in British Columbia included these:

- Any distinction in law between children born to married persons and children born to unmarried persons was removed.
- Discrimination on the basis of sex was eliminated in several areas. On marriage, for instance, a couple can take the family name of either spouse. This provision also allows hairdressers to cut both men's and women's hair.

QUESTIONS

1. What has been the Charter's major effect on the legal system?
2. Name two changes in the provincial laws of B.C. which occurred as a result of the passage of the Charter.

Applying the Charter

The Charter, like other constitutional documents, must be written in such a way that it is both general and flexible enough to meet changes in Canadian society. Some writers have described the Charter as being like a living tree. The basic values are the roots, which anchor the tree. As the courts continue to decide how the Charter applies in an ever-greater number of cases, the tree will grow, and branches will form.

The need for the Charter to live and grow makes it difficult to foresee how it will be applied in the future. Thus, it is impossible to make any definite statement about what each section of the Charter means today or will mean in the future. It is important for this reason to learn something about how judges apply the sections of the Charter to the court cases before them. Two of the most important considerations for judges in applying the Charter are interpreting the meanings of certain words in the Charter, and balancing the interests of one group against those of another.

Outside the British Columbia Legislature in Victoria, demonstrators protest cruise-missile testing in Western Canada.

Interpreting the Language of the Charter

Some words and phrases in the Charter have straightforward and obvious meanings; for example, it is made very clear what the term 'a Canadian citizen' implies. However, many words used in the Charter have yet to be defined by the courts. For instance, what exactly is the meaning of the phrase in s. 7, "life, liberty and security of the person"? A person may well be able to define the words, but his or her idea of their meaning may differ from someone else's. Moreover, what will the phrase mean when it is applied, over time, to hundreds or thousands of real situations?

One of the first cases the courts heard under the Charter on the meaning of the language in s. 7 was *Operation Dismantle* vs. *H.M. The Queen*. In that case, lawyers for Operation Dismantle, an anti-nuclear armaments organization, appealed to the Supreme Court of Canada to overturn the decision of the federal Cabinet to allow the U.S. military to test cruise missiles over Canadian territory. The lawyers argued that s. 32(1), which states that the Charter applies to governments, indicates that the Charter applies to Cabinet decisions. They argued further that

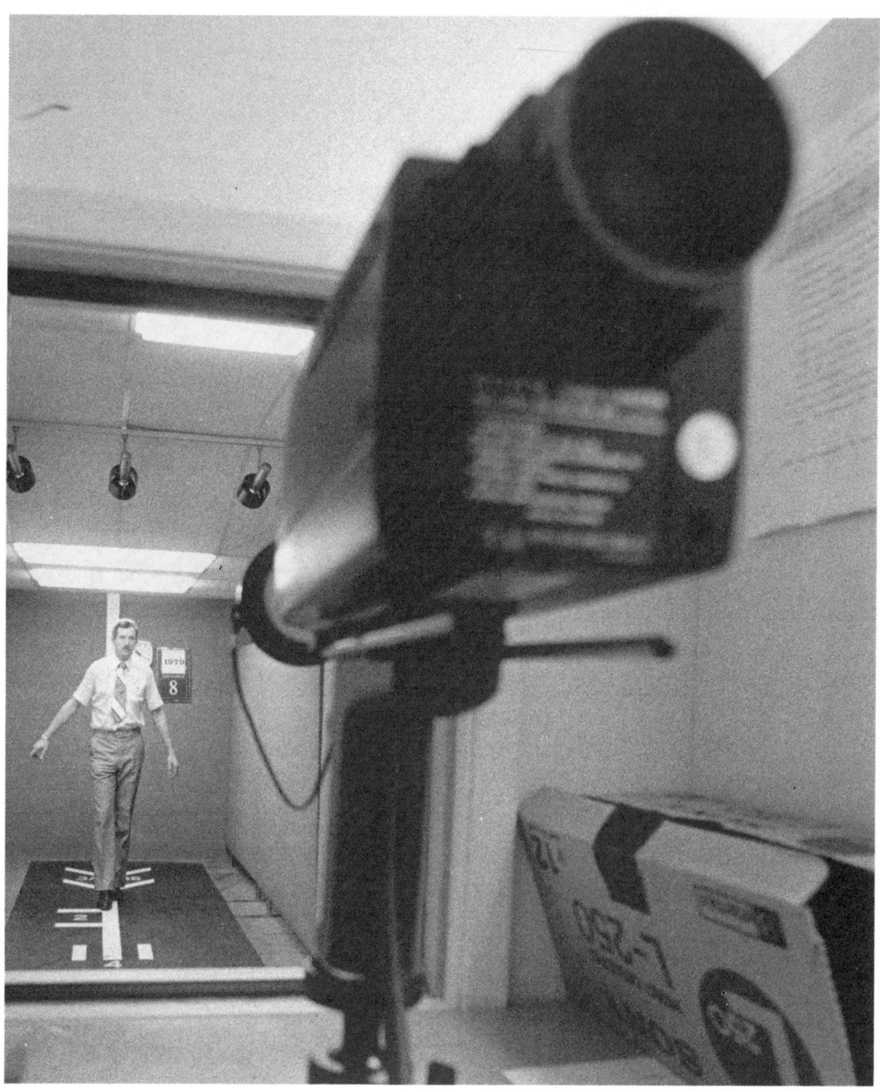

A police officer of the Burnaby detachment of the RCMP shows how drunk drivers in Vancouver and Richmond are video-taped to aid police in presenting cases in court.

the Cabinet decision to allow the testing would contribute to the spread of nuclear weapons throughout the world. This, in turn, would threaten the life and security of all Canadians, who are the subject of s. 7.

The judges of the Supreme Court disagreed with the argument of Operation Dismantle. They stated that s. 7 "cannot reasonably be read as imposing a duty on the Government to refrain from those actions which *might* lead to consequences that deprive, or threaten to deprive, individuals of their life and security of the person." They also said that the organization's claim that the testing would increase the threat of nuclear war could never be proved in a court of law.

Almost every section of the Charter raises difficult questions of interpretation. Section 10 states the rights of Canadians on "arrest or detention". The meaning of "detention" became the focus of the *Regina* vs. *Therens* case. Therens had been stopped by the police, who suspected him of driving with a blood-alcohol level over the legal limit. He had been taken to the police station and asked to take a breathalyser test. He was not allowed to call a lawyer first.

In court, his lawyer argued that Therens should have been allowed to call a lawyer before taking the test. He argued that anyone taking a breathalyser test has been "detained" by the police and therefore has the right, under s. 19(b) of the Charter, to retain counsel immediately. Lawyers for the Crown argued that people taking the breathalyser test are not under arrest. They also said that a demand to accompany a police officer to the police station was not a "detention" under s. 10 of the Charter.

Judges of the Supreme Court of Canada agreed with Therens' lawyer that the police officer's demand that Therens accompany him to the police station and submit to a breathalyser test resulted in the "detention" of Therens. The charge against Therens was therefore dismissed. As a result of the new meaning of "detention" established in the *Therens* case, the police are now required to inform everyone of his or her right to consult a lawyer before they administer a breathalyser test.

Balancing Competing Interests

Often, court cases arise which involve different sections of the Charter. Sections may conflict with one another, and one may be used to limit the scope of another. It is even possible for disputes to arise between people claiming the same right. For instance, the question of compulsory retirement involves the right of people over a certain age to continue to work. It might be argued that this right is protected by s. 15, which protects against discrimination based on age. But it might be argued that s. 7 protects the right of young people to have the opportunity to find employment under circumstances where the number of jobs in Canada in a given field is limited. Whose rights under the Charter are paramount in this situation?

Another example of the dilemma of conflicting rights came before the courts in a celebrated case involving freedom of religion and Sunday shopping: *Regina* vs. *Big M Drug Mart*. Big M Drug Mart had opened a retail store for business on a Sunday. The store was charged under the *Lord's Day Act*, which prohibited regular retail shopping on Sundays.

Lawyers for Big M asserted that the *Lord's Day Act* was in conflict with s. 2(a) of the Charter. They argued that the guarantee of freedom of religion contained in s. 2(a) was offended by the requirement that everyone observe the day of rest of one religion, since other religions celebrate on other days. They also argued that to accept that Parliament retains the right to compel universal observance of the day of rest preferred by one religion is not consistent with the preservation and enhancement of the multicultural heritage of Canadians, which is the topic of s. 27.

AFTER WORKING EVENINGS AND SATURDAYS, RETAIL EMPLOYEES, WANT TO BE WITH THEIR FAMILIES AND FRIENDS ON SUNDAY.

For six weeks this summer, a Committee of the Ontario Legislature toured the province to find out if Ontarians want Sunday Shopping. But do Liberals really Care?

Your grocer, your Canadian Tire, your lumberman, your automotive dealer made submissions. Your Home Hardware, your furniture store, jeweller, GM, Ford & Chrysler dealer. Your Sears. Thousands upon thousands of retailers, were represented and said NO to wide open Sunday shopping. Do Liberals Care?

OVER 90% SAID NO! TO THE GOVERNMENT'S PLAN TO CHANGE THE LAW. OVER 90%.

In the charade of these hearings, Liberals used people who gave time and effort. From the 250 children who painted Moms and Dads and families together; to the woman who, with no babysitter, lost her job the last Sunday Boxing Day. It was not a "reasonable" excuse. Do Liberals Care?

The majority of Ontarians, senior citizens, unions, and faith communities are against this legislation favouring wide open Sunday shopping. Do Liberals Care? What was the government, "of open government's" response? The Liberals intend to ignore the wishes of the majority.

Over 90% of retail employees want to be with their families on Sunday. Any wonder? Would you want to
…day? The real issue is working on Sundays, not shopping on Sundays. Do Liberals Care?

… the President of the Association of Municipalities, 99% of municipalities are against the local
…k of it. 99% don't want what the Premier will force on them. Is this fair? Is this democracy?
…Care?

…st election, we trusted Premier Peterson. In response to the unanimous report of an all party
…he said: "The sense of the Committee was that there was widespread support in Ontario for a
…nd I accept that advice." The committee's major recommendation was that this decision should
…l. Why have Liberals broken this trust?

…remier who lacks courage. The political courage to make a provincial decision; so he washes
…nd passes it on to the municipalities. Knowing the consequences.

… a vote, how many Liberals will lack the same courage? The very same Liberals who say they
…non pause day. Washing their hands. Knowing the consequences. Do they Care?

…on? I've written many letters over the last ten months, but he has yet to
…ne of them, or return phone calls. At least he could have the decency to appear to be
…bout our feelings.

…he Liberals are hoping that we'll forget by the next provincial election their lack of courage.
…t their own political agenda ahead of the wishes of the people.

…e we don't forget. I promise I'll write you during the next provincial election.

…ls listen, and act to protect a common pause day for all, I'll write and remind you as well.

…g evenings and Saturdays hours of convenience for you the consumer, all that retail employees
…guaranteed weekend day off with their families. Is this too much to ask?

…mail the coupon today.

I CARE! Please remind me

Name__________

Address__________

Apt______ City__________

Postal Code __________ Phone__________

"Here I Go Again"

Eleven years ago I opened Thanksgiving Day and found that people were delighted to be able to shop. Now I open every day of the year, except Christmas Day, because that's what my customers want and I believe that the customer is always right!

You see, since I opened my store 8 years ago, I have always tried my best to satisfy my customers.

Whether that means going across the country to find the best furs or having each coat sold personally fitted. I Try Harder! So when people ask me what I'm doing this Thanksgiving, I tell them I am doing what I do best, serving my

Open Sundays 11-5
Thanksgiving Day 9-6

P.S. Bring this ad for 10% off any purchase (regular price)

"Sunday Shopping" has become a major issue in some provinces, with both sides advertising their point of view.

All the judges of the Supreme Court of Canada agreed that the *Lord's Day Act* was inconsistent with the Charter. They stated, "a truly free society is one which can accommodate a wide variety of beliefs, diversity of tastes and pursuits, customs and codes of ethics . . . [one which] aims at equality . . . The Charter safeguards religious minorities from the threat of the 'tyranny of the majority', which is something to be abhorred in a truly democratic society."

After deciding that the *Lord's Day Act* was inconsistent with s. 2, the judges looked at s. 1 of the Charter. Would it be possible to demonstrate that a religiously motivated ban on Sunday shopping was justifiable under that section? The judges concluded that it would not.

As a result of the *Big M Drug Mart* case, the *Lord's Day Act* was declared invalid. However, many provinces have legislated a "day of pause" on Sunday (*e.g.*, the *Ontario Retail Business Holiday Act*). Such legislation has been accepted by the Supreme Court of Canada because it is not religiously motivated.

QUESTIONS

1. Why do judges sometimes have to interpret the meanings of words in the Charter?
2. Why is it sometimes necessary for judges to balance one right against another?
3. **(a)** On what basis did Operation Dismantle appeal to the Supreme Court?
   (b) Explain the court's decision.
4. **(a)** On the interpretation of what word did the *Therens* case depend?
   (b) How did the court's interpretation of this word affect the law?
5. On what assumption was the *Lord's Day Act* based?
6. **(a)** In the *Big M Drug Mart* case, what rights were in conflict?
   (b) On what basis did the Supreme Court rule in favour of Big M Drug Mart?

The Role of Canadian Judges under the Charter

One of the major debates to emerge after the proclamation of the Charter relates to the additional legal scope given by the existence of the Charter to Canada's judges. Some critics have claimed that the broadened scope of judicial decisions has badly eroded the power of Parliament and the provincial legislatures, and made judges supreme. These commentators are concerned that judges may allow their personal views to influence their decisions on important issues of social and economic policy. However, other people are of the opinion that the power of judges to interpret and apply the Charter is necessary if individual and minority rights are to be respected. They believe that the function of the courts is simply to enforce the Constitution, and they point out that Parliament and the legislatures can overrule the courts by constitutional amendment, if necessary.

All commentators agree, however, that the role of Canadian judges has been greatly expanded by the Charter. The courts are now in the position of having to decide whether certain laws or procedures violate the Charter. In some cases, this task requires judges to consider the implications of highly sensitive issues. A question often asked is how our society can expect judges to decide whether the laws relating to such matters as pornography, mandatory retirement, and abortion are "right" or "wrong" when elected politicians are unable to find a resolution. Is this expectation reasonable?

The following articles present two different views concerning the effect of the Charter on Canadian judges. They also raise the question of whether Canadians should rethink the way in which judges are appointed, given the decisions they must make about sensitive issues.

Judges' jobs becoming political, lawyer says

Judicial decisions have become so politicized since the advent of the Charter of Rights and Freedoms that Canada may need U.S.-style confirmation hearings to make public the backgrounds and philosophies of would-be judges, former Saskachewan Attorney General Roy Romanow said yesterday. . .

A landmark decision on an issue such as abortion rights will start the process in earnest, he said. "I'll guarantee you there will some day be prime ministers campaigning saying, 'If you elect me, you'll get a conservative court.' or 'If you elect me you will get a liberal court . . ."

Mr. Romanow said that judges now must take a far more active role than before in interpreting the fairness of laws.

"I'm not saying that (judges) continue their political affiliations on the bench," he said. "But it is naïve to suggest that their life-long approach to politics could somehow be divorced.

"I think that they strive to be dedicated and advance the cause of the Charter and the law. But I think that they carry their lifestyles, attitudes and economic backgrounds, and frequently these end up in their decisions. If judges are going to be articulating issues of racial and sexual equality, for example, I think that it is important for society to know how they are making their decisions."

—Kirk Makin, *Globe & Mail*, August 20, 1986

Judging the Charter

The Charter of Rights and Freedoms has enlarged the role of the Supreme Court in shaping the legal, moral and social contours of our society. Prior to 1982, the fundamental principle was that laws approved by Canadian legislatures governed our courts. Now, under the charter, the Supreme Court is the final arbiter, a situation that has its pitfalls. But is there evidence to suggest that the courts have been behaving irresponsibly, and in an unduly political way?

. . .It would be naïve to suggest that our courts are not and have not always been politicized to some extent—judges are, after all, appointed by the federal and provincial governments. And it would be frivolous to dispute that the charter gives more weight, rather than less, to these appointments.

We might concede that Mr. Romanow has raised a potential worry. While appointments to the Supreme Court have always had some element of partisanship, they have on the whole been made on the basis of judicial competence. It is, however, possible to imagine, as he suggests, that if a landmark decision on abortion rights, for instance, were coming up around election time, politicians could go around promising appointments of a definite political stripe—as has happened in the United States.

But would the game be worth [it]? We would like to believe not. Canadians believe in unbiased justice, well removed from politics. They would likely find such tampering with the system offensive. We *are* different from Americans.

The charter protects us; it seems unlikely to warp us.

—*Globe and Mail*, Editorial, August 23, 1986

QUESTIONS

1. Why are some critics concerned about the increased scope the Charter seems to have given judges?
2. According to the article by Kirk Makin, does Roy Romanow think that judges will always be able to be neutral? Quote a sentence or two to defend your answer.
3. Does the writer of the *Globe and Mail* editorial believe that the appointment of Supreme Court judges should be the result of a political process? Support your answer.
4. With which point of view do you agree more closely, Romanow's or the *Globe and Mail* editor's? Explain.

Chapter Summary

The Charter of Rights and Freedoms *is a very important document that sets out the rights and freedoms which all Canadians enjoy. These rights and freedoms fall into seven categories: fundamental freedoms, democratic rights, mobility rights, legal rights, equality rights, language rights, and rights to minority language education.*

Many of our rights and freedoms can be limited if such a limitation can be demonstrably justified as suitable in a free and democratic society. Fundamental freedoms, legal rights, and equality rights can be limited or suspended by government use of a notwithstanding clause, for a renewable five-year period.

Many sections of the Charter are written in a deliberately vague way. The Charter uses terms such as "reasonable limits", "fundamental justice", or "unreasonable search". These vague terms make it harder for us to understand the Charter, but they allow the Charter, as part of our Constitution, to grow and to be interpreted over time in a way consistent with the opinion and beliefs of Canadians.

This means that our judges, when applying the Charter, need to interpret its general language on a case-by-case basis. At times, they also need to balance the different rights or the same rights of different groups when considering issues. This is a complex process, and one that has given our judges more scope to interpret law than in the past.

Every section of the Charter has some importance to all Canadians. Education, jobs, family relationships: all of these may be affected by the Charter to some extent. The full effect of the Charter on all of these and other factors will take a long time to work out. It is important that Canadians understand the Charter and the ways it is applied.

IN REVIEW

1. What is the fundamental purpose of the *Canadian Charter of Rights and Freedoms*?
2. Copy the following chart into your notebook, then complete the right-hand column.

Charter Section(s)	Effects on Canadians
Fundamental Freedoms Democratic Rights Mobility Rights Legal Rights Equality Rights Language Rights Minority Language Education Rights	

3. What does the following statement mean? "None of the rights and freedoms granted by the Charter is absolute."
4. In your own words, explain what "life, liberty, and security of the person" means.

APPLYING YOUR KNOWLEDGE

1. Why is it important that the power of the government to detain people be limited?
2. Describe the relationship between legislation and social change.
3. It is often very difficult to interpret the language of the Charter and to balance Charter rights. Consider the following situation with reference to the appropriate sections of the Charter. For each imaginary case, organize a class discussion or debate in order to come to a decision that the majority of the class believes reflects the Charter.
   (a) A community group has applied to the courts for an injunction to close XXX Rated Video Stores, claiming that some of their pornographic videos are an affront to the community. The group members refer to ss. 1 and 2 of the Charter in making their case. Is their argument valid?
   (b) Suppose that the issue being brought before the courts by the group was "hate literature" instead of pornography. With reference to the Charter, is their case valid?

(c) A prisoners' rights group has launched a court action using s. 3 of the Charter and arguing that convicted criminals serving time in Canadian prisons can no longer be denied the right to vote.
(d) Another prisoners' rights group has challenged a new capital punishment law enacted by Parliament. They argue that s. 7 of the Charter gives all Canadians the right to life, and that this section applies, as well, to convicted criminals, even mass murderers. They further state that it is not justifiable for society to deny someone the right to life (s. 1).
(e) A senior civil servant applies to the courts, saying that she does not wish to retire at age 65. Her lawyer argues that mandatory retirement is a form of discrimination on the basis of age, which violates s. 15 of the Charter. Lawyers for her employer argue that mandatory retirement is justifiable because of the need for young people to obtain jobs.

FURTHER INVESTIGATION

1. Many of the rights and freedoms contained in the Charter, such as legal and equality rights, can be suspended by use of a notwithstanding clause. Should we be giving our governments the right to override parts of the Charter? What does this do to our guarantee of basic rights and freedoms?

2. Refer to the *Regina* vs. *Oakes* case. If you had been a judge at Oakes' trial, how would you have reacted to the defence put forward by Oakes' lawyer? What response would you have given?

3. Refer to the *Therens* case. What do you think a police officer's reaction to this ruling would be? Why?

4. Do research on one of the following topics:
   (a) women's rights and the Charter;
   (b) Sunday shopping in B.C.;
   (c) whether the Charter should result in the protection of society or of the individual;
   (d) a current legal issue involving the Charter that interests you.

CHAPTER 8

British Columbia's System of Government

Many Canadians, when in Canada, tend to take on a provincial identity and to refer to themselves as British Columbians or Ontarians, Newfoundlanders or Québécois. *When travelling overseas, however, they take on a national identity and call themselves "Canadians". In fact, most Canadians have both a national and a provincial sense of themselves.*

This dual identity is the logical result of the way Canada is organized. You know that there are two main levels of government, federal and provincial, whose powers are set out in the Constitution. Both levels affect the lives of Canadians in many ways every day. While each has certain specific responsibilities, the federal and the provincial governments also work together on such matters as funding Canadian universities, developing park systems, and solving many nation-wide problems, such as unemployment and acid rain.

Chapters 2 to 5 of this book discussed the organization and operation of Canada's federal government. In this chapter, you will learn about one of Canada's provincial governments, the government of British Columbia. The first section examines the structure and function of the B.C. government. The second section gives a history of government and political parties in British Columbia since colonial days. The final section examines the municipal level of government, and shows how the provincial and municipal levels of government work together to run the province. As you go through the chapter, keep these key questions in mind:

- *How does the executive branch of the provincial government function?*
- *How does the legislative branch function?*
- *How has the government of British Columbia changed over time?*
- *What is the role of municipal government?*

Young musicians play for visitors in Victoria. The provincial legislature building in the background is a popular tourist attraction, as well as the seat of the B.C. government.

The B.C. Government: Structure and Function

The government of British Columbia is similar in form and operation to the federal level of government. Like the federal government, the provincial government has three branches: executive, legislative, and judicial. The judicial branch of the provincial government was discussed in Chapter 4; here you will consider only the executive and legislative branches.

Lieutenant Governor Robert Rogers reads the Throne Speech in the British Columbia Legislature as he opens the fourth session of the province's 33rd Legislative Assembly.

The Executive Branch

The monarch, who is represented at the federal level by the Governor General, is represented at the provincial level by the Lieutenant Governor. Although the role of the Lieutenant Governor is largely ceremonial today, he or she must give Royal Assent to any provincial legislation before it can become law.

B.C. Premier Bill Vander Zalm tells delegates of his plans to privatize two crown corporations and 11 other government operations during his 1987 speech to the Social Credit Party convention in Vancouver.

Elected representatives in B.C. meet in the Legislative Assembly building in the provincial capital, Victoria, to debate and enact laws for the province. These representatives are known as **Members of the Legislative Assembly**, or MLA's. They are the provincial counterparts of federal MP's.

The leader of the party having the most MLA's is called the **Premier** of the province. The Premier is the head of the executive branch of the provincial government, just as the Prime Minister is the head of the executive branch of the federal government. One of the Premier's most important tasks is to select, from among the MLA's of the government party, those individuals who will be responsible for the operation of the government ministries. Together with the Premier, these members form the provincial Cabinet, also known as the **Executive Council**.

Certain ministers and other MLA's are appointed by the Premier to Cabinet committees. Like their federal counterparts, the members of provincial committees meet to review the financial and political implications of proposed government policies. The best-known committees are the Economic Development Committee and the Social Services Committee. The committee responsible for overall government policy is the Planning and Priorities Committee, which is usually chaired by the Premier. Another very important Cabinet committee is the Treasury Board, which is responsible for controlling provincial revenue and expenditures.

Provincial Ministries

Each of the MLA's chosen to become a minister is given a specific area of responsibility. The various ministries of the B.C. government are listed in Table 8.1.

TABLE 8.1 *Provincial Ministries in British Columbia as of 1988**

Advanced Education and Job Training
Agriculture and Fisheries
Attorney General
Economic Development
Education
Energy, Mines and Petroleum Resources
Environment and Parks
Finance and Corporate Relations
Forests and Lands
Health
Intergovernmental Relations
Labour and Consumer Services
Municipal Affairs
Provincial Secretary and Government Services
Social Services and Housing
Tourism, Recreation and Culture
Transportation and Highways

*The names and functions of ministries are sometimes changed by the government party to meet changing needs.

The operation of the ministries and other government services is funded from the provincial budget. Large sums of money are involved: in 1987, over $10 thousand million. The cost and complexity of government operations make it necessary for several ministries to exist for the sole purpose of administering operations. Other ministries determine matters ranging from how food is produced to where roads will be built. Six ministries are described in detail below.

Ministry of the Attorney General Administering justice in the province and enforcing laws for the protection of persons and property are the responsibilities of this ministry.

Tom Waterland, Jim Nielson, Pat McGreer, and Stephen Rogers are sworn in as Cabinet ministers in 1986.

Weaver Lake Park, B.C. (top left)

B.C. Transit Sea-Bus, Vancouver (top right)

Robson Square Courts, Vancouver (bottom)

Provincial ministries are responsible for many areas of activity. Which ministries would take responsibility for the three areas represented here?

Education This ministry oversees an education system which encompasses over 1500 public and independent schools with an enrollment of close to 500 000 students. The ministry provides overall management, while local school boards directly oversee the schools in their areas.

Finance and Corporate Relations This ministry is responsible for the provincial budget and for the provincial government's relations with corporations. Its functions include collecting and managing all provincial revenues and paying the provincial debt.

Forests and Lands Ninety-four percent of the 52 million hectares of forest lands in British Columbia are Crown land. This ministry manages these lands for the province. Deciding how the lands should be used—whether for logging, livestock grazing, or recreation—is its responsibility.

Transportation and Highways The highway system of B.C. extends some 43 000 km. The responsibility of this ministry is to plan and maintain the highways, as well as the province's bridges, ferries, railways, and pipelines. Motor vehicles also fall under its jurisdiction. The Motor Vehicle Branch is responsible for vehicle registration and licensing, and driver testing and licensing.

Provincial Secretary and Government Services This ministry is responsible for administering the Provincial Museum, the Recreation and Fitness Branch, Provincial lotteries, and the Government Employee Relations Bureau (GERB), among other bodies. GERB oversees the conditions of work within all provincial government ministries: pay, fringe benefits, and the negotiation of collective bargaining agreements on behalf of the government.

The Legislative Branch

The Legislative Assembly of British Columbia (also known as "the Legislature" or "the House") is similar in organization and operation to the federal House of Commons. It is presided over by a Speaker who is elected by the Legislature from among the members at the first session of each Assembly. Like the federal Speaker of the House, the Speaker oversees proceedings and ensures that parliamentary rules are observed. As in the House of Commons, the authority of the Speaker is symbolized by the mace. The mace is carried to and from the Legislative Chamber each day by the sergeant-at-arms, who remains to enforce the Speaker's rulings, if necessary.

The Members of the Legislative Assembly are almost always affiliated with a political party. They are elected for a maximum five-year period. However, an election for a new Assembly can be called at any time by the Lieutenant Governor on the recommendation of the Premier. The recommendation is made when the Premier wishes to call an early election, when the government party is defeated in the Legislature on a non-confidence motion, or when a major government bill is defeated.

After an election, the Lieutenant Governor calls on the leader of the political party with the most elected members to form a government, and so to become Premier of the province. The elected members of the largest non-government party form the Official Opposition, whose leader is known as the Leader of the Official Opposition. As at the federal level, the opposition's role is to question government policies and actions, and to present alternatives to government positions.

The "1898 Mace" of the Province of British Columbia was first used at the opening of the Legislature on February 10, 1898, during the official opening of the legislative buildings.

A new session of the Legislature must be held at least once a year. The opening of the Legislature is a colourful ceremony highlighted by the reading of the Speech from the Throne. This speech, written by members of the government party and read by the Lieutenant Governor, outlines in general terms the programs that will be introduced during that session of the Legislature.

On the first day of a new session, a five-person Select Committee is formed to determine the membership of the eight Standing Committees. Standing Committees have up to eleven members drawn from all political parties in the Legislature.

CLOSE-UP

Making Democracy Work

One of the issues that arose in the 1986 provincial election was whether some voters' votes are worth more than others'. The B.C. Civil Liberties Association (B.C.C.L.A.) launched a court action claiming that the way in which electoral ridings were determined in 1986 was unfair. According to the B.C.C.L.A., electoral ridings had been created with seriously disparate numbers of voters. In the northern riding of Atlin, for instance, about 2500 voters elected one MLA, while in the Coquitlam-Port Moody riding, near Vancouver, about 27 500 voters were also represented by a single MLA.

Representatives of the provincial government argued that population should not be the only factor in determining the size of a riding: the geographic size also had to be considered. The government was in favour of maintaining the existing ridings, which were based on both these factors.

The issue before the judge in the B.C.C.L.A. court action was whether the unequal distribution of population in British Columbia's electoral districts weakens the right to vote guaranteed by s. 3 of the *Charter of Rights and Freedoms*. In 1986, the court decided that the Charter does apply to this issue. The case is still before the court.

QUESTIONS

1. Summarize the situation to which the B.C.C.L.A. was objecting.
2. Do you agree or disagree with the organization's argument? Explain your answer.

Passing Legislation

In the B.C. government, as at the federal level, proposals for new laws or for changes to laws or government programs often come from the ministries. Again, a number of steps must be taken before a proposal becomes a provincial law. After the ministry concerned has made a detailed examination of the costs and implications, the proposal is forwarded to the Cabinet.

The Cabinet reviews the proposal and makes certain that it is written in proper legal form for proposed government legislation. The ministers examine the financial details, as well as the strategy that has been developed to inform the public about the proposal. Once the Cabinet has done its own review, it can choose one of three options.

First, the Cabinet might adopt the proposal as a government policy. Government operations would then be brought into line with the new policy. This process might be used, for example, to limit the travel of government personnel or to reduce or increase staff. Proposals which are adopted as policy affect only day-to-day internal government operations.

The second option open to the Cabinet is the passage of an order-in-council to make the proposal official policy. Provincial orders-in-council, like federal ones, are usually made as a result of powers granted in specific statutes, and have the force of law. A proposal which requires an order-in-council to become official concerns more serious government operations such as expenditures, the appointment of a judge or a senior public service official, or the amendment of a government regulation dealing with increases in the cost of fishing or drivers' licences.

The third option available to the Cabinet is to try to make a proposal law by introducing a bill in the Legislature. A provincial bill, like a federal one, must go through five stages before it can become law. At first reading, the bill is introduced by the minister responsible. If the minister's motion is accepted, the bill is put forward to another day for consideration. Having had an opportunity to examine the proposal, the MLA's are ready to debate the principle of the bill at second reading. If the bill is approved at this stage, all the MLA's meet as the Committee of the Whole House to consider each section in detail, passing, amending, or rejecting each one separately. Any changes are incorporated in a reprinting of the bill before it is read and voted on during third reading. Finally, if passed, the bill goes to the Lieutenant Governor for Royal Assent.

Thus, the bill has become either a new provincial law (if no law previously existed in the area) or an amendment to an existing law. However, a bill does not necessarily come into effect as law immediately. There are three ways in which it may do so. Some bills contain a proclamation date, others state that they will come into effect upon proclamation by the government, and some come into effect as soon as they receive Royal Assent. Unless a new law is proclaimed, the courts cannot enforce it, and the previous law remains in force.

Provincial Orders-in-Council

As a general rule, a draft order-in-council is prepared within the ministry responsible. Thus, an order-in-council affecting an aspect of the **School Act**, *such as setting the starting and closing dates for the current school year, is prepared by officials of the Ministry of Education. The draft order-in-council is then submitted to the Ministry of the Attorney General, to make certain that the proposed change or action is legal. Next, it is presented to the Cabinet by the appropriate minister. On Cabinet approval, the draft order-in-council is forwarded to the Lieutenant Governor for signature. Once signed, the document is a legally binding order-in-council of the B.C. government.*

A further legislative process often begins after a new law has been proclaimed and is in force. This is the process of making regulations. Regulations define the applications of the law, and are often much longer than the new law itself. They become part of the new law and have the same force.

The power to make regulations is delegated to bodies other than the Legislature by a section of the new law. Frequently, this power is given to the Cabinet, which passes regulations by order-in-council. Other bodies, such as the Workers' Compensation Board, may be governed by legislation which gives them the power to pass regulations.

QUESTIONS

1. Name two nation-wide problems which the federal and provincial governments work together to solve.
2. Who represents the monarch at the provincial level?
3. Compare the B.C. government and the federal government with regard to three of the following areas:
   (a) role of the Speaker;
   (b) defeat of the government party;
   (c) opening of a session;
   (d) Cabinet structure and operation;
   (e) passage of legislation;
   (f) structure of the executive branch.

The Workers' Compensation Board holds rehabilitation courses for workers injured on the job.

A History of Government in British Columbia

The government of British Columbia traces its roots to the 1840's. In 1849, the Colony of Vancouver Island was created by British Royal Charter. The colony was to be self-governing, with a Governor, an appointed Executive Council or Cabinet, and an elected Legislature. In fact, however, the Governor ruled alone for many years, with an appointed three-man Cabinet to assist him. In response to continuing pressure from the British to create a more democratic government, a seven-man House of Assembly was elected in 1856.

The Colony of British Columbia was created in 1858, to ensure that a British system of government would oversee settlement on the mainland. The majority of mainland residents came north from the United States after the gold rush of 1858. Fearing an American takeover at the polls if elections were held, Governor James Douglas (who was also Governor of the Colony of Vancouver Island) ruled by means of proclamations which had the force of law. This situation ended in January, 1864, when the first session of the Council of British Columbia opened. The Council consisted of a Cabinet of four government officials, four magistrates (judges), and five elected members.

Sir James Douglas

After the union of the Colonies of Vancouver Island and British Columbia in 1866, Governor Douglas proclaimed all English laws as they existed in 1858 to be the laws of the greatly enlarged Colony of British Columbia. He governed with the assistance of an appointed five-man Cabinet and a Legislative Council consisting of nine magistrates and nine elected representatives. The capital of the united colony was moved from New Westminster to its current location in Victoria in 1868.

Responsible government as we know it today was not achieved until the Colony of British Columbia became a province of the Dominion of Canada in 1871. Joining Confederation brought many changes. Immigration, fisheries, and defence (among other matters) became federal responsibilities, and the B.C. government was left with the same responsibilities as any other provincial government. The *British Columbia Constitution Act* of 1871 provided for the creation of an assembly of 25 persons, to be elected by a system of oral nomination and open voting. In that same year, the first Legislative Assembly, consisting mostly of merchants, lawyers, and landowners, was elected from the province's 12 electoral districts. It met for the first time on February 15, 1872. The first Premier, John Foster McCreight, chose eight of his colleagues to join him in the first Cabinet. (By 1987, the number of members in the B.C. Legislature had increased to 69, and the number of electoral districts in the province had risen to 52!)

John Foster McCreight

In the late 1800's, only white males over 21 who were Canadian citizens and owned property were allowed to vote. White women gained the right to vote in 1917, after a hard struggle. Native people and Chinese immigrants were excluded from voting in provincial elections by an Act of the provincial Legislature during its first session, in 1875. Around the turn of the century, voting rights were also denied to citizens of Japanese and East Indian origin. The right to vote was finally granted to Native people and citizens of Chinese and East Indian origin in 1947. Canadians of Japanese descent were not granted the right to vote until 1949.

The voting age was lowered from 21 to 19 in 1979, in order to enable more young people to participate in the democratic process. Today, anyone meeting the age, citizenship, and residency requirements of the *Provincial Elections Act* is entitled to register and vote in provincial elections.

Political Parties in British Columbia

Political parties played a very minor role in the government of British Columbia during the first five decades of the province's existence. At certain times, the Lieutenant Governor, as representative of the monarch, asked a member of the legislature to try to form a government. The member's success and, therefore, term of office depended on the number of supporters, but members often changed their loyalties. The primary commitment of most members was to the local interests of their electors, not to the loose coalition of MLA's and its leader. The first 30 years of the history of the province saw no fewer than 14 Premiers. The rapid change of Premiers and of member loyalties made it hard to govern in a province experiencing rapid growth. The politicking a Premier had to do to maintain support from MLA's often made it very difficult to develop government policies and programs to meet changing needs.

This era of political instability ended in 1903, when Richard McBride led his newly formed political party, the Conservatives, to victory over the newly formed Liberal and Socialist Parties in a provincial general election. The Conservatives governed for 12 years and were then replaced, in 1915, by B.C.'s first Liberal government. Both the Conservatives and the Liberals were committed to achieving rapid provincial growth by promoting a stable investment climate for big businesses and encouraging railway construction and timber development. However, the Conservatives relied on rural support, while the Liberals looked for support to the growing urban areas. The Socialist Party promoted the interests of the growing labour movement, and fought to improve the poor working conditions which existed throughout the province at the time.

Over the next decades, many political parties were formed, some of which existed for only a short period. Such parties are sometimes called

Sir Richard McBride

"fringe parties". The Provincial Party, for instance, was formed in 1923 by dissatisfied Conservatives who were upset with the existing Conservative Party leader and with what they saw as corruption in both the Conservative and the Liberal Parties. The Provincial Party contested two elections and then disbanded.

The Co-operative Commonwealth Federation (CCF) first elected members in B.C. in 1933, when it and some affiliated parties won over 30% of the vote on a socialist platform. Not a fringe party, the CCF continued to participate in B.C. politics, and in 1961 became the cornerstone of the New Democratic Party. In the 1937 election, voters heard the campaign speeches of two new parties: the Social Constructive Party and the Social Credit Party. The Social Constructive Party was formed by dissatisfied members of the CCF, who were unhappy with the CCF's aggressive program; it participated in only one election before it disbanded. The Social Credit Party contested the 1937 election and subsequent elections in the 1940's, without much success. However, its fortunes would soon change.

CLOSE-UP

Fringe Parties in B.C.

The following article from the *Vancouver Sun* gives a rather tongue-in-cheek assessment of the status of political parties in B.C. just before the provincial election of 1986.

FRINGE PARTIES STILL FIGHTING

The One-man Nobody Party is no more.

The Western National party is dead.

And the short-lived United party is a trivia question after being abandoned by founder and leader Graham Lea before it had a chance to contest an election.

But fringe politics are still alive in Lotusland as the province prepares to vote October 22.

When nominations closed Thursday, there were single candidates from the New Republic and Libertas parties, three libertarians and eight candidates carrying the People's Front banner.

The separatist Western Canada Concept, which flirted with respectability after winning a seat in Alberta a few years ago, is foundering.

It will run only one candidate, down from 18 in 1983.

The Western National Party ran two candidates in 1983, but leader Hanna Lehnert says the party's "pretty well dead."

The Communist Party is doubling its spending to $40 000 but will run just three candidates, its smallest contingent in years.

The best organized fringe party appears to be the neophyte [novice] Green Party, a loose grouping of environmentalists and disgruntled left wingers. The Greens will run nine candidates, up from the four they ran in 1983.

The Socreds and the NDP are the only parties to nominate full slates for the 69 seats.

A total of 237 candidates filed nomination papers by yesterday's deadline.

Louis Lesosky ran as the Nobody Party in Cowichan-Malahat in 1983, but can't be found this time around.

—*Vancouver Sun,* October 10, 1986

QUESTIONS

1. What seems to be the attitude of the writer of this article towards fringe parties?

2. Do you think independent candidates and small parties contribute to the political process? If so, what is their contribution?

Rhino Party

Green Party

Western Canada Concept Party

This cartoon appeared in the Colonist *in 1945.*

Cartoonists clarify issues by using humour to make a point. Think of a recent political issue at any level of government, and draw your own cartoon to illustrate the controversy.

From 1941 to 1952, British Columbia was run by a Liberal-Conservative coalition government formed to prevent a possible CCF victory. Also participating, but unsuccessful, in all provincial elections during this period were candidates from the Labour Progressive Party, a forerunner of today's Communist Party.

The 1952 election was conducted differently from previous elections. Amendments to the *Provincial Elections Act* in 1951 provided for the replacement of the old plurality form of election with a system of preferential voting known as the **single transferable ballot.** This system required voters to number the candidates in order of preference, thus providing an alternative vote. Conservatives and Liberals supported the change in order to prevent a possible CCF victory after the dissolution of their governing coalition in early 1952. Both parties believed that their supporters would choose the other as their second preference, allowing one of them to win. The new voting system made it possible for the Liberal and the Conservative Parties to contest the election independently, while ensuring that no other party could win—or so the Liberals and Conservatives thought.

The 1952 election results were a great surprise and disappointment for both parties. Neither had expected the majority of alternative votes to go to the newly reformed Social Credit Party. The party had undergone major changes in 1951, and hotly contested the 1952 elections with many candidates. Presenting itself as holding Christian and anti-socialist values, the Social Credit Party found support among former Liberal and Conservative voters who were disillusioned with the coalition government. When the vote was counted, the Liberal Party had just six seats; the Conservative Party, only four. The Social Credit Party, with 19 seats, squeezed out the CCF, which won 18 seats, to form the government. The party abandoned the transferable ballot system and returned to the plurality system in time for the 1956 election.

According to W.A.C. Bennett, the leader of the winning Social Credit Party, what occurred in B.C. in the mid-1950's was a "return to the two party system. . .a socialist party (the CCF) on the one hand and our Social Credit free enterprise party on the other." After 1952, each successive election became more of a contest between these two parties. The Liberals and Conservatives were reduced to provincial parties with few or no elected members. In 1961, as you have read, the CCF was reformed to become the New Democratic Party (NDP).

Bennett and the Social Credit Party governed B.C. for 20 years. Then, in 1972, the NDP, with Dave Barrett as leader, won its first provincial election. The NDP governed for only one term before a revitalized Social Credit Party, led by W.A.C. Bennett's son Bill Bennett, returned to power in 1975.

W.A.C. Bennett mingles with voters-to-be in Victoria, 1970.

Dave Barrett (left), gives his final speech as leader of the NDP in 1984.

Bill Bennett (right), son of W.A.C. Bennett

QUESTIONS

1. What prompted the creation of the Colony of British Columbia in 1858?
2. When did B.C. achieve responsible government?
3. Who had the right to vote in the late 1800's? By 1917? By 1947? By 1979?
4. Why did B.C. have so many Premiers in its first 30 years?
5. What development policy did B.C.'s early Conservative and Liberal Parties have in common?
6. Name two short-lived B.C. political parties.
7. Why did the Liberals and Conservatives form a coalition from 1941 to 1952?
8. **(a)** What change in provincial election procedures caused both the Liberals and the Conservatives to lose the 1952 election?
   (b) Why had the two parties assumed that one of them would win?

Municipal Government in British Columbia

So far in this book, you have learned about the federal and provincial levels of government in Canada. Now you will look at the municipal, or local, level. It is perhaps this level of government which is closest to most Canadians. In British Columbia, there are more than 1000 municipal officials to ensure that everything for their own communities, from the daily water supply to garbage disposal services, is maintained and improved.

The Canadian Constitution makes the creation of municipal governments a provincial responsibility. In other words, all B.C. communities, from cities to villages, are given their powers to govern at a local level by the provincial government. The B.C. government does this through two statutes: the *Municipal Act of British Columbia*, which sets out the powers of municipal councils and regional districts; and the *Vancouver Act*, which sets out the powers of the Vancouver City Council. Over 20 other provincial statutes, including the *Police Act*, the *Highway Act*, the *Schools Act*, and the *Fire Services Act*, also affect the governing of B.C.'s municipalities. The general rule is that municipal governments do not have authority to take any measures except what the provincial legislation allows. If there is ever a conflict between a provincial law and municipal by-law, the provincial law prevails.

The Structure and Operation of Municipal Government

The government of most municipalities in British Columbia consists of an elected **mayor**, who is the head of a municipal council made up of elected representatives called **aldermen**. ("Alderman" is the legal term for a member of a municipal council, regardless of sex. This is because it derives from the Old English word *aldermann* or *eldermann,* meaning "elderperson" or "chief".) *The Municipal Act* sets out the rules for the size of councils, as shown in Table 8.2.

TABLE 8.2 *Size of Council by Size of Municipality*

*Type of Municipality**	*Mayor*	*Aldermen*	*Full Council*
Village/Town	1	4	5
District/City	1	6	7
District/City (population over 50 000)	1	8	9

*Villages: population under 2500; towns: population 2500–5000; cities: population over 5000; districts: large geographically defined areas, most having a low population density (under 5 persons per hectare)

Mayors and aldermen are elected for a fixed term of office, unlike federal MP's and provincial MLA's, whose terms depend on varying election dates. Again, unlike both MP's and MLA's, municipal council members are usually not affiliated with a traditional political party. Most candidates in municipal elections run for office by promoting two or three individually chosen campaign themes. However, some municipalities have community groups which run groups of candidates with a certain political program for council or the school board. These groups are called **civic parties**.

The function of municipal councils is to develop policies and then adopt by-laws based on these policies. Each council has its own

Tents were used for a Vancouver City Council meeting in 1886, after a fire which destroyed most of the city's buildings.

Vancouver Municipal Council of 1986 holds an informal meeting.

procedure for passing by-laws, but the procedures are broadly similar throughout British Columbia. Like other laws, by-laws usually go through a committee stage, then through three readings. The three readings generally take place at the same sitting of a municipal council. Before a by-law is finally passed, there is a mandatory reconsideration which must occur at least one day after third reading. A by-law usually comes into effect when it is adopted and signed, although occasionally one will set a proclamation date. Once passed, a by-law, like any law, is enforceable by the courts. However, as you read earlier, in any case of conflict between a provincial (or federal) law and a by-law, the higher law prevails.

Certain types of by-laws, such as those that affect zoning, must go to a public hearing prior to adoption, in addition to undergoing the normal procedure described above. Other types, including those that require borrowing money for major projects such as bridges or parks, must go to a public vote, as well, before they can be adopted. Still others require the approval of the provincial Cabinet or the Minister of Municipal Affairs.

The legislative activities of municipal councils are diverse, and bylaws affect many aspects of people's lives both directly and indirectly. Most council activities can be divided into two categories. The first is the provision of services, including water, sewers, garbage collection, local roads, police, firefighting, and parks and recreation. The second has to do with regulations, such as the licensing of local businesses, the inspection of buildings, and the subdivision and use of land. Municipal councils obtain the revenue needed for all their activities from diverse sources. In the early 1980's, about one-half of the $1.5 thousand million of municipal revenues collected in British Columbia came from property taxes, including taxes on businesses. Grants from the provincial and federal governments and money obtained in connection with regulation (the sale of building permits and various types of licences, for example) accounted for the rest. Table 8.3 summarizes the breakdown of municipal expenditures during the early 1980's.

TABLE 8.3 *Local Government Expenditures*

General administration	10%
Fire, police, court services	27%
Transportation services, buses, roads	13%
Garbage and waste and other environmental health concerns	4%
Public health and social assistance	3%
Environment	2%
Recreation and culture	14%
Debt costs	8%
Other	19%

Municipal councils obtain some of their revenues from the sale of building permits and vendor licenses.

The Greater Vancouver Regional District coordinates a wide variety of services including sign regulation, fire protection, bus transit, and garbage collection/ recycling programs.

Regional Districts

Some areas of British Columbia, such as the lower mainland, are densely populated and so have many municipal councils. Other areas, such as Atlin, are geographically large but have a sparse population and therefore few municipal councils. Without careful management, local services could be duplicated unnecessarily in areas of heavy population, or underfunded where the population is low. To avoid duplication and to make certain that essential services are available, 28 regional districts were created in the late 1960's to coordinate the provision of municipal services. The Greater Vancouver Regional District is the largest, with over 1.5 million people: almost half the population of B.C.

The regional districts operate in diverse ways which reflect their geography and population. Taken together, they oversee a very wide range of services, including airports, air-pollution control, animal control, bus transit, cemetery operations, civil defence, emergency programs, fire protection, flood control, garbage collection and disposal, recycling programs, health centres, house numbering, mosquito control, local and regional parks, recreation programs, lighting, senior citizens' housing, water supply, and sign regulation.

Other Local Authorities

Working with the other levels of government is a small number of local authorities with jurisdiction over specific areas.

School Districts B.C. is divided into 75 school districts, each one governed by a school board consisting of locally elected people. Making use of a provincially approved budget, these boards are responsible for running the schools.

Improvement Districts There are over 500 improvement districts in B.C., organized by groups of citizens and businesses in rural areas to provide one or more services. Such services may include water supply, fire protection, or garbage collection and disposal. The improvement districts are administered by boards of trustees consisting of locally elected people serving three-year terms.

Library Boards These bodies run either local or regional libraries. The Greater Vancouver Library Federation, for example, is operated by directors from member municipal boards. It is funded mainly by the provincial government and partly by the member boards.

CLOSE-UP

Working Together to Preserve Agricultural Land

Even though both the provincial and the municipal levels of government have tens of thousands of employees, it would be impossible for them to administer the province effectively without working together. While doing so, they must always look to the future and consider the effect of present actions on future generations.

One of the most important areas of local and provincial coordination—and occasional disagreements—is the preservation of B.C.'s agricultural land. Agriculture is an important industry in British Columbia, yet each year the province imports over 50% of the food consumed. As world populations continue to increase, B.C.'s present food suppliers (based mainly in California) may have less surplus for export, and the price of the surplus will be considerably higher. At some time in the future, British Columbians may have to grow more of their own food.

The NDP provincial government, concerned about this situation, passed several orders-in-council in December, 1972 and January, 1973. Popularly known as the "land freeze", the orders-in-council set aside large tracts of land for present and future agricultural use. Most of this land later became part of the Agricultural Land Reserve (ALR). In April 1973, the *B.C. Land Commission Act* was adopted by the Legislature. The *Act* established an Agricultural Land Commission comprised of five or more appointed technical experts to administer the new land-control system.

Before the land freeze occurred, an estimated 4000 ha to 6000 ha of farmland were disappearing each year under subdivisions, roads, and parking lots. The loss of cropland on such a scale was alarming, because only 5 percent of the province's land area is arable. Top-quality agricultural land makes up a mere one-half of one percent (about 400 000 ha) of the total land area of B.C. The problem of land loss was aggravated by the fact that the best arable land happens to be located near major urban centres, where competition for different types of land use is usually most intense.

The ALR comprises those lands within the province which can produce food. Today, it covers approximately 4.7 million hectares. ALR land is found in every regional district and includes both private and Crown land: forests, farms, and vacant land. Some

FIGURE 8-1 *Map of B.C. Agricultural Land*

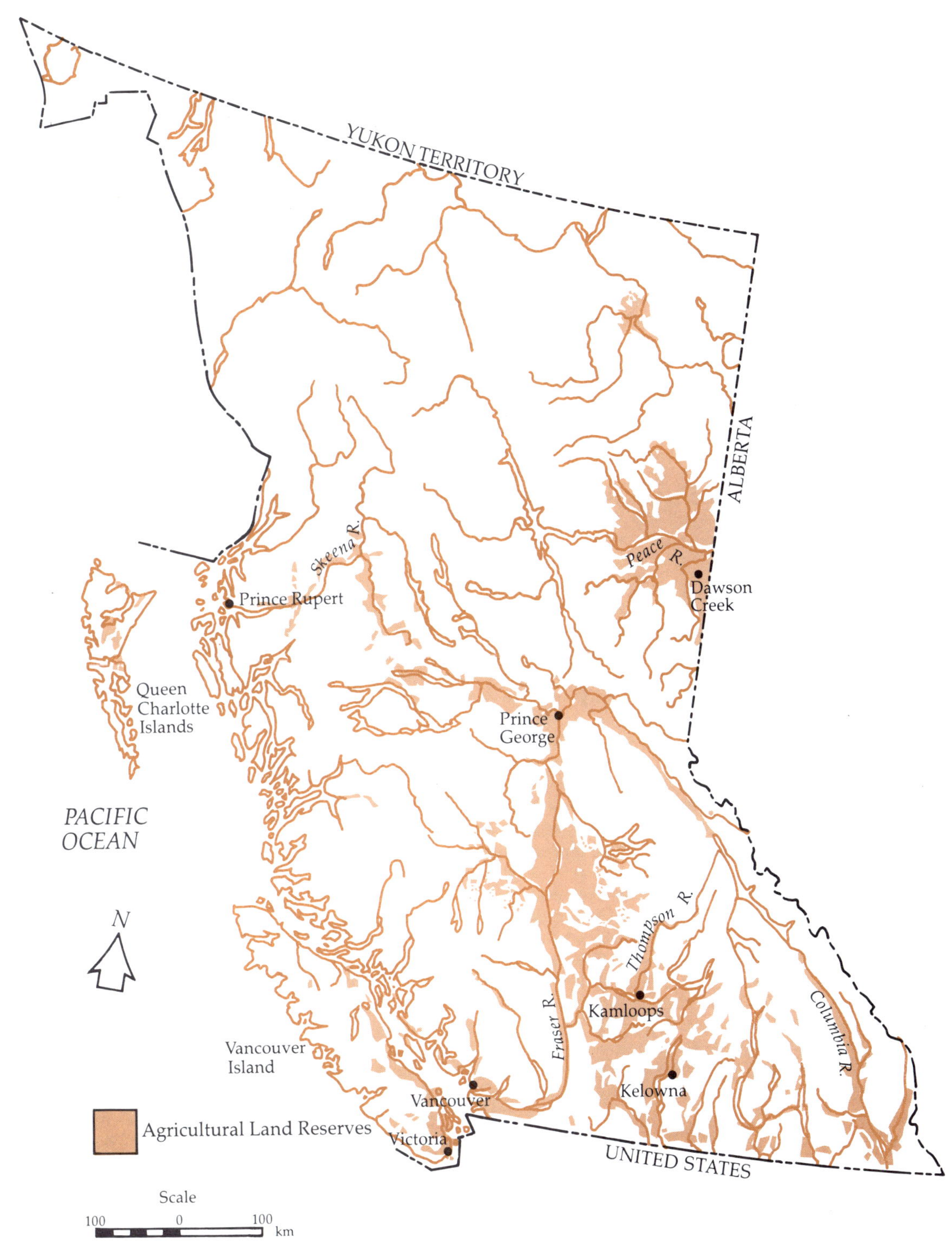

ALR units are vast tracts of many thousands of hectares, as in the Peace River area, while others are small pockets of only a few tens of hectares, as in the Gulf Islands.

The ALR was established with the participation of all 28 regional districts. Each district prepared an ALR plan, using suggestions from the provincial government as a starting point and modifying them on the basis of knowledge of the local situation. In addition, public hearings were held to obtain input from residents. The proposed land reserves were then reviewed by the various resource ministries of the provincial government and by the Environment and Land Use Committee of the Cabinet (ELUC).

Several years of joint government work succeeded in producing policies favouring agricultural land preservation. They are now part of the Regional, Settlement and Community Plans of all local government agencies in B.C. Nevertheless, the pressure on the land reserve is enormous. The use of the ALR is restricted; all developers are expected to plan in accordance with the provincial policy of preserving agricultural land. Thousands of requests to change the designation of land are heard annually by the Agricul-

"What a crop failure . . . 500 acres of condominiums."

tural Land Commission. The commissioners treat each application on its own merits, reviewing the information in their file, looking at photographs if available, considering the recommendations of the regional district or municipality involved, and actively debating the issues raised by the application.

In 1977, the Social Credit provincial government amended the *Land Commission Act* to allow a new kind of appeal: Private landowners who have been turned down by the Land Commission can apply to the Minister of Agriculture for permission to appeal to ELUC. If the minister approves, ELUC hears the appeal and a final decision is made in a closed meeting. Because ELUC is a Cabinet committee, its reasons for allowing an appeal are confidential. Normally, a tribunal which makes decisions about legal rights is required to make its reasons public.

In October 1979, ELUC announced that it was releasing from the ALR for industrial use a block of 253 ha of farmland in Langley, a municipality just east of Vancouver. As soon as the media learned of the exclusion, it became a major public issue. Why was a committee of politicians over-ruling the Land Commission, whose members had been appointed on the basis of their technical knowledge and experience in land-use planning? Were developers using their political connections to get land released from the reserve? Questions such as these made headlines, prompted a ground swell of public protest, and gave the opposition parties an opportunity to complain loudly. The protest later died down, but the public concern over whether ELUC was making decisions based on fair reasons or on political loyalties had been made very clear.

Pressures on the land reserve come from municipalities, land developers, and public and private corporations such as B.C. Hydro and forestry companies. Some municipalities have argued that they must have their fair share of industrial land, even at the expense of the ALR, because industrial land provides high tax revenues. Others have wished to promote tourism or suburban development, or to locate highways and factories on the most accessible land, which is often the best agricultural land as well.

The management of the land resource is a clear example of how important it is for provincial and municipal governments to work together. Balancing the competing demands on land use—the need to ensure the food supply and the desire of both levels of government to get the most revenue possible from the land—is not easy. The issue is occasionally political and often very emotional. It is certainly an issue that affects every citizen of British Columbia.

QUESTIONS

1. Imagine that you have been appointed to the Agricultural Land Commission and are hearing requests to exclude parcels of land. List the factors that you would need to consider when deciding on an application.

2. If you were a local council member working with the provincial government on your community's development, what arguments would you present to the Agricultural Land Commission when applying for permission to build an industrial estate on land which has been designated part of the ALR?

QUESTIONS

1. Which level of government is given responsibility for municipal governments by the Constitution?

2. How are citizens protected from being subject to conflicting local and provincial laws?

3. What is the chief function of municipal councils?

4. Look again at Table 8.3. Why is no expenditure shown for education?

5. How are schools in British Columbia administered?

6. **(a)** What are civic parties?
(b) Give one argument in favour of and one argument against civic parties.
(c) With which viewpoint do you agree more closely? Why?

Chapter Summary

Canada's constitution divides the responsibility for governing between the federal and provincial governments. As a result, the actions of two levels of government affect us every day.

The provincial government operates in a very similar way to the federal government. The areas of responsibility and the names are different (e.g., prime minister instead of premier) but the method of government follows the same rules. Like Canada's federal government, B.C. has both legislative and executive branches of government and an independent judicial branch which relies on both provincial and federal government cooperation.

The provincial government delegates many of its responsibilities to local governments. Local governments take responsibility for local planning and the day-to-day operation of our communities. Some of this they do alone. Many tasks are done jointly through regional districts and other agencies.

The development of our society relies on the working together of the local, provincial and federal governments. The day-to-day operation of our hospitals, universities, and many other institutions depends on this co-operation.

IN REVIEW

1. Copy this table into your notebook, and complete the right-hand column.

Ministry	Responsibility
Attorney General	
Education	
Finance and Corporate Relations	
Forests & Lands	
Transportation and Highways	
Provincial Secretary and Government Services	

2. Some historians claim that the area now known as British Columbia should have become American. What historical or geographical factors can you identify to support this view?

3. Suggest one advantage and one disadvantage to having Victoria as the capital of B.C.

4. Study the list of the typical range of services provided by regional districts (page 191). On what basis does the provincial government appear to have assigned responsibilities to the regional districts?

5. Summarize the development of responsible government in British Columbia, from the creation of the colony in 1849 to the meeting of the first Legislative Assembly in 1872.

6. Give a brief history of each of the following parties in B.C. politics:
(a) the Co-operative Commonwealth Federation (later the NDP);
(b) the Social Credit Party.

APPLYING YOUR KNOWLEDGE

1. Why is the Ministry of Finance and Corporate Relations often considered the most prestigious ministry?
2. Why is it that an order-in-council is not able to overturn a law?
3. Why does the provincial government delegate the right to pass regulations to bodies such as the Workers' Compensation Board?
4. What do you think would motivate a group of people to form a political party?
5. Why do provincial laws require certain by-laws to be considered by a public hearing before adoption?

FURTHER INVESTIGATION

1. The Social Credit Party has been in power in B.C. for 33 of the last 36 years. Do you believe that it is beneficial for a single party to be in power for so long? Explain your reasoning.
2. What might result if opposition parties were not represented on standing committees?
3. Undertake research on one of the following topics:
   (a) how the provincial government budget is spent;
   (b) why various ethnic groups were denied the right to vote until as late as 1949;
   (c) the basic differences in economic and social policies between the Social Credit Party and the NDP;
   (d) the Green Party of B.C.;
   (e) the Agricultural Land Reserve.

GLOSSARY

adjournment debate Generally, the last event of the parliamentary day, when three Members of Parliament are given up to 7 min each to raise issues usually concerning items unresolved in Question Period. One 3 min reply to each item is allowed.

administrative law The area of public law which regulates the activities of various government agencies and prescribes the relationship between these agencies and the public.

advance poll A poll set up for people who for some reason cannot vote on election day; it is usually held a week before the regular election.

affirmative action Programs for disadvantaged persons or groups which give them job preference. These programs are permitted by law because they promote opportunities for people who often suffer discrimination.

alderman An elected representative of a municipal council. (The term "alderman" is correct regardless of the sex of the representative.)

amending formula A method by which changes (*amendments*) can be made to an Act, law, statute, or regulation.

amendment A change made to an Act, law, statute, or regulation.

assistant deputy ministers Several of these officials report to the deputy minister of a government department. Each has a specialized area of responsibility. In turn, various branches and divisions of a government department report to the assistant deputy ministers.

assizes Trials conducted by Provincial Supreme Court judges travelling "on circuit" around a province.

backbenchers Members of Parliament, from the opposition parties and the government party, who have no Cabinet responsibilities and thus occupy seats in the rear areas of the Commons chamber.

benches The front rows of the Commons chamber, reserved for the Prime Minister and his Cabinet.

bill A piece of proposed legislation. A bill that is passed by Parliament becomes a law.

bureaucracy The collective item for the huge network of public service departments, Crown corporations, and other agencies that make up the government's administrative structure.

by-election A local election held when a Member of Parliament dies or resigns between national elections.

Cabinet A body of MP's and Senators chosen by the Prime Minister from his own party. Members of the Cabinet are called *ministers*. The Cabinet is the most important group in the legislative and executive branches of government because it exercises a vital role in both creating and implementing government policy.

Cabinet committee The Cabinet generally has about 10 Cabinet committees made up of six to 12 ministers each. Key ministers sit on several committees.

Cabinet secrecy Unlike House of Commons and Senate debates and the proceedings of parliamentary committees, the records of Cabinet meetings are not made public.

Cabinet solidarity The united front presented by Cabinet ministers. Cabinet decisions are always collective: thus a minister who disagrees with his or her colleagues must keep the disagreement private. In case of extreme disagreement, the minister will resign his or her seat.

candidate A person who runs for election in a federal constituency. Usually, candidates are representatives of a political party. The candidate who wins the most votes in a constituency becomes the Member of Parliament for that constituency.

capitalism The economic system where business, rather than government, is the major producer of goods and services. This system highly values the concept of economic freedom.

case citation The title of a legal case. For example, "*Regina* vs. *Dudley and Stephens*" is a case citation.

caucus The gathering of all of a party's Members of Parliament. Caucus meetings allow the party's leader and MP's to settle their disagreements privately. Proceedings of these meetings are not made public.

centralist In favour of increased federal, in contrast provincial, power.

civic parties Parties of candidates that are formed and supported by community groups.

civil law Civil law, also called *private law*, incorporates all laws affecting the relationships between individuals, between individuals and private organizations, and between organizations. Civil law can be divided into several categories, including contract law, property law, labour law, and family law.

classical liberalism An ideology based on a strong belief in economic and intellectual freedom, that was the forerunner of today's reform liberalism. Classical liberals believed that government should not become involved in the economic and intellectual life of the community any more than necessary.

Clerk of the Privy Council The head of the Privy Council Office (the part of the federal public service that acts as the "eyes and ears" of the Cabinet). The Clerk is the chief public servant in Canada, and is one of the most influential people in government, appointed by, and reporting directly to, the Prime Minister. He or she is responsible for the coordination of Cabinet meetings and for conveying Cabinet decisions to the bureaucracy.

closure A convention that allows the government party to use its majority to place a time limit on further debate on a bill.

(to) codify To consolidate and systemize (laws). The first codified set of Roman laws dates back to about 500 B.C.

committee of the whole The committee composed of the entire House of Commons. Sessions of the committee of the whole are reserved for consideration of special types of legislation, such as study of the government's annual budget.

common law A system of law based on the rule of precedent, or judgments in previous cases. This system developed in Britain and is one of the bases of the Canadian judicial system. The approach used today is to examine the decisions of judges in previous similar cases, and then to extract general principles applicable to the specific legal problem which is before the court.

conflict of interest Under the rule of conflict of interest, a judge cannot preside over any case in which he or she has a personal interest, financial or other. Thus, judges usually will not hear cases involving people who were former clients, or cases being presented by their former legal partners.

constituency The population of a particular geographical area designated a political unit for the purpose of voting. Each Member of Parliament represents a constituency. This area is also called a *riding* or *seat*.

constituency association The bottom level of a party's extra-parliamentary wing, consisting of the majority of party members. There is one association to represent each (major) political party for each constituency in the country.

constituency vote The vote of all electors in a given constituency.

convention An unwritten tradition that is widely observed in practice. The Canadian Constitution consists partly of written documents, and partly of conventions.

criminal law The area of public law concerned with offences against the public interest. Criminal law deals with human conduct that is considered harmful both to society as a whole and to its individual members, such as homicide, sexual assault, and theft.

Custom of Paris The code of law, based on the Justinian Code, that was developed in France during the Middle Ages. This was the law that the earliest French settlers brought with them to Québec; it has been one of the principal influences on the development of the Québec Civil Code.

decentralist Favouring increased provincial, rather than federal, power.

(to) de-index To stop adjusting social welfare payments to keep pace with inflation.

democracy Literally, "rule by the people". The word is generally applied to any system of government in which citizens can freely elect representatives.

departments Various government divisions also called *ministries* such as Finance, Justice, Transport, and Foreign Affairs.

deputy minister The chief public servant within a government department. This person usually has years of experience in the public service and has made a career of serving in a particular department. The deputy minister is the expert to whom the minister for that department turns to for advice.

deputy returning officer In an election, each polling station is manned by a deputy returning officer responsible for checking all voters against the list of voters prepared for the poll, giving each voter a ballot, and making sure that all completed ballots are dropped into a special locked box.

dictator The leader of a dictatorship; a person in power who rules as he or she sees fit, without being answerable to the people.

dictatorship A system of government in which the leader (dictator) rules according to personal decisions and suppresses all opposing opinions.

economic equality The right of every member of society to have adequate food, clothing, and shelter.

economic freedom The right of individuals to own property, run a business, invest money, or advertise a product.

election writ The document issued by the Chief Electoral Officer that sets a federal election in motion.

enumeration The preparation of the voters' list before a federal election. The term is derived from a Latin word that means "to count" or "to number".

enumerators The people who number Canadian voters by recording names, addresses, and occupations in order to prepare a voters' list before an election.

equality The right of all individuals in a society to equal treatment before the law.

executive branch The branch of government that implements (carries out) government policies.

Executive Council In provincial government, a body made up of the Premier and members of the provincial Cabinet.

extra-parliamentary wing That group of party members, officers, and workers who are not Members of Parliament.

Family Division The division of a Provincial Court that has authority over matters relating to family disputes and legal difficulties.

first reading The short statement by a cabinet minister which introduces a proposed piece of legislation to the House of Commons. This statement explains what the legislation is intended to do, and asks that the bill be printed. At this stage, there is no debate—just a presentation of information.

freedom The right of the individual to determine his or her own course of action consistent with the laws and regulations of the state.

Governor General The representative of the monarch in Canada. This official is a native-born Canadian nominated by the Prime Minister and then officially appointed by the monarch. A Governor General's term usually lasts 5 years, during which he or she performs many ceremonial duties.

head of state The ultimate source of legislative authority in a nation. In Canada, the head of state is the monarch: the King or Queen.

House of Commons In Canada, the component of Parliament which consists of the elected representatives from all federal constituencies.

House of Commons committee A committee consisting of 10 to 15 MP's, from all parties in the House, who have special knowledge of or interest in the subject of a bill. After a bill is originated in the Cabinet and introduced to the House of Commons, it is reviewed by one of these committees.

ideology A political doctrine or concept. Liberalism, conservatism, socialism, communism, and fascism are all examples of ideologies.

independents Members of Parliament who do not belong to political parties.
intellectual equality The right of everyone in a society to hold and exercise views within the law, and to be protected, by law, from unacceptable expressions of intellectual freedom.
intellectual freedom The right of individuals to believe in and think about what they wish.
interventionist Taking a positive role in the direction and control of the economy of a country (government) or of other aspects of corporate life.
judicial branch The branch of government that adjudicates (interprets and applies) laws.
Justinian Code The legal document produced about 500 A.D. under the Emperor Justinian when he decided to consolidate (or *codify*) Roman laws passed from early times to his own reign.
law A bill that passes all the necessary Parliamentary stages and is proclaimed.
leader of the Official Opposition The person elected by the Official Opposition to lead its party in Parliament.
leader of the opposition The person elected by each opposition party to lead its party in Parliament.
left wing An ideology that supports progress.
legal realism The approach to law which argues that the situation in which a law was broken, and the opinions of the public and government authorities on the matter, must be considered.
legislative branch The branch of government that makes laws.
local-hiring policy A policy that allows only residents of a given province to work in certain industries in that province.
majority government When a party wins more than one-half of the total number of seats in the House of Commons in a federal election, it forms a majority government.
mandate When a party wins an election, its leader can claim that it has received a mandate; that is, that the voters have shown that they want the elected party to form a government, and its leader to head that government as the Prime Minister.
mayor The head of a municipal council.
Members of the Legislative Assembly (MLA's) Elected representatives of a provincial government. (MLA's are the provincial counterparts of federal MP's.)
Members of Parliament (MP's) The constituency representatives elected to the House of Commons in a federal election.
ministers Members of the Cabinet who are responsible for the various government ministries or departments. There are three categories of Cabinet ministers: ministers in charge of permanent, regular departments (e.g. Finance, Justice); ministers of state; and ministers without portfolio.
ministers of state Ministers who are usually in charge of relatively small, often temporary, departments linked to a major department. For example, the Minister of State for Small Business and the Minister of State for Tourism are "junior" ministers responsible for subdepartments of the Department of Regional Industrial Expansion.
ministers without portfolio Ministers who have no specific responsibilities for a particular government department or ministry. They are often appointed to the Cabinet so that a particular province or region may have its quota of Cabinet representation.
ministries See *departments.*
minority government When a party wins more seats in the House of Commons that any other party in a federal election but less than half the total number of seats, it forms a minority government.
monarch The King or Queen who is head of state in a nation.
national association The top level of the extra-parliamentary wing of a party. This body coordinates the activities of the provincial associations and acts as a link between the parliamentary and extra-parliamentary wings.
national conventions A convention held roughly every two years by the national association of each major political party in Canada, where selected party members meet to elect party officials and to discuss party policy.
nationalism The common spirit of a group of people who are united by culture, politics, or place of birth, or by combinations of the three. Nationalism is characterized by loyalty and devotion to a nation, and by a sense of national consciousness.
natural law An approach to law that looks to the "state of nature": the circumstances in which a law has been broken, rather than following the letter of the law.
nomination The selection of candidates by members of each political party, in each constituency. Candidates tend to be long-time workers for their party and are generally selected at a nomination meeting held in their riding. Party members who are present at the meeting vote until one of the people seeking the nomination receives a majority of the votes cast.
Official Opposition The party that elects the greatest number of representatives to Parliament, except for the government party.
opposition Members of Parliament from all parties who are not members of the government party make up the opposition.
opposition days Time set aside in Parliament for the opposition to raise issues and express views. For example, the 8 days following the Throne Speech and the 6 days following the government budget speech are set aside for opposition speeches.
order-in-council The authority by which most Cabinet decisions are carried out. This is expressed in a Cabinet document, signed by the Governor General, which orders a particular course of action and has the force of law. For example, appointments to government office are normally made through orders-in-council.
Order Paper The agenda of the House of Commons—the document that states what the House purposes to do. The process of converting the ideas of the government into law begins when specific legislation is placed on the Order Paper.
parliamentary wing The wing of a political party which consists of all of its Members of Parliament. The most highly visible and publicized section of the party.
partisan A person with close ties and loyalty to a particular political party.
party vote The vote of party members or their delegates in a given constituency that chooses an electoral candidate to

represent their party. Each party would prepare a slate of candidates for each province and territory.

passive role Judges are expected to play a passive role in court cases: that is, they must be neutral, open-minded observers who listen carefully to all the evidence presented. This approach helps them to be as objective as possible in making their decisions. Thus judges rarely take an active part in a trial.

patriation The transfer of control over Canada's original constitution (the *BNA Act*) from the British government to the Canadian government, in 1982. After patriation, the document was renamed the Constitution of Canada.

policy What a party purposes to do if it is elected, and what it does do once it has been elected.

political party A group of people organized for the purpose of participating in government. In Canada, a government is formed by the political party that wins a federal election.

polling stations Places where constituents vote in an election.

popular vote A measure of the public's support of party candidates in an election, expressed as the percentage of total ballots that are cast for candidates of a particular party (rather than the number of seats won in the House of Commons).

portfolios Departmental responsibilities. Ministers are said to "hold portfolios".

positivist The approach to law that interprets the written language of a statute literally.

precedents Decisions of judges in previous court cases. Common law is based on a system of law that judges similar cases on the basis of precedents.

preliminary hearing When a person who is accused of committing a crime elects trial by jury, he or she goes through a preliminary hearing conducted in the Provincial Court to determine whether there is enough evidence for the case to go to trial in a higher court.

Premier In Canada, the leader of the provincial party that sends the most elected representatives to the provincial legislature. This official is the head of the executive branch of the provincial government, just as the Prime Minister is the head of the corresponding branch of the federal government.

pressure groups See *special interest groups*.

Prime Minister In Canada, the leader of the party that forms the government of the country.

Principal Secretary The head of the Prime Minister's Office, whose task is essentially to advise the PM as to how government policy will affect the party's popularity. This official is one of the most influential people in the government because of his or her vital role as an advisor to the PM.

private law See *civil law*.

private members' business Time alloted in the House of Commons to give any MP—usually a backbencher—a chance to express an opinion or to raise a matter that concerns his or her constituents.

private ownership The basis of capitalism, which recognizes the right of citizens to economic freedom.

(to) privatize To allow private investors to buy shares in a government-owned company.

proportional representation An electoral system in which representation is based on the popular vote.

(to) prorogue To declare a session of Parliament over. In Canada, it is the Governor General who prorogues Parliament.

provincial association One of the levels of the extra-parliamentary wing of a party. There is one association for each province. Its main role is to coordinate the activities of the various constituency associations within the province.

public law One of the two major groups into which all law can be divided. (The other is *civil*, or *private*, law.) Public law covers all laws that concern the general public. It deals with the relationships between individuals and the government, as well as those among the various branches of government. It can be broken down into three areas: criminal law, constitutional law, and administrative law.

puisne (pronounced *puny*) A lesser, or junior, judge of the Supreme Court of Canada. The Supreme Court is composed of the Chief Justice and eight puisne judges, who represent the different regions of Canada.

Question Period The 45-minute time slot set aside for MP's to raise questions in the early afternoon of a Commons day. The procedure is for an opposition MP to direct a question at the Prime Minister or a minister. The questions cannot be about a specific bill on the agenda; instead, they usually concern a current event.

recount If the vote in a particular constituency is very close (differing by 100 votes or fewer), the runner-up candidate may request a recount. A recount may be undertaken when suspicious circumstances surround the balloting.

reform liberalism An ideology that is strongly committed to economic equality. Supporters believe that this equality can be brought about by limited government intervention in the economy. Reform liberalism has developed from classical liberalism's commitment to progress and intellectual freedom.

responsible government Responsible government exists when the executive branch of government (which is appointed) is answerable to, and must act on the decisions of, the legislative branch (which is elected).

returning officers These are election officials who report to the Chief Electoral Officer. They are in charge of compiling the list of voters' names "returned" to the constituency office, and the election results "returned" in that constituency on election day.

reverse onus Onus placed on a person accused of a crime to prove him - or herself innocent. The opposite of the principle prevailing, in Canada that accused persons are presumed to be "innocent until proven guilty".

riding See *constituency*.

rights Individuals' claims to freedom or to equality. Rights are valued differently by governments that adhere to different political ideals.

right wing An ideology that supports tradition and is opposed to progress.

routine An "announcements period" during a Commons day, when the Speaker of the House makes rulings on the proceedings so far, and determine those that are to come next.

Royal Commissions These temporary advisory bodies, also called *Task Forces* are appointed by an order-in-council for a term of about 3 years. Their role is to study special issues and make appropriate recommendations to the government. Members of these bodies travel across Canada to sound out public opinion on an issue, and then publish a report. Royal Commissions address issues that are of concern to many sectors of government; they are not connected to any particular department, but are, instead, directly responsible to the Cabinet.

rule of precedent The practice of deciding cases in a common way on the basis of common principles. The rule of precedent is the basis of Canada's system of common law.

seat See *constituency.*

second reading The debate stage in the passing of a bill. The minister responsible for the legislation gives a detailed speech on why the legislation is needed and what it will do. Debate may last for several days. Eventually, a vote is taken, and if it passes, the bill is approved by the House of Commons in principle. The vote also sends the bill to a committee for further study.

Senate A component of Canada's Parliament, consisting of 104 appointed Senators. The Senate has the least important role in deciding Canada's laws. In theory, it has the power to veto (stop) any bill passed in the House of Commons, but it rarely does so. Since the Senate represents vast political experience, its advice is valued by the House of Commons.

Senate committee The stage in the legislative (lawmaking) process to which a bill passes from the House of Commons. A committee will consist of 10 to 15 Senators who have special knowledge of, or interest in, the subject of a bill.

session of Parliament The term which Parliament is active, usually lasting a year or more. The Prime Minister decides when a session has come to a close.

shadow Cabinet A group of MP's selected by each opposition party's leader to be critics of a specific ministry on the government party side.

single transferable ballot A system of preferential voting that requires voters to number the candidates in their order of preference. (B.C.'s 1952 election was conducted on this basis.)

Small Claims Division The division of a Provincial Court that hears civil disputes in which the sum involved is fairly small (under $3000, in 1988). People usually present their own case in Small Claims Court.

solidarity A united front. A party's members are supposed to show solidarity in the House of Commons.

Speaker of the House The Member of Parliament (usually belonging to the government party) who acts as the "referee" in the House of Commons. The Speaker is responsible for applying and enforcing the rules of Commons procedure in an impartial way. All comments or questions made in the House of Commons must be addressed through the Speaker, rather than directly from one MP to another.

special interest groups Groups (also called *pressure groups*) that form in a reaction to government policy. They are concerned about economic, professional, social, or other specific issues and try to influence government policy of these matters. Examples are the Canadian Labour Congress, the Canadian Medical Association, and the Native Council of Canada. These groups are active between, as well as during, elections.

standing committees Committees that are usually matched with the major ministries. For example, committees on Justice and Legal Affairs; Labour; Manpower and Immigration. All parties are represented on committees, but the government party dominates. The two most important tasks of standing committees are the study of legislation and the study of public expenditures.

Standing Order 19 (S.O. 19) A procedure adopted in 1982 which instituted a half-hour period in the Commons week during which any member may make a statement no more than 60 s long on an issue of particular importance to him or her.

statute A law that originates with, and is passed by, the government, rather than being based on the French Civil Code or on British common law.

statute law Laws passed by all three levels of government—federal, provincial, and local—are known as statute law and represent by far the greater proportion of the laws made in Canada.

supply days A minimum of 25 days (in addition to opposition days) "supplied" to the opposition during each session of Parliament.

suspensive veto The power only to suspend or delay legislation, rather than to reject it completely. In recent years, it has been suggested that the Senate's right to veto be modified to a suspensive veto.

Task Forces See *Royal Commissions.*

third parties In Canada, political parties apart from the Progressive Conservatives and the Liberals. These consist of the NDP, the Progressives, the Social Credit Party, and the *Créditistes.* None has ever won enough seats to form a federal government; only the NDP is currently active at the federal level.

third reading Once a bill is agreed to by a House of Commons committee, it is formally placed before the House of Commons. This stage is usually routine. Once the bill has passed third reading, the House of Commons is finished with the proposed legislation, and it goes to the Senate for passing.

totalitarian A government that is in total control of all aspects of political, social, and cultural life is said to be totalitarian.

Treasury Board A key executive agency linked with the Cabinet, which consists of the President of the Treasury Board, the Minister of Finance, and four other ministers. The role of the Treasury Board is to monitor and evaluate the budgets of the various government departments.

universal suffrage The right of all adult citizens to vote, regardless of wealth, status, or sex.

veto The power to reject legislation. In theory, the Senate has always had the power to veto a bill from the House of Commons, but only in extremely rare cases has it exercised this power.

Youth Court Division The division of a Provincial Court that hears criminal trials of persons between the ages of 12 and 17 years (in B.C.), under the special procedures that Parliament has established for young offenders.

INDEX